Frommer's

Maui
day BY day®
5th Edition

by Shannon Wianecki

FrommerMedia LLC

Contents

Published by:

Frommer Media LLC

ISBN: 978-1-62887-370-2 (print); 978-1-62887-371-9 (ebk)

Editorial Director: Pauline Frommer
Editor: Holly Hughes
Production Editor: Lindsay Conner
Photo Editor: Seth Olenick
Cartographer: Roberta Stockwell
Front cover photos, left to right: Couple kayaking © Epic Stock Media/Shutterstock; Island of Maui © Joe West/Shutterstock; Plumeria flowers and banana leaf © enciktat/Shutterstock.
Back cover photo: Surfer girls © Epic Stock Media.

For information on our other products and services, please go to Frommers.com/contactus.

Frommer's also publishes its books in a variety of electronic formats. Some content that appears in print may not be available in electronic formats.

Manufactured in China

5   4   3   2

About This Guide

Organizing your time. That's what this guide is all about.

Other guides give you long lists of things to see and do and then expect you to fit the pieces together. The Day by Day guides are different. These guides tell you the best of everything, and then they show you how to see it *in the smartest, most time-efficient way.* Our authors have designed detailed itineraries organized by time, neighborhood, or special interest. And each tour comes with a bulleted map that takes you from stop to stop.

Hoping to sunbathe on a secluded beach or to explore Haleakalā National Park? Planning on snorkeling Molokini, driving the winding road to Hāna, or relaxing at one of Maui's beachside spas? Whatever your interest or schedule, the Day by Days give you the smartest routes to follow. Not only do we take you to the top attractions, hotels, and restaurants, but we also help you access those special moments that locals get to experience—those "finds" that turn tourists into travelers.

The Day by Days are also your top choice if you're looking for one complete guide for all your travel needs. The best hotels and restaurants for every budget, the greatest shopping values, the wildest nightlife—it's all here.

Why should you trust our judgment? Because our authors personally visit each place they write about. They're an independent lot who say what they think and would never include places they wouldn't recommend to their best friends. They're also open to suggestions from readers. If you'd like to contact them, please send your comments our way at feedback@frommers.com, and we'll pass them on.

Enjoy your Day by Day guide—the most helpful travel companion you can buy. And have the trip of a lifetime.

About the Author

Shannon Wianecki has been exploring Hawaii's hidden treasures since her "small kid" days. She contributes to numerous publications worldwide including *Smithsonian, BBC Travel,* and *Hana Hou!, the* Hawaiian Airlines magazine. In 2016, the *Hawaii Ecotourism Association* named her Travel Writer of the Year and she has twice been a finalist for Best Independent Journalist in Hawaii. When she isn't busy writing about rare plants or fascinating local characters, she's out looking for them with her four-legged sidekick, Spike. She resides on Maui's north shore.

An Additional Note

Please be advised that travel information is subject to change at any time—and this is especially true of prices. We therefore suggest that you write or call ahead for confirmation when making your travel plans. The authors, editors, and publisher cannot be held responsible for the experiences of readers while traveling. Your safety is important to us, however, so we encourage you to stay alert and be aware of your surroundings.

Star Ratings, Icons & Abbreviations

Every hotel, restaurant, and attraction listing in this guide has been ranked for quality, value, service, amenities, and special features using a **star-rating system.** Hotels, restaurants, attractions, shopping, and nightlife are rated on a scale of zero stars (recommended) to three stars (exceptional). In addition to the star-rating system, we also use a **kids icon** to point out the best bets for families. Within each tour, we recommend cafes, bars, or restaurants where you can take a break. Each of these stops appears in a shaded box marked with a coffee-cup-shaped bullet .

The following **abbreviations** are used for credit cards:

AE	American Express	DISC	Discover	V	Visa
DC	Diners Club	MC	MasterCard		

Frommers.com

Frommer's travel resources don't end with this guide. Frommer's website, **www.frommers.com,** has travel information on more than 4,000 destinations. We update features regularly, giving you access to the most current trip-planning information and the best airfare, lodging, and car-rental bargains. You can also listen to podcasts, connect with other Frommers.com members through our active-reader forums, share your travel photos, read blogs from guidebook editors and fellow travelers, and much more.

A Note on Prices

In the "Take a Break" and "Best Bets" sections of this book, we have used a system of dollar signs to show a range of costs for 1 night in a hotel (the price of a double-occupancy room) or the cost of an entree at a restaurant. Use the following table to decipher the dollar signs:

Cost	Hotels	Restaurants
$	under $130	under $15
$$	$130–$200	$15–$30
$$$	$200–$300	$30–$40
$$$$	$300–$395	$40–$50
$$$$$	over $395	over $50

How to Contact Us

In researching this book, we discovered many wonderful places—hotels, restaurants, shops, and more. We're sure you'll find others. Please tell us about them, so we can share the information with your fellow travelers in upcoming editions. If you were disappointed with a recommendation, we'd love to know that, too. Please write to: Support@FrommerMedia.com

16 Favorite **Moments**

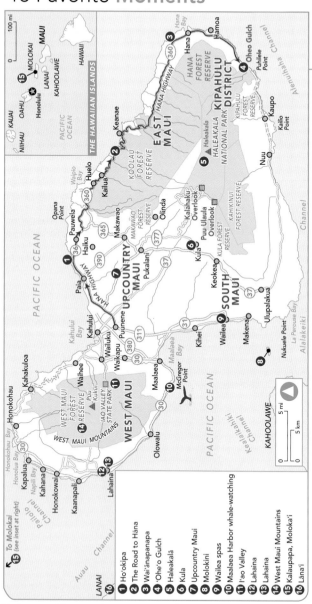

THE HAWAIIAN ISLANDS

KAUAI
NIIHAU
OAHU
Honolulu
MOLOKAI
LANAI
KAHOOLAWE
MAUI
HAWAII

1 Ho'okipa
2 The Road to Hana
3 Wai'anapanapa
4 'Ohe'o Gulch
5 Haleakalā
6 Kula
7 Upcountry Maui
8 Molokini
9 Wailea spas
10 Maalaea Harbor whale-watching
11 I'ao Valley
12 Lahaina
13 Lahaina
14 West Maui Mountains
15 Kalaupapa, Moloka'i
16 Lāna'i

Previous page: Hikers savor the panorama atop Haleakalā Crater.

To experience the true magic of Maui, just step outside to watch the sun crack like a golden egg on the horizon, inhale the perfume of delicate ginger blossoms, listen to the clattering of bamboo in the rain forest, or witness the sky full of the same stars that guided the first Polynesians to these Islands. A few more of my favorite Maui experiences are described below.

❶ Watch windsurfers ride the waves at Ho'okipa. This famous beach draws waveriders from around the globe to ride, sail, and pirouette over the waves. Watching them flip into the air while rotating 360 degrees is the best free show in town. *See p 78.*

❷ Smell the sweet scent of ginger on the road to Hana. At every twist on this winding road you are greeted by exotic tropical blossoms, thundering waterfalls, breathtaking vistas, and a glimpse at what Maui looked like before it was " discovered." *See p 10.*

❸ Walk the coast trail at Wai'ānapanapa. This trail will take you back in time, past lava cliffs, mysterious caves, a *hala* forest, an ancient *heiau* (temple), an explosive blowhole, native Hawaiian seabirds, and the ever-changing Pacific. *See p 91.*

❹ Take a dip in a waterfall at 'Ohe'o Gulch. These fern-shrouded waterfall pools spill seaward at 'Ohe'o

Gulch, on the rain-shrouded eastern flanks of Haleakalā. *See p 73.*

❺ Greet the rising sun from atop Haleakalā. Dress warmly and drive the 37 miles (60km) from sea level up to 10,000 feet (3,048m), where you can watch the sunrise. Breathing in the rarefied air and watching the first rays of light streak across the sky is a mystical experience. *See p 87.*

❻ Head to Kula to bid the sun aloha. This town perched on the side of Haleakalā is the perfect place to watch the sun set over the entire island, with vistas across the isthmus, the West Maui Mountains, and Moloka'i and Lāna'i in the distance. *See p 65.*

❼ Explore upcountry Maui. On the slopes of Haleakalā, cowboys, farmers, ranchers, and other country people make their serene, neighborly homes, worlds away from the bustling beach resorts. *See p 64.*

❽ Snorkel off Molokini. Calm, protected waters in the islet's crater, plus an abundance of marine life,

Windsurfing at Ho'okipa Beach.

A beachside massage is the perfect way to relax.

make Molokini one of Hawai'i's best places to snorkel. Paddle with turtles, watch clouds of butterflyfish flitter past, and search for tiny damselfish in the coral. *See p 98.*

⑨ Get pampered in paradise. Maui's spas have raised the art of relaxation and healing to a new level. A massage on the beach will smooth out the kinks, while you bask in the sounds of the ocean, smell the salt air, and feel the caress of a warm breeze. *See p 34.*

⑩ Watch for whales. From mid-December through the end of March, humpback whales can be seen from shore jumping, breaching, and slapping their pectoral fins. *See p 107.*

⑪ Explore I'ao Valley. When the sun strikes Iao Valley in the West Maui Mountains, an almost ethereal light sends rays out in all directions. This really may be Eden. *See p 60.*

⑫ Visit a historic port town. In the 1800s, whalers swarmed into Lahaina and missionaries fought to stem the spread of their sinful influence. Before that, Hawaiian royalty ruled this coast. *See p 50.*

⑬ Experience Art Night in Lahaina. Every Friday, under a canopy of stars, the town's galleries open their doors and serve refreshments. Wander in to see what's going on in Maui's creative community. *See p 116.*

⑭ Fly over the remote West Maui Mountains. The only way to see the inaccessible, prehistoric West Maui Mountains is by helicopter. You'll fly low over razor-thin cliffs and flutter past sparkling waterfalls while descending into canyons and valleys. *See p 101.*

⑮ Ride a mule to Kalaupapa. Even if you have only 1 day to spend on Moloka'i, spend it on a mule. Trek from "topside" Moloka'i down a narrow, dizzying switchback trail to Kalaupapa National Historic Park below. *See p 62.*

⑯ Take a day trip to Lāna'i. Sailing from Lahaina Harbor, you can admire Maui from offshore, go snorkeling in the clear waters of Lāna'i, tour this tiny former plantation island, and still catch the last ferry back. *See p 152.* ●

One of Lahaina's quirky characters.

Strategies for Seeing Maui

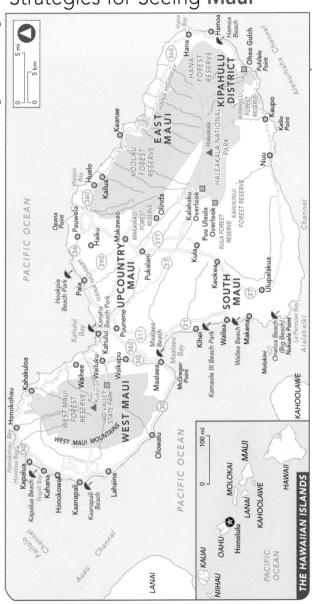

Previous page: Nature-watching in ʻĪao Valley.

Maui may be an island, but it's a good-sized island and your vacation time is precious. There really is just one cardinal rule: relax. Maui is not a place to "see" but a place to experience. If you are too busy rushing to tick things of your to-do list, you won't experience the magic of the island. Here are my suggestions for making the most of your time.

Rule #1: Remember you are on vacation

Don't jam your days with activities; allow time to relax, to stop and smell the plumerias. That said, if you arrive jet-lagged, use it to your advantage! Get out and watch the sunrise while you're still on East or West Coast time. Book an early morning snorkel trip. Remember: Exposure to sunlight can help reset your internal clock—another good reason to soak up the ambient Vitamin D.

Rule #2: Expect driving to take a lot longer on Maui

Maui lacks adequate public transportation, so you'll need a car to get around. But plan to stretch your legs as much as possible. Don't just rubberneck from your car window; get out and inhale the salty, flower-scented air, revel in the panoramic views, and listen to the sounds of surf crashing or mynah birds arguing over squashed guavas. Sure, you could drive the 50-mile-long (80km) Hāna Highway in as few as 2 to 3 hours, but that would miss the

Take some time to stop and smell the plumerias.

point of the journey entirely. One last thing: Maui does have traffic jams. From 7 to 9am and 4 to 6pm the main roads are bumper-to-bumper with commuters. Plan accordingly. Sleep in late and get on the road after the traffic has cleared out, or watch the sunset and then go to dinner.

Fly Direct

If possible, fly nonstop and directly to the island of Maui (the airport is in Kahului and the airport code is OGG). Not only is it easier, but it will also save you time. Yes, there are flights from the U.S. mainland through Honolulu and then on to Maui, but the "on to Maui" bit generally means getting off a plane in the big, big Honolulu International Airport and transferring to another terminal. Going through the fun-filled security procedures (taking off your shoes again!) and then checking in and waiting (sometimes up to 2 hours) for your flight to Maui is no way to begin a vacation.

Maluaka Beach.

Rule #3: If your visit is short, stay in one place

Unless you're visiting for a week or longer, try not to hotel hop. With the exception of Hāna, all the towns on Maui are within easy driving distance. Checking in and out of hotels is inconvenient—there's the schlepping of the luggage (and the corresponding tips to the parking valet, the bellman, and so on), the waiting in line to check in, and unpacking, only to repeat the entire process a few days later. Your vacation time is too precious.

An endangered grey-crowned crane, native to Africa, at the Kula Botanical Garden.

Rule #4: Pick the key activity of the day and plan accordingly

To maximize your time, decide what you really want to do that day, then plan all other activities in the same geographical area. For example, if you want to go golfing in Kapalua, plan to hit a beach and eat dinner nearby—that way you won't have to trek back and forth across the island.

Rule #5: Remember you are on the island of aloha

Maui residents aren't in a rush and you shouldn't be either. Slow down. Smile. Say "aloha" (hello, goodbye, and I love you all rolled into one) and "mahalo" (thank you). Remember that you are a guest here. Ask questions. Eat unfamiliar fruits. Practice standing up on a surfboard even if it makes you scream. Learn as much as you can about local history—it's fascinating and knowing even a little will enrich your time here.

Rule #6: Use this book as a reference, not a concrete plan

The best vacations are a mix of careful plans and total spontaneity. Pick and choose the tours you want to take and then let the weather and the new friends you make dictate some diversions. ●

2 The Best Full-Day Tours

The Best of Maui in Three Days

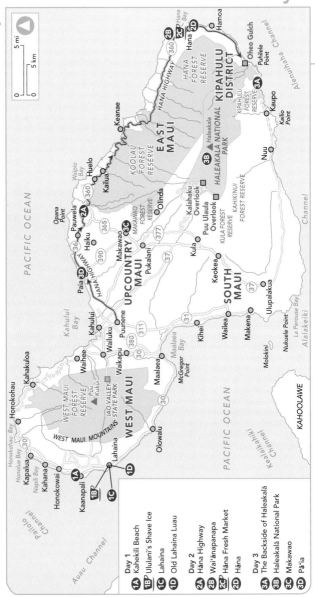

Day 1
1A Kahekili Beach
1B Ululani's Shave Ice
1C Lahaina
1D Old Lahaina Luau

Day 2
2A Hāna Highway
2B Wai'ānapanapa
2C Hāna Fresh Market
2D Hāna

Day 3
3A The Backside of Haleakalā
3B Haleakalā National Park
3C Makawao
3D Pā'ia

Previous page: The Garden of Eden botanical garden near Hana.

For a smallish island, Maui has wildly diverse ecosystems and communities—there's a lot to see and experience. If you only have 3 days, concentrate on some of Maui's most quintessential experiences: a beach, a luau, the scenic Hāna Highway, and the view from the top of Haleakalā, a 10,023-foot-high (3,048km) dormant volcano. START: **Kahekili Beach.**

Travel Tip

For detailed descriptions of the beaches in this chapter, see chapter 5. For hotel reviews, see chapter 10. For more on the recommended restaurants, see chapter 8.

To get to Kahekili Beach from Lahaina/Ka'anapali, take Hwy. 30 north towards Kapalua. Turn left on Pu'ukoli'i Street and follow it to the shaded parking lot.

1A ★★★ Kahekili Beach. Check in to your hotel, and then head for Kahekili Beach, named for an ancient Maui king. You'll feel like royalty when you sink your toes into the deep sand here. Don't overdo the sun on your first day. Bring water, sunscreen, and a hat. If you're feeling adventurous, rent snorkel equipment—the reef here is vibrant. Otherwise, simply bask like a turtle on the sand and enjoy the perfect temperature. See p 79.

Retrace your route back to Hwy. 30 and turn right, continuing into Lahaina town.

1B Ululani's Shave Ice. Cool off with this uniquely Hawaiian treat. Snow-fine ice shavings are topped with tropical fruit syrups. Try lilikoi and coconut with ice cream or a "snow-cap" (sweet condensed milk). *790 Front St, Lahaina* ☎ *808/877-3700. $.*

1C ★★ Lahaina. After an hour or two at the beach, spend a couple of hours walking this historic oceanfront town, which was once the royal capital of Hawai'i, and later a favorite spot for both whalers and missionaries. Today, you can browse its array of unique storefronts, restaurants, and nightlife spots. See the walking tour on p 50 for more information.

1D ★★★ Old Lahaina Lū'au. To really feel as though you are in Hawai'i, immerse yourself in

The Old Lahaina Lū'au immerses guests in Polynesian culture.

Polynesian culture at this beach-front lūʻau. The festivities begin at sunset and feature Tahitian and Hawaiian dancing and chanting. The food is a mix of Pacific Rim and traditional Hawaiian, from imu-roasted kalua pig to baked mahi-mahi to teriyaki sirloin steak. *1251 Front St. www.oldlahainaluau.com. ☎ 800/248-5828 or 808/667-1998. $115 adults, $78 children 12 and under. See p 127.*

From Lahaina take Hwy. 30 south to Hwy. 380 and turn right (east). In Kahului, Hwy. 380 becomes Dairy Road. Turn right (east) on Hwy. 36.

2A ★★★ Hāna Highway. You'll probably wake up early on Day 2, your first full day in Hawaiʻi, so take advantage of it and get out as quickly as you can and onto the scenic Hāna Highway. Allow at least 3½ to 5 hours for the journey. Pull over often, get out to take photos, smell the flowers, and jump in the mountain-stream pools. Wave to everyone, move off the road for those speeding by, and breathe in Hawaiʻi. For a detailed description of this route, see p 66.

After MM 16, Hwy. 36 becomes Hwy. 360 and starts with MM 0. Just past MM 32 is:

2B Waiʻānapanapa State Park. Just before reaching Hāna town, stop at this state park and hike down to the black-sand beach and cave pool. See p 91.

The dramatic black sands of Waiʻānapanapa State Park.

Back on the Hāna highway, a couple of miles down the road between MM 34 and 35 is:

2C² Hāna Fresh Market. This small, outdoor farmer's market and deli (open every day) has hot breakfast and lunch made with locally grown produce (including coffee). I highly recommend the frittata—and the lattes are divine. Get a picnic lunch before you leave.

About ½ mile (.8km) after MM 35, you come to the outskirts of Hāna; veer right at the police and fire station.

2D ★★★ Hāna. While you're here, make sure to hit three of my favorite spots, the **Hāna Cultural Center and Museum,** the **Hasagawa General Store,** and **Hāna Coast Gallery.** Spend the night in Hāna. For more detailed information on Hāna's sights, see p 66. For where to stay in Hāna, see p 142.

3A ★★ The "Back Side" of Haleakalā. On Day 3, pack up to leave Hāna and head out towards the lush **Kīpahulu District of Haleakalā National Park.** Bring snacks, water, and charged camera batteries to capture the stunning vistas you will encounter. Stop at the waterfalls in Kīpahulu (save your park receipt for entrance to the summit later). Continue on the

Waterfalls at Kīpahulu.

3B ★★★ Haleakalā National Park. Cruise up to the 10,000-foot (3,048km) dormant volcano, **Haleakalā.** You won't have time for a hike, but spend at least an hour gazing into the crater's moonscape. See p 88 for details. *www.nps.gov/hale.* ☎ 808/572-4400. Daily 7am–4pm.

Retrace your route down Hwy. 378 to Hwy. 377, where you turn right and head north to Hwy. 37. Turn right onto Hwy. 37 and, at the next light, turn right onto Makawao Avenue to drive to the town of Makawao. To get to Pā'ia from Makawao, head downhill on Baldwin Avenue.

cliff-hanging road through the dry, cattle country of **Kaupō**. (The road turns to gravel in a few spots, but it isn't too bad. Drive slow and watch for cows.) Stop for ice cream at **Kaupo Store.** Proceed on Pi'ilani Hwy. 31 into the rolling green hills of 'Ulupalakua. Take a spin through **MauiWine** and the **'Ulupalakua Ranch Store.** (p 65, **5**).

Pi'ilani Hwy. 31 becomes Kula Hwy. 37 after 'Ulupalakua. Follow it to Kekaulike Hwy. 377 and turn right. Turn right again onto Haleakalā Hwy. 378 to go to the top of Haleakalā.

3C ★★ Makawao. Tour the old cowboy town (see p 33 for details), and plan a sunset dinner in **3D ★★ Pā'ia** (p 122) before heading back to the airport. If you're feeling luxurious, make reservations at **Mama's Fish House**. See p 147, **11** and **12** for more information. See p 129.

From Hwy. 36 in Pā'ia, drive west to Kahului, turning right on Airport Road.

Maui Driving Tips

Hawai'i residents know the highways by their Hawaiian names; very few know the highway numbers. I've included both the Hawaiian highway name and number on the maps, but the directions in this book mainly refer to the highway number. You'll also see the abbreviation MM, which stands for "mile marker." Below is a quick reference to the names and numbers of Maui's highways.

Hwy. 30: Honoapi'ilani Highway
Hwy. 31: Pi'ilani Highway
Hwy. 36 and Hwy. 360: Hāna Highway
Hwy. 37: Haleakalā Highway and the Kula Highway
Hwy. 311: Mokulele Highway
Hwy. 377 and Hwy 378: Haleakalā Highway
Hwy. 380: Kuihelani Highway

The Best of Maui in One Week

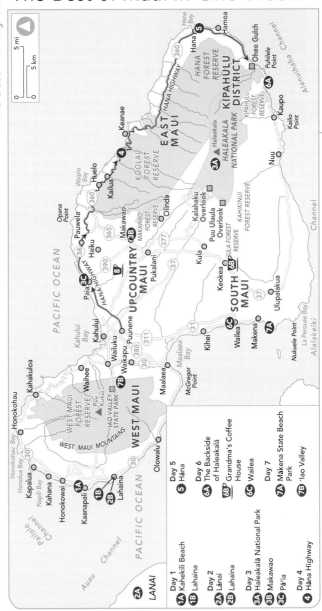

Day 1
1A Kahekili Beach
1B Lahaina

Day 2
2A Lānaʻi
2B Lahaina

Day 3
3A Haleakalā National Park
3B Makawao
3C Pāʻia

Day 4
4 Hāna Highway

Day 5
5 Hāna

Day 6
6A The Backside of Haleakalā
6B Grandma's Coffee House
6C Wailea

Day 7
7A Mākena State Beach Park
7B ʻIao Valley

I recommend staying at least a week on Maui to take in this sensuous island at a slow, leisurely pace. This weeklong itinerary adds a few new favorites to the 3-day tour: sailing to the island of Lāna'i; spending an extra day in Hāna; and, depending on your preference, a final day on the beach, at a spa, or shopping for souvenirs. I suggest working your way around the island to avoid unnecessary commuting: spend the first 2 nights in West Maui (Lahaina/Ka'anapali/Kapalua), night 3 in Pā'ia, nights 4 & 5 in Hāna, and the last night in South Maui (Kīhei/Wailea). If that's too much hotel-hopping for you, pick one home base to drive back and forth from. START: **Kahekili Beach.**

Travel Tip

West Maui is the area from Lahaina north, including Ka'apanali, Honokowai, Kahana, Nāpili, and Kapalua. South Maui includes Kīhei, Wailea, and Mākena.

To get to Kahekili Beach from Lahaina/Ka'anapali, take Hwy. 30 north towards Kapalua. Turn left on Pu'ukoli'i Street and follow it to the shaded parking lot.

1A ★★★ **Kahekili Beach &**
1B ★★ **Lahaina.** See Day 1 in "The Best in 3 Days," above.

Go south on Hwy. 30 to Lahaina. Turn right at the light on Dickenson Street. Look for the REPUBLIC PARKING sign on the right.

2A ★★★ **Lāna'i.** Get out on the water early with **Trilogy** (p 99), my favorite sailing-snorkeling trip in Hawai'i. Pack your swimsuit, sunscreen, hat, and plenty of water. You'll spend the morning sailing to the island of Lāna'i, snorkeling, and touring the island. Breakfast and lunch are included.

2B ★★ **Lahaina.** After sailing back to Lahaina, in the afternoon you'll have time to shop for souvenirs or relax in Lahaina. For dinner, I'd book a table on the ocean at sunset at the **Mala Ocean Tavern** (p 129). If you still have energy, watch the Cirque-de-Soleil inspired performance of **'Ulalena** (p 138).

Take Hwy. 30 south along the West Maui coast. Turn right on Hwy. 380, right again on Hwy. 36, then another right on Hwy. 37. Just after Pukalani, turn left on Hwy. 377. Turn left again at the

Sailing to Lāna'i.

sign for Haleakalā National Park and take Hwy. 378 to the top. Allow at least 2 hours.

3A ★★★ Haleakalā National Park. After 2 days on the water, turn *mauka* (toward the mountain) for a cooler climate on Day 3. Head up the 10,000-foot-high (3,048m) dormant volcano, Haleakalā. You can hike in the crater (p 85), speed down the mountain on a bicycle (p 101), or simply wander about the park. If you want to watch the sunrise from this height (a near-religious experience) you must reserve your spot in advance (see p 87). Wear layers. Save your park entrance receipt to access the Kīpahulu District later. *www.nps.gov/hale.* ☎ 808/572-4400. Daily 7am–4pm.

Retrace your route down the mountain, and turn right at the light on Makawao Avenue. To get to Pā'ia from Makawao, head downhill on Baldwin Avenue.

3B ★★ Makawao & 3C ★★★ Pā'ia. See p 13. Stay in one of the boutique inns nearby to get an early start for the following day's adventure; see p 142 for options.

4 ★★★ Hāna Highway. On Day 4, pack your bags, stock up on snacks, water, and driving music, and head to Hāna. See p 12, 2A through 2D.

5 ★★★ Hāna. With another whole day to spend here, I recommend lounging at **Hāmoa** or **Kaihalulu** beaches (see chapter 5), with great swimming and snorkeling at either beach, or touring **Pi'ilanihale Heiau** (p 71), one of the largest ancient Hawaiian temples in the state. You'll be grateful to spend a second night in Hāna.

Get on the road by 10am for Day 6. Head west on Hwy. 360 to 'Ulupalakua, allowing at least 1 hour driving time. After Kaupō, Hwy 360 becomes Hwy. 31.

6A ★★ The "Back Side of Haleakalā." See page 33.

6B Grandma's Coffee House. Need refreshment? I love the homegrown coffee, fresh-baked pastries, and live music on the lanai (porch) at this tiny wooden coffee house. 9232 Kula Hwy. (Hwy.37), Kēōkea (about 6 miles/9.7km past MauiWine in 'Ulupalakua). ☎ 808/878-2140. $.

After 'Ulapalakua, Hwy. 31 becomes Hwy. 37. Follow it across the island to Hāna Hwy. 36 and turn left. Take the next left onto Hansen Road and follow it until it end at Mokulele Hwy. (Hwy. 311). Turn left and head south. Hwy. 311 becomes Hwy 31, Pi'ilani Hwy., which ends at Wailea. The drive will take a little more than an hour.

Wines from MauiWine.

Valley State Park. The 8-mile (13km) trip will take about 30 to 40 minutes.

7B ★★ ʻĪao ʻValley. If you have extra daylight before your flight, swing up through this historic verdant valley on your way back to the airport. Bring a picnic lunch and hike the trails or pack a swimsuit and plunge into the cool mountain streams that run through the **ʻĪao** Valley park. One feature you won't miss: the black basalt **ʻĪao** Needle, jutting upward some 2,250 feet (686 meters). Park gates are open 7am to 7pm daily; entry fee is $5 per car. For more details, see p 44, **6** and p 60, **2**.

Return the way you came on ʻĪao Valley Road. Continue straight as the road turns to Main Street then West Kaʻahumanu Ave. 30. Turn right on Hāna Hwy, then left on Airport Road. The 8-mile (12.9km) trip will take about 25 minutes.

ʻĪao Valley.

Wailea Beach.

6B ★★★ Wailea. For your last night on Maui, stay in one of the tony resorts on the island's palm-fringed south shore. (See p 145 for lodging suggestions.) Walk the oceanfront path (p 56), or simply relax on Wailea Beach (p 82), drinking in the romantic sunset views.

7A ★★★ Wailea & Mākena Depending on how much time you have on your final day, you relax at **Mākena State Beach Park** (p 81), snorkel with tropical fish at **Ulua** (p 81), or get pampered in a spa. Spagoers have terrific spas to choose from (p 36) and shoppers should check out some of my favorite stores at the nearby **Shops at Wailea** (p 119).

To go from Wailea to ʻĪao Valley, head north on Hwy. 31 and turn right on Hwy. 30. In the town of Wailuku, turn left at the light onto Main Street, which becomes ʻĪao Valley Road, and ends at ʻĪao

The Best of Maui in Two Weeks

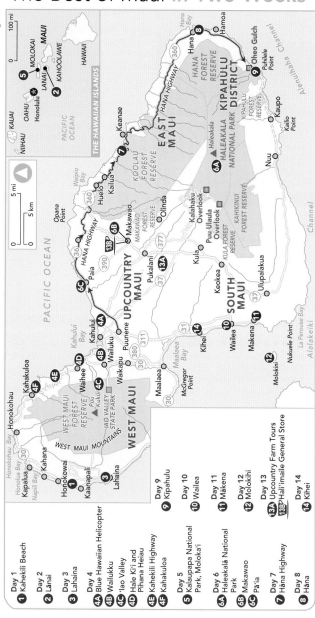

Day 1
1 Kahekili Beach

Day 2
2 Lānaʻi

Day 3
3 Lahaina

Day 4
4A Blue Hawaiian Helicopter
4B Wailuku
4C ʻĪao Valley
4D Hale Kiʻi and Pihana Heiau
4E Kahekili Highway
4F Kahakuloa

Day 5
5 Kalaupapa National Park, Molokaʻi

Day 6
6A Haleakalā National Park
6B Makawao
6C Pāʻia

Day 7
7 Hāna Highway

Day 8
8 Hāna

Day 9
9 Kipahulu

Day 10
10 Wailea

Day 11
11 Makena

Day 12
12 Molokihi

Day 13
13A Upcountry Farm Tours
13B Haliʻimaile General Store

Day 14
14 Kihei

Two weeks on Maui separates the visitors from the adventurers and gives you time to really get to know this exotic isle. This tour is similar to the 1-week tour above with a few additional stops: flying to Moloka'i and riding a mule into the dramatic Kalaupapa Peninsula; seeing Maui from a helicopter; snorkeling in the old volcanic crater of Molokini; touring Maui's farms; and kayaking off historic Mākena. To reduce driving time, plan on spending 6 nights in West Maui, 3 nights in Hāna, and 4 nights in South Maui. START: **Kahekili Beach.**

On Day 1, head to the picture-perfect **① ★★★ Kahekili Beach** (see p 79) on the West Maui coast. On Day 2, plan to spend the day on the ocean—well equipped with swimsuit, sunscreen, a hat, and plenty of water—with a boat trip from Lahaina to **② ★★★ Lāna'i** (see p 152).

Turn right on Hwy. 30 to Lahaina town.

③ ★★ Lahaina. After a day on the remote island of Lāna'i, head for the bustling town of Lahaina. Plan to arrive in this historic town early, before the crowds. I recommend a big breakfast—at **Mala Ocean Tavern** (p 129) or **Lahaina Coolers** (p 128)—then put on your walking shoes and take the self-guided **historic walking tour** of the old town (p 50), do some browsing in the quaint stores (p 112), and watch the surfers skim the waves in front of the library.

Skimboarders ride the waves in Lahaina.

Travel Tip—Rush Hour

Plan ahead to avoid Maui's rush hour, which lasts from 7 to 9am and from 4 to 6pm. Roads can be packed bumper-to-bumper—not a fun way to spend your vacation!

From the West Maui coast, take Honoapi'ilani Hwy. 30 through Mā'alea and then branch northeast on Kuihelani Hwy. 380, which becomes Airport Road. Follow the signs towards the heliport, turning right on Kala Road. Make a left on Leleipio Place.

④A ★★★ Maui from above. Day 4 gets you a bird's-eye view of the island. Flying over Maui in a helicopter will give you an entirely different perspective of the island, from canyons and lush rainforests to plunging waterfalls and mountain peaks. Of all the helicopter companies, I think **Blue Hawaiian Helicopter** (p 102) offers the most comfortable, informative, and thrilling tours.

After your flight, head to Wailuku. Return to Airport Road. Turn right (northwest) on Hāna Hwy. 36. Follow Hwy. 36 until it merges with Hwy. 32 (Ka'ahumanu Ave.), which will take you into Wailuku (the street name changes to Main St. in Wailuku).

Meander around the old town of **④B ★★ Wailuku** (see the walking tour on p 60). Visit Native Intelligence (p 118) and stop at the Bailey House Museum (p 44). Continue up

Kahakuloa Head on the North Shore.

Main Street, which becomes 'Īao Valley Road, to the end, where you will be in ④C ★★ **'Īao Valley** (p 44). Hike the trails or pack a swimsuit and plunge into the cool mountain streams that run through the 'Īao Valley park.

From here, retrace your route back to Main Street in Wailuku. From there, make a left on N. Market Street, then a right on Mill Street, which ends at Lower Main Street. Turn left and, as you near the coast, go left again onto Waiheu Beach Road (Hwy. 340). Take the second left onto Kuhio Place and then take your first left on Hea Place.

At the end of the street are the ancient temples of ④D **Hale Ki'i** and **Pihana Heiau** (see p 71). If you aren't too tired, take the long route back to West Maui via the ④E **Kahekili Highway** (see p 44 for its storied history): Return to Waiheu Beach Road (Hwy. 340), turn left, and when the road ends, make a right onto Kahekili Highway (also Hwy. 340). Follow Hwy. 340 northeast about 12 winding miles (19km) to visit the ancient Hawaiian village of ④F **Kahakuloa** (see p 44). From there it is another 21 miles (34km) on Hwy 340 then Hwy. 30 to return to Lahaina.

To fly to Moloka'i for the day, go to Kahului Airport. From West Maui, take Hwy. 30 to just past Mā'alaea and veer right onto Kui-helani Hwy. 380, which becomes Airport Road.

⑤ ★★★ **Kalaupapa National Park.** For an unforgettable all-day adventure, hop over to Moloka'i to visit the beautiful, haunting **Kalaupapa Peninsula.** Meet up with **Damien Tours** to explore this extraordinary island, which is now a National Historic Park. You can either hike or ride a mule down the world's tallest sea cliffs, and then take a bus tour of historic sites, most relating to its 19th-century role as a compulsory "home" to sufferers of Hansen's Disease, also known as leprosy. See p 62 for more details.

From West Maui, take Hwy. 30 south, pick up Hwy. 380 just past Mā'alea, and turn right on to Hwy. 36. Take another right on Hwy. 37 and follow it southeast through Pukalani. Turn left on Hwy. 377, then right at the sign to the Haleakalā National Park on Hwy. 378 and take it to the top. The summit is 40 to 50 miles (64–80km) from West Maui. Allow at least 2 hours.

⑥A ★★★ **Haleakalā National Park.** Cool off and dress warmly for Day 6 at the summit of this 10,000-foot volcano. For details on exploring this volcano, see p 89 and 101; if you have time, you'll want to add on the rural towns of ⑥B ★★ **Makawao** (p 64) and ⑥C ★★ **Pā'ia** (p 33).

To reach Hāna Highway from Lahaina/Ka'anapali, take Hwy. 30 south to Hwy. 380 and turn right (northeast). In Kahului Hwy. 380

becomes Dairy Road. Turn right (east) on Hwy. 36, otherwise know as the Hāna Highway.

7 ★★★ **Hāna Highway.** On Day 7, pack your bags and head out to heavenly Hāna along the famous Hāna Highway (see p 66 for a complete driving tour). Stop in **Pā 'ia** for snacks at **Mana Foods** (p 67). Visit the napping sea turtles at **Ho'okipa Beach Park** (p 78). From here on out, cell service is nil. You'll spend the next few days unplugged and blissed out in East Maui's rain-forested hinterlands.

8 ★★★ **Hāna and**
9 ★★★ **Kīpahulu.** In addition to the activities in Hāna listed on p 70 **5**, visit the **Kīpahulu District of Haleakalā National Park** (see p 88 for full information). Pack a pic-nic lunch and hike to **Waimoku Falls,** above 'Ohe'o Gulch (see p 87).

After 'Ulapalakua, Hwy. 31 becomes Hwy. 37. Follow it across the island to Hāna Hwy. 36 and turn left. Take the next left onto Hansen Road and follow it until it ends at Mokulele Hwy. (Hwy. 311). Turn left and head south. Hwy. 311 becomes Hwy 31, Pi'ilani Hwy., which ends at Wailea. The drive will take a little more than an hour.

10 ★★ **Wailea.** Spend a day relax-ing in this tony resort area: Indulge yourself at a spa (p 34), lounge on Wailea Beach (p 82), or browse the Shops at Wailea (p 119).

Haleakalā's crater.

A mule ride on Molokai is an unfor-gettable adventure.

To get to Mākena Beach from Wailea, h take Hwy. 31 south, which ends at Wailea 'Ike Drive. Turn left at the intersection onto Wailea Alanui Road, which becomes Mākena Alanui Road. Turn right on Mākena Road to Mākena Bay. From there to La Pérouse Bay con-tinue on Mākena Road until it ends, then take off on foot for a couple of miles to reach the bay.

11 ★★★ **Mākena.** Take things easy on Day 11 by venturing out to wild, untamed Mākena and beyond. Consider exploring this scenic coast by kayak—the water is calm and clear enough that you can see the fish, and you are protected from the wind (see "Kayak Tours," p 106). After a couple of hours of kayaking and snorkeling at **Mākena Landing**, break for a picnic lunch. If you have energy to spare, hike over to **La Pérouse Bay,** along the rugged

Upcountry, the Ali'i Kula Lavender Farm welcomes visitors.

verdant farmlands. (See the driving tour on p 38 for fuller details). Book a multi-farm trip with **Maui Country Farm Tours** (p 39), a luncheon at **O'o Farm** (p 40), or investigate a few farms on your own. Cheese aficionados will love sampling fromage at the **Surfing Goat Dairy Tour** (p 39). The **Ali'i Kula Lavender Farm** (p 40), will revive your senses with its fragrant herb gardens.

🔞 Heading down the mountain, stop for dinner in the middle of the pineapple fields at **Hāli'imaile General Store.** See p 127.

Head south on Hwy. 31, South Kīhei Road.

⓮ **Kīhei.** After 13 days of exploring Maui, spend your last day doing whatever you love best in the laidback town of Kihei, whether it's shopping, beach hopping the 5 miles (8km) of white-sand beaches (see p 76), visiting the wildlife preserve (see p 57), or taking a whale-watch tour (p 107). Pick up a lei on your way to the airport to carry the scent of Maui with you home. ●

shoreline, and see the **'Ahihi-Kina'u Natural Area Reserve** (p 97). Return for a luxurious dinner at **Ka'ana Kitchen** or **Spago** (p 128 and 132).

The boat trip to Molokini departs from Mā'alaea Harbor. Travel on Hwy. 31 north, turn left on Hwy. 30. The left-turn exit to Mā'alaea comes up within a mile.

⓬ ★★★ **Molokini.** On Day 12, the deep sea beckons. Board a boat to Molokini Crater, that tiny crescent on the horizon. You'll see dazzling corals and schools of fish in 100 feet of crystal clear water. If it's whale season, you'll be treated to a show on the way over or back. I recommend taking one of **Trilogy's** tours (p 99).

Kula Hwy. 37 is the main road through Maui's upcountry. You can reach it either from the Hāna Hwy. 36 along the Hāna coast or from Pi'ilani Hwy 31 on the South Maui coast.

⓭ ★★ **Upcountry farm tours.** Return to the slopes of Haleakalā on Day 13 for a tour through Maui's

One of Kīhei's beaches.

Maui with Kids

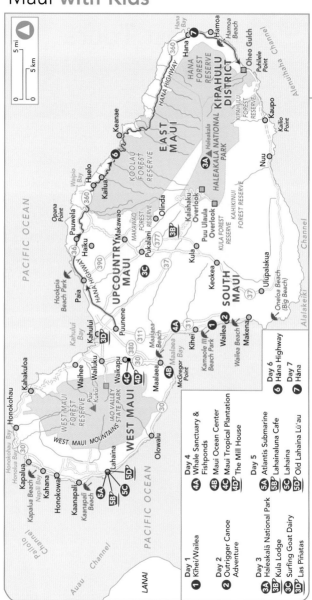

0 5 mi
0 5 km

PACIFIC OCEAN

Honokohau Bay
Honokohau
Honolua Bay

Kapalua Bay
Kapalua Beach
Napili Bay
Kahana
Honokowai
Kaanapali Beach
Kaanapali

Kahakuloa

WEST MAUI
FOREST
RESERVE

WEST MAUI MOUNTAINS STATE PARK

Puu
Kukui

IAO VALLEY
STATE PARK

Olowalu

Lahaina

Honolua Bay (30)

LANAI

Auau Channel

Pailolo Channel

Waihee
Waikapu
Wailuku
Waiehu

Kahului Bay
Kahului

Puunene

Maalaea
McGregor
Point

Maalaea Bay
Maalaea
Kihei

Kamaole III
Beach Park

Wailea Beach
Wailea
Makena

Oneloa Beach
(Big Beach)

SOUTH
MAUI

Keokea
Kula

Ulupalakua

Kula
KULA FOREST
RESERVE

Puu Ulaula
Overlook

Kalahaku
Overlook

HALEAKALA NATIONAL
PARK

Haleakala

KIPAHULU
FOREST
RESERVE

Kaupo

Kaulio
Point

Nuu

KAHIKINUI
FOREST RESERVE

Alalakeiki Channel

Alenuihaha Channel

Puhilele
Point

Oheo Gulch

KIPAHULU
DISTRICT

Hamoa Beach
Hamoa

Hana

Hana Bay

HANA
FOREST
RESERVE

EAST
MAUI

KOOLAU
FOREST
RESERVE

Keanae

Kailua
Huelo
Pauwela

Waipio Bay
Opana Point

Haiku
Makawao

Olinda

MAKAWAO
FOREST
RESERVE

UPCOUNTRY
MAUI

Pukalani

Kahakuloa

HANA HIGHWAY 360

Paia

Hookipa
Beach Park

HANA HIGHWAY 36

390

377

37

31

311

380

30

PACIFIC OCEAN

1 Day 1
Kihei/Wailea

2 Day 2
Outrigger Canoe
Adventure

Day 3
3A Haleakalā National Park
3B Kula Lodge
3C Surfing Goat Dairy
3D Las Piñatas

Day 4
4A Whale Sanctuary &
Fishponds
4B Maui Ocean Center
4C Maui Tropical Plantation
4D The Mill House

Day 5
5A Atlantis Submarine
5B Lahainaluna Cafe
5C Lahaina
5D Old Lahaina Lū'au

6 Day 6
Hāna Highway

7 Day 7
Hāna

Previous page: Sea jellies on display at the Maui Ocean Center.

The number-one rule of family travel is *don't plan too much,* especially with young children, who will be fighting jet lag, trying to get adjusted to a new bed (and most likely new food), and may be hyped up to the point of exhaustion. The 7-day itinerary below is a guide to the various family-friendly activities available on Maui; I suggest staying in a convenient South Maui (Kīhei or Wailea) condo or resort for the first 5 nights. Then venture out to Hāna for an unforgettable last night. START: **Kīhei/Wailea.**

Travel Tip

See chapter 10 for hotel recommendations and chapter 8 for detailed reviews of the restaurants mentioned in this chapter.

❶ Kīhei/Wailea Beach & Pool.

The first thing kids will want to do is hit the water. **Wailea Beach** (p 82), fronting the Four Seasons and the Grand Wailea resorts, is a safe place to start. If your youngsters aren't used to the waves, consider sticking to the swimming pool at your hotel. (If you're staying at the Grand Wailea, with its fantasy water park, they'll be ecstatic with this choice.) You'll probably want an early dinner with food your kids are used to. My family-friendly picks in Kīhei: **Nalu's South Shore Grill** (p 130) or **Peggy Sue's** (p 130). Get to bed early.

Canoe trips may leave from Polo or Wailea Beach, or from Olowalu, halfway to Lahaina on Honoapi'ilani Hwy. 30.

After a long plane ride, the beach is a great first stop for kids and adults.

❷ ★★★ Outrigger Canoe

Adventure. Day 2 is the prime time to build upon your family's cooperation and teamwork. Climb into a six-person outrigger canoe and learn how to paddle in sync while you explore the South Maui coastline amidst surfacing sea turtles, curious manta rays, and, in winter months, humpback whales. Several resorts, such as the Fairmont Kea Lani, have their own canoes and guides. My favorite company to paddle with is **Hawaiian Paddle Sports** (p 105). After a few hours on the water, reward your brave ocean explorers with shave ice at **Ululani's** (p 132) and sushi at **Sansei** (p 131)—maybe even with a little karaoke fun.

Allow 1 hour and 45 minutes to reach the Haleakalā summit from South Maui. Go north on Pi'ilani Hwy. 31 to Mokulele Hwy. 311. Turn right on Hansen Road, merge onto Hāna Hwy. 36, then turn right onto Haleakalā Hwy. 37. Turn left onto Hwy. 377 and left again onto Hwy. 378.

❸Ⓐ ★★★ Haleakalā National

Park. Today is the day to tackle the 10,000-foot (3,048m) dormant volcano at Maui's heart. Depending on the age of your children, you can either hike in the crater, speed down the mountain on a bicycle, or just wander about the park. See p 84 in chapter 6 for details. *www. nps.gov/hale.* ☎ *808/572-4400. Daily 8am–3:45pm.*

3B **Kula Lodge.** Either on the way to or from Haleakalā, stop off at this upcountry lodge to let your kids pile into its renowned huge breakfasts. See p 128.

From the summit, retrace Hwy. 378 to Hwy. 377 to Hwy. 37 and turn left onto Ōma'opio Road. Look for the SURFING GOAT DAIRY sign on the left about 4 miles (6.4km) down. Allow 1 hour and 10 minutes.

3D **Surfing Goat Dairy.** Your kids will love petting and playing with the four-legged kids of the goat variety. If you time it right, you can help with the evening chores and milking—at 3:15pm Monday through Saturday. See p 39.

Continue down the mountain on Ōma'opio Road, which after MM 5 joins Pulehu Road (Hwy. 370). When the road ends, turn right on Ho'okele Street, left on Hāna Hwy, then right on Dairy Road to Las Piñatas of Maui.

3E **Las Piñatas of Maui.** Kids can stick to the comfort zone with cheese quesadillas while the grown-ups can go nuts over cilantro-jalapeño-battered fish tacos. 395 Dairy Rd., Kahului. ☎ 808/877-8707. $.

Shark tanks enthrall youngsters at the Maui Ocean Center.

4A **Whale Sanctuary & Fishpond.** Today's the day to study Maui's rich marine life. Head up coastal S. Kihei Road, which parallels Hwy. 31, and stop by the **Hawaiian Humpback Whale Sanctuary Visitor Center** (726 S. Kīhei Rd.; http://hawaiihumpbackwhale.noaa.gov; ☎ 808/831-4888) to learn about the giants of the sea. Next door, the **Ko'ie'ie Fishpond** is a prime example of ancient Hawaiian aquaculture.

Head north on S. Kihei Rd., which merges into N. Kīhei Rd. Turn left onto Honapi'ilani Hwy 30.

4B **Maui Ocean Center.** On your way north, the kids may enjoy stretching their legs along the **Kealia Boardwalk** (just north of

Goats at the Surfing Goat Dairy.

Ziplining at the Maui Tropical Plantation.

MM2 on North Kīhei Rd.). Then continue to the **Maui Ocean Center** to spend a couple of hours gazing at the ocean life in this big aquarium. *See p 28.*

Return to Honoapi'ilani Hwy 30 and head north to the Maui Tropical Plantation in Waikapū.

4C Maui Tropical Plantation. Explore the plantation's verdant grounds, take a 40-minute tram ride through exotic flora and fruit, and soar on a speedy zipline that will amuse even jaded teenagers. *See p 60.*

4D The Mill House. The menu might be a little adventurous for youngsters, but they'll love the train engines, gears, and fantasy fountains decorating this eclectic restaurant. Adults will love the refined cuisine and handcrafted cocktails. *At Maui Tropical Plantation, 1670 Honoapi'ilani Hwy., Waikapū* ☎ *808/270-0333. $$$.*

Head north on Pi'ilani Hwy. 31. Turn left onto North Kīhei Road, then left onto Honoapi'ilani Hwy. 30. Turn left onto Prison Street, right onto Front Street, and find parking.

5A Atlantis Submarine. In Lahaina you can take the kids

underwater in a Jules Verne–type fantasy, the **Atlantis Submarine**). You'll plunge 100 feet (30m) under the sea in a state-of-the-art, high-tech submarine and meet swarms of vibrant tropical fish up close as they flutter through the deep blue waters. Atlantis offers trips out of Lahaina Harbor, every hour on the hour from 9am to 2pm. *658 Front St. www.goatlantis.com.* ☎ *800/ 548-6262 or 808/667-2224. $115 adults, $48 children 11 and under (children must be at least 3 ft/9m tall). Book online to save 10%.*

5B Lahainaluna Cafe. Grab fancy grilled cheese sandwiches, hot dogs, and soba noodle salads from this casual courtyard restaurant, and then reward yourself with shave ice from Ululani's (p 132) next door. *790 Front St, Lahaina.* ☎ *808/757-8286. $.*

5C Lahaina. In the afternoon, wander around Lahaina (see walking tour p 50). Even if you don't visit all the attractions, be sure to hit the kid-friendly highlights, including the giant **Banyan Tree**, the **Old Lahaina Courthouse**, and the **Old Prison**. Then pick a nearby beach—gentle **Launiupoko County Wayside Park** (p 81) for younger children to paddle around, or long

A Great Way to Spend a Rainy Day

If it rains during your vacation, take the kids to **Maui Ocean Center** (www.mauioceancenter.com; ☎ 808/270-7000), located at 192 Mā'alaea Rd. in Mā'alaea. Introduce the *keiki* (children) to the underwater world, without getting wet. This terrific aquarium starts with the reef world, where you can see the animals living in the reefs surrounding Maui. Then the exhibits go deep—very deep—to feature big pelagic fish like 100-pound tunas and sleek barracudas. But most kids' favorite exhibit has to be the shark tanks, where you can watch these kings of the deep prowl through the water. ***Budget hint:*** Save money by booking online.

Ka'anapali Beach (p 79) for teenagers to swim or snorkel.

5D **Old Lahaina Lū'au.** Book seats far in advance for the **Old Lahaina Lū'au** (p 127) in the evening. Your drive back to the hotel will take about 30 minutes to Kihei, or 45 minutes to Wailea-Makena.

Head north on Pi'ilani Hwy. 31 to Mokulele Hwy 311. Turn right on Hansen Road, then right on Hāna Hwy. With stops, this drive will take the whole day.

6 **★★★ Hāna Highway.** Get an early start, pack your bags, and head out to heavenly Hāna. (see detailed driving tour p 66). Stop in **Pā'ia** for snacks at **Mana Foods** (p 67). Visit the napping sea turtles at **Ho'okipa Beach Park** (p 78). Pull over often and let the kids get out to take photos, smell the flowers, and jump in the mountain-stream pools. Stop for ice cream at **Coconut Glen's** (see p. 69) and dig your toes into the black sand at **Wai'ānapanapa State Park** (p 91). Spend the night in Hāna (see tour p 70).

7 **★★★ Hāna & Home.** Hopefully you've scheduled a flight later

The Atlantis Submarine.

in the day, so that you can make the most of your last day on Maui. Pick one activity to experience before leaving Hāna, depending on your children's ages and interests: bodysurfing at **Hāmoa Beach** (p 78), hiking to waterfalls in the **Kīpahulu District of Haleakalā National Park** (p 12), or spelunking in **Ka'eleku Cave** (205 Ula'ino Rd.; www.mauicave.com; ☎ **808/ 248-7308**). Return to Kahului Airport on Hāna Highway.

Swimming holes beckon along the Road to Hāna.

Family-Friendly Events

Your trip may be more exciting with the added attraction of attending a celebration, festival, or party on Maui. Check out the following events:

- **Chinese New Year,** Lahaina (☎ **888/310-1117**). In 2018, lion dancers will be snaking their way around Maui towns, celebrating the Chinese Year of the Dog. Lahaina rolls out the red carpet with a traditional lion dance, accompanied by fireworks, food booths, and a host of activities.
- **World Whale Day,** Kalama Park, Kīhei (www.mauiwhalefestival. org; ☎ **808/249-8811**). In early to mid-February, this daylong celebration features a parade of whales, entertainment, a crafts fair, games, and food.
- **Whale & Ocean Arts Festival,** Lahaina (www.visitlahaina.com; ☎ **888/310-1117**). Kids love this mid-March event with marine-related activities, games, and a touch-pool exhibit.
- **Annual Lei Day Celebration,** islandwide (www.gohawaii.com/ maui; ☎ **808/875-4100**). May Day is Lei Day in Hawai'i, celebrated with lei-making contests, pageantry, arts and crafts, and concerts.
- **King Kamehameha Celebration,** islandwide (www.visitlahaina. com; ☎ **888/310-1117**). June 10 is a state holiday with a massive floral parade, a *ho'olaulea* (party), and much more.
- **Fourth of July Parade & Rodeo,** Makawao. (www.facebook. com/MakawaoTownParade; ☎ **808/879-8047**). Hawaiian cowboys ride up Baldwin Avenue on the first Saturday in July, on their way to an exciting rodeo.
- **Maui County Fair,** War Memorial Complex, Wailuku (www. mauifair.com; ☎ **800/525-MAUI** [6284]). At the end of September or early October, this traditional county fair features a parade, amusement rides, live entertainment, and exhibits.

Romantic Maui

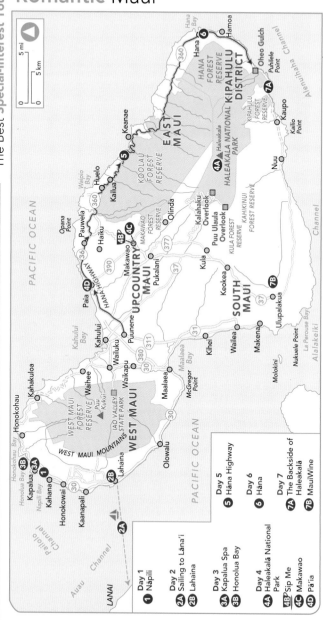

Day 1
1 Nāpili

Day 2
2A Sailing to Lāna'i
2B Lahaina

Day 3
3A Kapalua Spa
3B Honolua Bay

Day 4
4A Haleakalā National Park
4B Sip Me
4C Makawao
4D Pā'ia

Day 5
5 Hāna Highway

Day 6
6 Hāna

Day 7
7A The Backside of Haleakalā
7B MauiWine

Maui's sensual landscape makes it the perfect place to fall in love. The scent of flowers, the sound of tumbling waves, and the island's intoxicating beauty beckon lovers. If you're discovering Maui as a twosome for a week, I suggest spending the first 3 nights in Nāpili, 1 night in Pā'ia and the final 2 in Hāna. START: **Nāpili.**

① ★★★ **Nāpili.** Check into the Nāpili Kai Resort (p 148), go for a swim in the turquoise bay, and get dressed for your private **Na Hoku Dinner**—a four-course torchlit feast for two set on a romantic perch overlooking the ocean. Book the dinner in advance.

Head south on Honoapi'ilani Hwy. 30 to Dickenson Street and find parking near Lahaina Harbor. It's a 22-minute drive. Allow extra time for traffic.

②A ★★★ **Sailing to Lāna'i.** Climb aboard **Trilogy** (p 99), my favorite sailing outfit, and chase the horizon to Lāna'i. On the half-day excursion, the crew hands you hot cinnamon rolls and coffee as soon as you step on board, and after the 9-mile (14km) trip to Lāna'i, you'll snorkel in the island's protected waters and land for a barbecue lunch. Upon your return, spend the remainder of the day strolling through **②B** historic **Lahaina** (see tour p 50). Dine at **Gerard's** (p 126) or **Lahaina Grill** (p 128).

Head north on Lower Honoapi'ilani Rd., turning left onto Bay Dr. to get to Spa Montage.

③A ★★★ **Kapalua Spa Morning.** A visit to any of the island's spas would be a treat, but **Spa Montage** (1 Bay Dr., Kapalua; www. montagehotels.com/spamontage; ☎ 800/548-6262 or 808/665-8282) has a few perks for couples: a co-ed spa pool and gorgeous garden *hale* (houses) with romantic rock tubs. Plus, it's only 2 minutes up the road. After indulging in luxurious massages or body treatments, take

a walk along the **Kapalua Coastal Trail** (accessed from multiple points along the coast, between the Merriman's Maui parking lot and D.T. Fleming Beach.)

Take Office Road inland to connect with Honoapi'ilani Hwy. 30. Turn left and continue on to Honolua Bay at MM #32 and Nakalele Blowhole at MM #38.5. Return the same way.

③B **Honolua Bay.** At MM 32, leave the highway to explore this jeweled bay. Linger a little on the forest path; snorkel in the bay (or watch surfers if the waves are up). Then continue on to see the **Nākālele Blowhole**. (The cars crowding the roadside at MM 38.5 are the tip-off.) Stay a safe distance from the explosive saltwater geyser. Turn around and look at the lava rock walls facing the blowhole. You'll see a perfect photo-op: a **heart-shaped rock.** It's actually a heart-shaped window in the rock that frames the dramatic coast—a perfect place to document your love. Dine at one of Kapalua's fine restaurants

Butterfly fish greet snorkelers in Honolua Bay.

Find the heart-shaped hole in the rock by the Nākālele Blowhole.

(see chapter 8 for ideas) and tuck in early for a big day tomorrow.

Allow 2.5 hours to drive to the summit of Haleakalā. Head south on Hwy. 30, then go right on Hwy. 380, right on Hwy. 36, and right again on Hwy. 37. Then follow Hwy. 377 to Hwy. 378.

4A Haleakalā. To-do list for the night before: pack your belongings, amass every stitch of warm clothing available, order an early morning delivery of hot coffee or cocoa from room service, and set your alarm clock. In the wee hours before dawn, drive to **Haleakalā National Park** in time for sunrise on the summit of this dormant volcano. (You must reserve your spot online several days in advance.) The two of you, swaddled in sweatshirts and beach towels (it's cold at 10,000 ft./3,048m), will watch the multitude of stars slowly fade and first sunbeams of the new day appear—guaranteed to be a magical memory. *See p 87.*

Retrace your route down Hwy. 378, turn right onto Hwy. 377, and go north to Hanamu Rd. and turn right. At the end of Hanamu Rd., turn left onto Olinda Rd. Follow Olinda into Makawao town, where

Getting Maui'd

Maui weddings are magic. Not only does the entire island exude natural beauty and romance, it also has an experienced industry in place to help you with every detail.

Most Maui resorts and hotels have wedding coordinators who can plan everything from a simple, relatively low-cost wedding to an extravaganza that people will talk about for years. Remember that resorts can be pricey—be frank with your planner if you want to keep costs down. Independent companies such as **White Orchid Wedding** (1961 E. Vineyard St., Wailuku; www.whiteorchid wedding.com; ☎ **800/240-9336**) and Sugar Beach Events (85 N. Kīhei Rd., Kīhei; www.sugarbeachevents.com; ☎ **808/856-6151**) have exclusive access to stunning venues and can help you select photographers, caterers, and florists.

You can plan your own island wedding, even from afar, without spending a fortune. The chef/owner of CJ's Deli & Diner in Ka'anapali offers useful tips for DIY brides on his blog: www.cjsmaui.com/blog. For a marriage license, go online to https://emrs.ehawaii.gov/emrs/public/home.html. A license costs $60 and is good for 30 days.

Watching windsurfers at Ho'okipa Beach.

it becomes Baldwin Ave. Take Baldwin down to Pā'ia.

4B Given your pre-dawn start, you may be needing a caffeine boost by now. Try **Sip Me** (3617 Baldwin Ave. Makawao; www.sipmemaui.com; ☎ 808/573-2340), which opens at 6am, or **Pā'ia Bay Coffee** (115 Hāna Hwy., Pā'ia; www.paiabaycoffee.com; ☎ 808/579-3111), which serves great espresso and breakfast starting at 7am. Follow the signs in the Nalu Place alley.

Makawao & Pā'ia Spend the rest of the day exploring **4C** Makawao, Maui's *paniolo* (Hawaiian cowboy) town and **4D** Pā'ia, the hippy surf town on the north shore. Shop, relax in one of several cafés, or go for a dip at beautiful **H.P. Baldwin Park** (p 78). Drive out to **Ho'okipa Beach Park** (p 78) to watch the windsurfers and see the napping sea turtles. Double back for dinner at the incomparable **Mama's Fish House** (p 129). Stay at a nearby boutique inn or vacation rental. See Chapter 10 for suggestions.

Head east on Hwy. 36 toward Hāna. With stops, this 44.5 mile (72km) drive will take a whole day.

5 Hāna Highway. Keep your swimsuit handy, put the top down, and turn the radio up. Plan on spending the entire day cruising the curves of Maui's most famous road. Stop at waterfalls, go for a swim in tranquil pools, buy five passionfruit for a dollar at a roadside stand, share a picnic, and enjoy every spontaneous moment. Lush, tropical Hāna is the perfect place for romance, and it's well worth spending a couple of nights here. *See p 66.*

6 Hāna. Ready for some relaxing beach time? Choose between the fiery red beach at **Kaihalulu Beach** (p 79), the perfect crescent bay at **Hāmoa Beach** (p 78), or the freshwater pools at **'Ohe'o Gulch** (p 87), where you can sit and soak while watching the waves rolling ashore. Around sunset, walk the ancient coastal trail in **Wai'ānapanapa State Park** (p 91). For more detailed information on Hāna's sights, see the tour on p 70. Splurge for dinner at the **Preserve Kitchen & Bar** at Travaasa Hāna (p 131).

Continue past Hāna on Hwy. 360, which becomes Hwy. 31 at Kaupō, to 'Ulupalakua. Allow 45 minutes to an hour.

7A The "Back Side" of Haleakalā. Pack snacks and water before leaving Hāna to explore the "backside" around Maui past Kaupō. See p 12 for details. When you reach 'Ulupalakua, duck into **7B MauiWine** (p 41). Sample a few of Maui vintages, and toast your romance on the grounds of the old estate.

A wedding chapel in Maui.

Relax & Rejuvenate on Maui

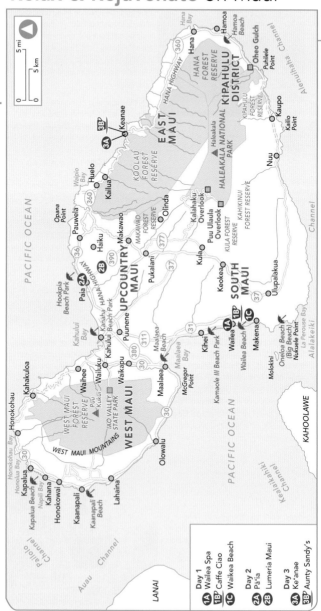

Day 1
- 1A Wailea Spa
- 1B Caffe Ciao
- 1C Waikea Beach

Day 2
- 2A Pa'ia
- 2B Lumeria Maui

Day 3
- 3A Ke'anae
- 3B Aunty Sandy's

Maui's near-perfect weather, unspoiled beaches, lush tropical vegetation, and invigorating tradewinds are just the recipe to soothe your body, mind, and spirit. Below are some of my favorite ways to relax over a 3-day weekend. START: **Wailea.**

Open-air spa at the Four Seasons Resort.

1A Wailea Spa Day. There are wonderful spas to choose from at several resorts all over Maui (see box p 36), but in my opinion, the best place to start is in Wailea, by booking a massage, either at the opulent **Spa Grande at the Grand Wailea Resort** or in a thatched hale (house) at the **Four Seasons Resort Maui** (p 146). The Four Seasons spa is wonderful, but I love the smell of salt in the air and the gentle whisper of the wind while experiencing Hawaiian *lomilomi* (massage).

1B Caffe Ciao (in the Fairmont Kea Lani, 4100 Wailea Alanui Dr., Wailea; www.fairmont.com/kea-lami-maui; ☎ 808/875-4100) is one of my favorite South Maui spots for a casual lunch. The deli & bakery at the Kea Lani resort serves wonderful roasted veggie sandwiches, açaí bowls, and pastries almost too pretty to eat.

1C Wailea beaches. After your spa treatment, walk along the beach path, looking for whales and inhaling the fragrance of the native flowers growing on the rocky coastline. Float in the warm, tropical waters at one of several beaches nearby (see chapter 5 for more details). For an elegant finish, dine at **Morimoto Maui** (p 129).

Take Wailea 'Ike Dr. up to Pi'ilani Hwy. 31. Continue on Mokulele Hwy. 311 towards Kahului. Turn right on Hansen Road, and merge onto on Hāna Hwy. 36. Continue to Pā'ia.

2A Pā'ia. On day two, head out to Pā'ia, the plantation-town-turned-hippy-haven on Maui's north shore (see shopping map, p 114). A dilapidated sugar mill looms over Baldwin Avenue like a steam punk sculpture, evidence of the industry that built this town 100-plus years ago. In the 1960s hippies dropped out here, and in the '80s windsurfers moved in, having discovered nearby **Ho'okipa** (p 78), one of the world's best places to catch air from the sea. Today you'll find eclectic cafés, yoga studios, and bikini shops crowding the intersection of Baldwin and

Relax, Breathe Deep & Say "Sp-Ahh"

Hawai'i's spas are airy, open facilities that embrace the tropics. Here are your best options on Maui:

- **Spa Grande at the Grand Wailea Resort** (www.grandwailea. com; ☎ 800/888-6100 or 808/875-1234): Hawai'i's most opulent spa combines Japanese-style *furo* baths and Swiss-jet showers with traditional Hawaiian treatments and island-inspired products. You can easily spend half a day luxuriating in the two-story marble bathhouse and toning muscles in the state-of-the-art fitness center. It's great for bachelorette parties. Day passes include a complimentary mango scrub.

- **Spa Montage at Kapalua Bay** (www.montagehotels.com/ spamontage; ☎ 808/665-8282): This freestanding spa facility in Kapalua has perks for couples: a co-ed spa pool, a huge yoga/ fitness studio with an ocean view, and private treatment *hale* (houses) with romantic rock tubs. Day passes are available.

- **The Spa at the Four Seasons Resort Maui at Wailea** (www. fourseasons.com/maui; ☎ 800/334-MAUI [6284] or 808/874-8000): Imagine the sounds of the waves rolling on Wailea Beach as you are soothingly massaged in the privacy of your cabana, tucked into the beachside foliage. This is the place to come to be absolutely spoiled.

- **The Spa at Travaasa Hana** (www.travaasa.com/hana; ☎ 888/ 820-1043): Hāna is relaxing in its own right, but when you add a lava rock hot tub and expert *lomilomi* (Hawaiian massage) therapists to the equation, it's next level.

- **Waihua Spa at Ritz-Carlton, Kapalua** (www.ritzcarlton.com/ kapalua; ☎ 800/262-8440 or 808/669-6200): *Waihua* translates as "healing waters." The treatments at this serene 17,500-square-foot (1,626 sq. m) spa are rooted in ancient Hawaiian techniques and theories on healing.

- **Willow Stream Spa at the Fairmont Kea Lani Maui** (www. fairmont.com/kea-lani-maui; ☎ 808/875-2229): This intimate spa offers a mud bar and Hawaiian rain showers. The fitness center next door is open 24 hours with a personal trainer on duty.

Hāna Highway. Willie Nelson sometimes drops by to play a surprise set with his son Lukas Nelson at **Charley's** (p 137). The Dalai Lama himself visited Pā'ia, to bless the gleaming white and gold stupa at the **Maui Dharma Center** (81 Baldwin Ave; ☎ 808/579-8076). Pop in and give the prayer wheel a reverent spin.

Head up Baldwin Ave. to Lumeria, 3.4 miles (5.5km) up on the left.

㉕ Lumeria Maui. Check into this retreat center (p 148) and try out one of the many complimentary classes: yin yoga, Tibetan bowl sound bath, Kundalini meditation, or 5 Rhythms dance. For dinner,

The Maui Dharma Center in Pāʻia.

return to Pāʻia for savory crepes or deep-flavored curries at **Café Des Amis** (p 126).

From Lumeria, take Baldwin Ave. back to Pāʻia and turn right onto Hāna Hwy. 36. Park on the roadside just after MM 16 and before the turnoff to Keʻanae Rd.

3A Keʻanae. Enjoy a delicious organic breakfast at Lumeria's

onsite restaurant **Wooden Crate** (complimentary with your room rate), then head out on the Hāna Highway for a rainforest tour. Park at the **Keʻanae Arboretum** and pass through the turnstile. This easy 2-mile (3.2km) stroll through a rainforest is a wonderful way to relax and commune with nature. I'd allow at least 2 hours here, longer if you bring your swimsuit and plunge into the swimming hole near the end of the trail. You start off on a flat trail where you can see the plants that have been introduced to Hawaiʻi (all with identification tags). The rainbow eucalyptus, while not native to these Islands, are downright magical. After your hike, drive down **Keʻanae Road** to explore the peninsula. Let the salty breeze tousle your hair at the shore.

3B Visit **Aunty Sandy's** (210 Keʻanae Rd., Keʻanae ☎ 808/248-7448) welcome shack for some homemade still-warm banana bread. Buy two loaves, since the first won't make it home.

Keʻanae Arboretum.

Maui's **Farmlands**

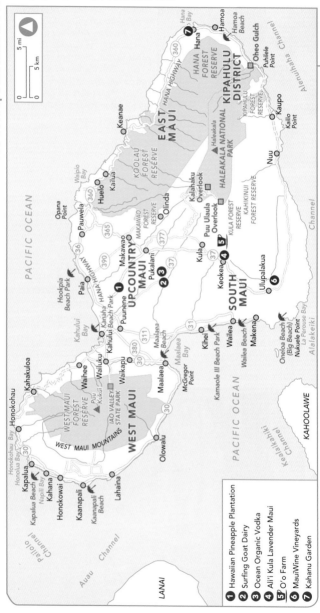

1. Hawaiian Pineapple Plantation
2. Surfing Goat Dairy
3. Ocean Organic Vodka
4. Ali'i Kula Lavender Maui
5. O'o Farm
6. MauiWine Vineyards
7. Kahanu Garden

When people think of Maui, flowers or pineapple often come to mind, but Maui's fertile soil grows lush fields of everything from sweet onions to lavender, coffee, chocolate, and every tropical fruit you can imagine, including dragonfruit. The island even has its own vodka farm! Below is a 1- or 2-day tours of Maui's bounty. START: **Hāli'imaile**.

Taste of Maui

To visit the farms listed here, as well as others, book a guided bus tour with **Maui Country Farm Tours** (www.mauicountryfarmtours.com; ☎ 808/283-9131). Marilyn Jansen Lopes and her husband, Rick, share their rich knowledge of the history of Maui's sugar mills, coffee plantations, family farms, and vineyards. Tours start at $150 and include lunch.

❶ Hawaiian Pineapple Plantation. Start with Hawai'i's golden fruit by taking the 1½-hour Maui Pineapple Company tour. Learn about the prickly fruit's history and how to grow, harvest, and pack it. Sample sweet slices along the way. ① *1½ hr. Across from the Hāli'imaile General Store, Hāli'imaile Rd., Hāli'imaile. http://mauipineappletour.com. ☎ 808/665-5491. Daily tram tours starting at 9:30am or 11:45am. Adults $67. From Hāli'imaile, head west to Haleakalā Hwy. 37. Turn right at the light and continue to ' Ōma'opio Road. Turn left and*

drive 4 miles to Ikena Kai Place. Watch for Surfing Goat Dairy signs nailed to trees.

❷ kids Surfing Goat Dairy. In Kula, just beyond the sugar-cane fields and on the slopes of Haleakalā, lies this dairy, where some 140 dairy goats blissfully graze the 42 acres (17ha) and contribute the milk for the 24 different cheeses that are made every day. Choose from the 2-hour **Grand Dairy Tour** ($25), where you can learn how to milk a goat, make cheese, and sample the different varieties; or drop by for the 20-minute casual dairy tour ($10, children $7). ① *20–120 min. 3651 Ōma'opio Rd., Kula. www.surfinggoatdairy.com. ☎ 808/878-2870. Open Mon–Sat 10am–3:15pm, Sun 10am–1pm.*

Return to Ōma'opio Road and turn left. Ocean Organic Vodka is less than 1 mile down.

❸ Ocean Organic Vodka. In Never heard of a vodka farm? Neither had I until this one opened just below Surfing Goat Dairy, halfway up

The Maui Pineapple Tour explores the history of Maui's famous fruit.

Wow! Look at the Size of That Fish

Enormous fish swim around the island of Maui. The largest caught in Maui waters, a Pacific blue marlin, tipped the scale at 1,200 pounds. To see some of these giants, wander down to the docks at Lahaina or Māʻalaea just after noon or around 5pm when sportfishing boats return with their catch. In September or October, some 75 teams compete in the island's largest fishing tournament, the **Lahaina Jackpot Fishing Tournament;** nightly fish weigh-ins at the

Fishing in Maui.

Lahaina Harbor start at 4pm. For more information contact the **Lahaina Yacht Club** (835 Front St., Lahaina; www.lahainayachtclub. org or www.lahainajackpot.com; ☎ **808/661-0191**).

Haleakalā. (The views alone are worth the price of admission.) Sustainably harvested sugarcane is blended with deep ocean mineral water to make fine-quality liquor at this solar-powered distillery Those 21 and over get to sample various spirits (and vodka-filled truffles!) and take home a souvenir shot glass. ⏱ *20–120 min. 4051 Ōmaʻopio Rd., Kula. www. oceanvodka.com.* ☎ *808/877-0009. Open daily 9:30am–5pm, Tours $12, Lunch $27 with 24-hour notice.*

Return up Ōmaʻopio Road to Hwy. 37 and turn right. Take the second left after Rice park onto Keak-aulike Hwy. 377, drive about ¼ mile around a bend, and take a quick right up Waipoli Road.

❹ Aliʻi Kula Lavender Maui.
Here, a choice of terrific tours take you to see the varieties of lavender that bloom year-round. I enjoy the daily 50-minute Walking Tour, which explores the grounds. You can add a Lavender Gourmet Lunch Basket

and taste the wonderful fruits of this farm as you gaze out over the breathtaking view. Walking Tour $10 in advance or $12 on site. ⏱ *30–50 min. for tour. 1100 Waipoli Rd., Kula. www.aliikulalavender.com.* ☎ *808/878-3004.*

❺ Oʻo Farm.
About ⅓ mile west of the lavender farm on Waipoli Rd., this bucolic orchard and biodynamic farm hosts scrumptious breakfast tours and gourmet lunches. Oʻo Farm supplies its sister restaurants in West Maui: Pacifico, **Feast at Lele** (p 126), and ʻAina Gourmet Market. Pluck your own coffee cherries, learn how beans are roasted, and then sit under a vine-covered canopy for a feast by chef Daniel Eskelsen. It's BYOB and costs $58—a deal if you make this your main meal of the day. ⏱ *2½ hours. 651 Waipoli Rd., Kula. www.oofarm. com.* ☎ *808/667-4341. Tours and lunch Mon–Thurs, 10:30am–2pm.*

From Kula take Hwy. 378 to Hwy. 377, then make a left turn on Hwy. 37. The winery is 9 miles (14.5km) down the road.

6 MauiWine Vineyards. Plan to arrive in time for a free tour (10:30am and 1:30pm) of Maui's only winery. Not only will you get to see the historic grounds, including the tasting room—once a guest cottage built for King Kalakaua in 1874—but you'll also learn about the six different varietals grown on the slopes of Haleakalā. ⏱ *1 hr. 14815 Pi'ilani Hwy., 'Ulupalakua. www.mauiwine.com.* ☎ *877/878-6058. Tasting room open daily 10am–5:30pm.*

Take Hwy. 31 east to Hāna. Just before MM 31, turn down Ula'ino Road toward the ocean. Allow about 2 hours driving time.

7 Kahanu Garden. The world's largest collection of breadfruit trees—a staple food for Pacific islanders—thrives here. The garden has some 130 distinct varieties gathered from 20 tropical island groups. You'll also view a Canoe

The world's largest collection of breadfruit trees, at Kahanu Garden.

Garden, filled with the many useful plants that the early Polynesian settlers brought by sea to Hawai'i: sugar cane, banana, sweet potato, taro, turmeric, and paper mulberry (used to make *kapa* cloth). The 3-acre stone *heiau* (temple) behind the garden testifies to ancient Hawaiian power. ⏱ *1–2 hr. Ula'ino Rd. www.ntbg.org/gardens/kahanu.* ☎ *808/248-8912. Mon–Sat 9am–2pm. Self-guided tours $10; guided tours: $25; children 12 and under free.*

Maui's Farmers' Markets

For the freshest Maui fruits, flowers, and produce (at budget prices), bring your re-usable bag to the closest farmers' market.

The best by far is the **Upcountry Farmers Market ★★★** (55 Kiopa'a St., Pukalani, in the Kulamalu Town Center parking lot; www.upcountryfarmersmarket.com). Every Saturday from 7 to 11am you'll find local honey, fresh-shucked coconuts, pickled veggies, and heaps of bright Maui-grown produce, plus ready-to-eat foods, flower bouquets, and gorgeous hand-carved cutting boards. Also on Saturday, in Kahului the **Maui Swap Meet ★★** (see p 120) rewards shoppers with produce from Ono Farms and other local growers.

In South Maui, the **Farmer's Market of Maui-Kīhei** is open from 8am to 4pm daily at 61 S. Kīhei Rd. On the West Side, try the **Honokowai Farmers' Market,** on Lower Honoapi'ilani Rd., across from the Honokowai Park. It's open Monday, Wednesday, and Friday, from 7 to 11am.

Maui's History & Culture

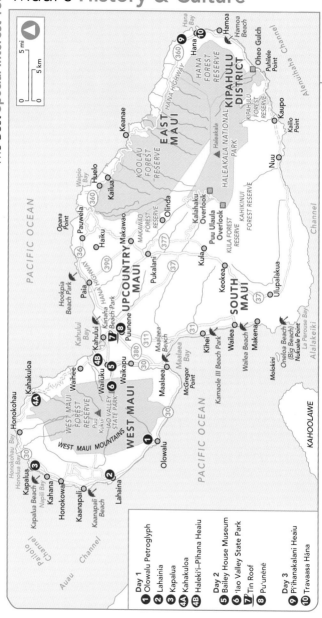

Day 1
1. Olowalu Petroglyph
2. Lahaina
3. Kapalua
4A. Kahakuloa
4B. Haleki'i–Pihana Heiau

Day 2
5. Bailey House Museum
6. 'Iao Valley State Park
7. Tin Roof
8. Pu'unēnē

Day 3
9. Pi'ihanakalani Heiau
10. Travaasa Hāna

Walk back in time on Maui, to when Polynesian wayfinders first settled the island around 1,000 years ago, to when whiskey-soaked whalers and prim missionaries arrived in the 1800s, and to the hard-scrabble days of sugar plantations and cattle ranches in the 1900s. This 3-day itinerary moves from West Maui to Central Maui to Hāna. Wailuku is a convenient home base for all three, or you can hotel-hop as you go (see chapter 10). START: **Olowalu.**

On Honoapi'ilani Hwy. 30 near MM 15, turn north on Luawai St. Drive .7 miles (1.1km). Follow signs to petroglyphs.

1 ★ **Olowalu Petroglyphs (Pu'u Kilea).** Start your voyage into Hawaiian history at this off-the-beaten-path archeological site. A cliff-face in the small village of Olowalu holds clues to the past: the shapes of people, animals, and sailing canoes chiseled into the rocks. Observe the ancient artwork in silence; let the grandeur of the West Maui Mountains overtake you. *Note:* Don't touch the petroglyphs or climb onto the rocks.

Continue north on Honoapi'ilani Hwy. 30, a 15-minute drive.

2 ★★★ **Lahaina.** This storied town, whose name translates as "merciless sun," dates back to at

least A.D. 700. Head over to the **Baldwin Home Museum** to begin the Lahaina walking tour (p 50), which covers the days of the whalers and missionaries and their effect on Lahaina. At night, immerse yourself in Hawaiian culture by attending the **'Ulalena** performance (p 138) or the **Old Lahaina Lū'au** (p 127).

Take Hwy. 30 north to Kapalua, a 20-minute drive.

3 **Kapalua.** Travel further back in time at the **Ritz-Carlton, Kapalua,** where the remains of hundreds of ancient Hawaiians were discovered during the resort's construction. This discovery sparked a cultural resurgence within the Native Hawaiian community. People came together to re-inter the sacred 'iwi (bones) and hotel was relocated inland. You'll find a plaque here

Baldwin Home Museum.

detailing the history. *Admission free; see p 149 for resort details.*

Continue north, past Kapalua, on Kahekili Hwy. 30 (which becomes Hwy. 340.). As the road bends, turn left on Waiehu Beach Road. Turn right on Kuhio Place (into a subdivision) and then take the first left on Hea Place, following it to the end. Allow 45 minutes to 1 hour to reach Wailuku.

④ ★★ Kahekili Highway (Hwy. 340). Along this highway (named for the great chief Kahekili, who built houses from the skulls of his enemies), nestled in a crevice between two steep hills, is the picturesque village of **④A Kahakuloa** with its red-roofed church and vivid green taro patches. Life here has not changed much during the past few decades. Continue into **④B Wailuku** to see an ancient site built in 1240 from stones carried up from the 'Īao Stream below. **Haleki'i-Pihana Heiau State Monument** sits forgotten atop a suburban hillside. Chief Kahekili lived here, as did the most sacred princess, Keōpūolani. When Kamehameha the Great came to wage war, 8-year-old Keōpūolani fled across the mountains to Lahaina. Kamehameha chased her all the way to the island of Moloka'i, where he married her to absorb her *mana* (power). Haleki'i ("house of images") has stacked rock walls and a thatched top, whereas Pihana Heiau ("gathering place of supernatural beings") is a pyramid-shaped mound of stones. If you sit quietly nearby (never climb on any *heiau*), you'll see that the view alone explains why this spot was chosen.

Return to Waiehu Beach Rd (Hwy. 340). Turn right onto Lower Main St. Shortly after St. Anthony School, turn right onto Lower Main

A church in Kahakuloa Village.

St. (same name, different road), which merges with Main St. Follow it up past High St. to the Bailey House Museum.

⑤ ★★ Bailey House Museum. Explore Central Maui on day two, starting with the 1833 home of missionary and sugar planter Edward Bailey, containing one of my favorite troves of Hawaiiana, with everything from foreboding *ki'i* (temple images) and rare collections of tree-snail shells, to latter-day relics like Duke Kahanamoku's 1919 redwood surfboard. ⏱ *30–45 min. 2375-A Main St. www.mauimuseum. org. ☎ 808/244-3326. Admission $7 adults, $5 seniors, $2 children 7–12, free for children 6 and under. Daily 10am–4pm.*

Continue up Main Street, which becomes 'Īao Valley Road, to the end.

⑥ ★★ 'Īao Valley State Park. It's hard to imagine that peaceful 'Īao Stream was the site of one of Maui's worst battles. In 1790 King Kamehameha and his men fought here to conquer the island. When the battle ended, so many bodies blocked the stream that the battle site was named Kepaniwai, or "damming of the waters." The park

Kings, Queens, & Deities

Discover the royal and supernatural history of Lahaina with **Maui Nei Native Expeditions ★★** (505 Front St., Lahaina, www. mauinei.com; ☎ **808/661-9494**). Your native Hawaiian *kumu*, or guide, will chant, tell stories, and reveal obscure sites of great importance to the Hawaiian monarchy. If you haven't viewed the queen's birthing stone or visited the former home of a powerful *mo'o* (lizard goddess), you haven't really seen Lahaina. Two-hour walking tours cost $50 and support the restoration of Moku'ula, one of the most significant archeological sites in all of Hawai'i—currently hidden beneath an unused ball field.

and stream get their names from the 'Īao Needle, a phallic rock that juts an impressive 2,250 feet (686m) above sea level. 'Īao in Hawaiian means "supreme cloud." **Note:** At press time, the park was closed for repair after major flooding.
🕐 *30–45 min. end of 'Īao Valley Rd. Entry fee $5 per car. Daily 7am–7pm.*

7 **Tin Roof.** Pop into this new local favorite for a taste of plantation-era cuisine. (See p 132) *360 Papa Pl., Kahului. www.tinroofmaui. com.* ☎ *808/868-0753.*

Retrace your route to Main Street and continue straight through Wailuku and Kahului. Turn right at the light onto South Pu'unēnē Avenue, and continue until Hansen Road. Museum is on the left.

8 **★ Pu'unēnē.** In the center of Maui, the town of Pu'unēnē (goose hill) has essentially disappeared. Once a thriving sugar plantation with numerous homes, churches, a school, and a hospital, Pu'unēnē is now just a post office, a shuttered sugar mill, and the **Alexander & Baldwin Sugar Museum** (Pu'unēnē Ave./Hwy. 350 and Hansen Rd.;

www.sugarmuseum.com; ☎ **808/ 871-8058**). Inside the humble museum, you'll learn how sugar was grown, harvested, and milled, and the inside story of how Samuel Alexander and Henry Baldwin (founders of Hawa 'i's largest and last sugar plantation, HC&S) managed to acquire huge chunks of land from the Kingdom of Hawai'i,

A display at the Alexander & Baldwin Sugar Museum.

The Best Special-Interest Tours

then ruthlessly fought to gain access to water on the other side of the island, making sugar cane an economically viable crop. ⏱ *30 min. Admission $7 adults, $5 seniors, $2 children 7–12, free for children 6 and under. Daily 9:30am–4pm.*

Head east on Hansen Road. Merge onto Hāna Hwy. 36. Continue east 45 miles (72.4km) to Ula'ino Rd. Turn left, drive 1.7 miles (2.7km) to Kahanu Garden.

9 ★★★ Pi'ilanihale Heiau. Stroll through **Kahanu Garden** (p 71) to stand in awe of the largest and one of the most important *heiau* (temples) in all of Polynesia, named after the great Pi'ilani dynasty. If the terraced 3-acre platform doesn't immediately impress you, imagine hand-carrying each basalt rock from Hāna Bay 5 miles away, as the Hawaiians did during construction 800 years ago. Tour the lush grounds, sit in the shade of the thatched canoe house, and imagine the lives of seafaring chiefs.

Return to Hāna Hwy. (now Hwy. 360), turn left and head 3.5 miles (5.6km) east into the town of Hāna, to Travaasa Hana.

10 Travaasa Hana. In the hotel lobby, you'll find rare Hawaiian artifacts: chiefly necklaces made of braided human hair with whale-tooth pendants, carved koa bowls, and dog-tooth anklets. During lunch at one of the resort's two restaurants, gaze at **Kau'iki Hill**, the birthplace of Queen Ka'ahumanu. If you ask nicely, your server might share *mo'olelo* (stories) of the area. *5031 Hāna Hwy. www.travaasa.com/maui.* ☎ *808/359-2401.* ●

The ancient Pi'ilanihale Heiau in Kahanu Garden.

West Maui

West Maui has map legend:

- **1A** Olowalu
- **1B** Leoda's Kitchen & Pie Shop
- **2** Lahaina
- **3** Ka'anapali
- **4** Kapalua

West Maui has it all: Rain-carved mountains, sandy beaches, fish-filled reefs, and plenty of action on shore. The stretch of coastline from the historic port of Lahaina to Kapalua is the island's busiest resort area (with South Maui a close second). Traffic jams frequently clog Honoapi'ilani Hwy., the only passage to this side of the island. START: **Olowalu.**

Travel Tip

I've used the highway number, not the name of the highway, when detailing how to get around on Maui. The abbreviation MM stands for "mile marker." For more information, see "Maui Driving Tips" on p 13.

1A **kids** **Olowalu.** Most visitors drive right past this tiny hamlet, halfway to Lahaina. Stop at MM 14 for one of my favorite snorkeling spots—over a turtle-cleaning station about 150 to 225 feet (46–69m) out from shore, where turtles line up to have cleaner wrasses (small fish) pick parasites off their shells. Further offshore, manta rays are known to congregate. Take care not to step on live coral and wear ocean-friendly sunscreen. After exploring the underwater world, head across the street to view the **Pu'u Kilea** petroglyphs— ancient rock carvings of sailors, canoes, and animals. See p 43 for directions. Fuel up at **Leoda's.**

Previous page: The Ke'anae Peninsula is a tempting detour along the Road to Hāna.

1B Leoda's Kitchen & Pie Shop
The gourmet sandwiches, hot dogs, and burgers are sinfully delicious, but save room for pie! The macadamia nut praline is intergalactic. *820 Olowalu Village Rd.* ☎ *808/662-3600. $.*

Take Hwy. 30 north 7 miles (11km).

2 ★★★ kids Lahaina. Spend half a day exploring Lahaina's surf boutiques, museums, and shave ice shops. Kids might take special interest in the fossils, dinosaur eggs, and sharks' teeth at the **Whaler's Locker** (780 Front St., ☎ 808/661-3775). See p 50 for a full walking tour of the town.

Take Hwy. 30 for 3 miles (4.8km) north of Lahaina.

3 Ka'anapali. Hawai'i's first master-planned resort consists of pricey midrise hotels lining nearly 3 miles (4.8km) of gold sandy beach. Golf greens wrap around the slope between beachfront and hillside properties. You can't miss the huge (almost life-size) metal sculpture of

a mother whale and two nursing calves that greets you at **Whalers Village,** a seaside mall that has adopted the whale as its mascot. For information on the stores here, see p 112. As you stroll down the beach path, at the **Hyatt Regency Maui** (p 147) you can spy on South American penguins playing in the lobby.

Continue north on Hwy. 30 for 7 miles (11km) and turn onto Office Rd.

4 ★★ Kapalua. Follow Highway 30 through the small seaside villages of Honokowai, Kahana, and Nāpili, and then head for the ocean shore along Office Road, bordered by elegant Cook pines. This is the domain of the luxurious **Ritz-Carlton Kapalua** (p 149). Kapalua Resort has a long list of amenities: a golf school, two golf courses (p 94), multiple swanky condos and restaurants, a collection of perfect beaches, and a rainforest preserve with hiking trails and a zipline tour—and all are open to the general public.

Whalers Village.

Lahaina

1 Baldwin Home Museum
2 Pioneer Inn
3 Banyan Tree
4 Courthouse
5 Maui Swiss Café
6 Malu'ulu O Lele Park
7 Waiola Church and Cemetery
8 Hongwanji Mission
9 Old Prison
10 Luakini Street
11 Ono Gelato
12 Wo Hing Temple
13 Hale Pa'i
14 Lahaina Jodo Mission

Between the West Maui Mountains and the deep azure ocean, Lahaina has managed to preserve its 19th-century heritage while still accommodating 21st-century guests. It has been at various times the royal capital of Hawai'i, the rowdy center of the whaling industry, the home of austere missionaries who tried to save the Hawaiians' souls, and the site of sugar and pineapple plantations. Today, it's one of the most popular towns in Maui for visitors to explore. START: **Baldwin Home Museum on Front Street.**

Travel Tip

Purchase a $10 Passport to the Past for entry to 4 popular museums: Baldwin Home, Wo Hing, A&B Sugar, and Bailey House. Buy the Passport at any of these museums.

1 **kids** **Baldwin Home Museum.** Step into this coral-and-rock house and travel back in time. Built in 1835, it belonged to Rev. Dwight Baldwin, a missionary, naturalist, and self-trained physician

who saved many Native Hawaiians from influenza and smallpox. Baldwin's rudimentary medical tools (on display here) bear witness to the steep odds he faced. He was rewarded with 2,600 acres in Kapalua, where he grew pineapple, then an experimental crop. On Friday night, docents dressed in period attire offer candlelit tours. Pick up a Lahaina walking map here, then visit the gift shop in the **Masters' Reading Room** next door. ◷ *30 min. 120 Dickenson St.*

Pioneer Inn.

(at Front St.). www.Lahaina restoration.org. ☎ *808/661-3262. Admission $7 adults, $5 seniors, kids ages 12 and under free. Admission also grants access to Wo Hing Temple (p 52). Daily 10am–4pm.*

2 Pioneer Inn. Lahaina's first hotel looks much as it did when it was built in 1901 by George Freeland, of the Royal Canadian Mounted Police, who tracked a criminal to Lahaina and then fell in love with the town. The scene of some pretty wild parties at the turn of the 20th century, the Pioneer is still open for business. Get a cold drink at the old bar or sit outside and watch the goings-on at the harbor. ⏱ *30 min. 658 Wharf St. www.pioneerinnmaui.com.* ☎ *808/661-3636.*

3 kids Banyan Tree. With octopus-like limbs, this enormous tree is so big that you can't fit it in your camera's viewfinder. It was only 8 feet (2.4m) tall in 1873, when Maui sheriff William O. Smith planted it. Now it's the largest banyan in the U.S., more than 60 feet (18m) tall, with 16 major trunks, and it shades ⅔ of an acre (.27ha) in Courthouse Square. ⏱ *15 min. At the Courthouse Bldg., 649 Wharf St.*

4 Courthouse. This 1860 building has served as a courthouse, customs house, post office, tax collector's office, and jail. On August 12, 1898, locals watched the Hawaiian flag come down and the American flag rise in its place, marking annexation to the U.S. Visit the **Lahaina Heritage Museum** upstairs to see fine exhibits on the history of Lahaina and whaling. The basement jail is now an art gallery. ⏱ *20 min. 648 Wharf St., Lahaina. www.visit Lahaina.com.* ☎ *808/661-3262. Free admission. Daily 9am–5pm.*

5 Maui Swiss Café. This is a great place for tropical smoothies, strong espresso, and affordable snacks. Sit in the somewhat funky garden area, or (my preference) get your drink to go and wander over to the seawall to watch the surfers. *640 Front St.* ☎ *808/661-6776. $.*

6 Malu'ulu O Lele Park. Not much to look at now, this ball field sits atop one of the most significant archeological sites in all of Hawai'i: **Moku'ula**, a former island where the highest-ranking ali'i (chiefs) took refuge. Beneath the grass, the royal residence and a glittering fishpond—home to a powerful *mo'o* (lizard goddess)—await excavation and restoration. (Learn more on a tour with **Maui Nei Native Expeditions**, p 45). ⏱ *5–10 min. Front/ Shaw sts.*

7 Waiola Church and Cemetery. Hawai'i's first stone church,

A gravestone in Waiola Cemetery.

built in 1828, was razed twice by hurricane winds and twice by fire—and rebuilt from the ground up each time. In the cemetery beside the church are the graves of two powerful women: Princess Keōpūolani—considered the highest-born, most sacred of all the Hawaiian *ali'i* (royals)—and Queen Ka'ahumanu, the two most influential wives of King Kamehameha I. Both women converted to Christianity and broke the ancient system of *kapu* (restrictions) by sitting down to eat with men, an act that signified the end of the old ways. ⏱ *10–15 min. 535 Waine'e St.*

8 Hongwanji Mission. Originally built in 1910 by members of Lahaina's Buddhist sect, this temple hosts a marvelous Obon festival in the summer. The reverend, who lives next door, takes time to talk to visitors and will give tours of the church to those interested. ⏱ *5 min., longer if you get a tour inside. Waine'e/Luakini sts.*

9 Old Prison. Stuck-in-Irons, or Hale Pa'ahao, is the Hawaiian name for this humble penitentiary. Drunken sailors were sent here, along with reckless horse riders. Wander inside and see the cells,

complete with shackles. ⏱ *5 min. Waine'e/Prison sts.*

10 Luakini Street. Sometimes to experience Hawai'i you have to feel with your heart, and not look with your eyes. That is true of this place. Back in 1837 this street was the route for the funeral procession of Princess Nahi'ena'ena, sister of kings Kamehameha II and III. A convert to Protestantism, she fell in love with her brother at an early age. Just 20 years earlier, their relationship would have been encouraged as a way to preserve the purity of the royal bloodlines. The missionaries, however, condemned it as incest. In August 1836 the couple had a son, who lived only a few hours; Nahi'ena'ena never recovered and died in December of that same year. Her funeral route became known as Luakini—meaning a *heiau* (temple) where chiefs prayed and human sacrifices were made—in reference to the gods "sacrificing" the beloved princess. Originally at Moku'ula (p 51), her mausoleum is now at Waiola Church (p 51). Stop on this street in the shade of one of the big breadfruit trees, and try to imagine the sorrow and fear of a population in transition. The old ways were dying—and the new ways seemed foreign and frightening.

11 Ono Gelato. This classy creamery makes Italian gelato with locally sourced passionfruit, mango, and coffee. The back patio hangs out over the surf—the best spot to chill in town. Bonus: free Wi-Fi. *815 Front St., Lahaina.* ☎ *808/495-0203. $.*

12 Wo Hing Temple. I adore this temple; it's small but filled with unexpected treasures. Starting in 1852, sugar planters began drafting

Wo Hing Temple.

Chinese contract labor to work in the sugarcane fields. The growing Chinese community built this temple and social hall in 1912. Today it hosts a lovely altar, gift shop, and rustic old cookhouse, complete with old woks. Duck inside to view some of the first movies ever made—Thomas Edison's footage of Hawai'i shot in 1898 and 1903! Check the calendar for Chinese New Year and kite-flying festival dates. ⏲ *20 min. 858 Front St.* ☎ *808/661-3262. Admission $7 adults, free for children ages 12 and under. Sat–Thurs 10am–4pm; Fri 1–8pm.*

⓭ **Hale Pa'i.** Little known fact: Lahaina was home to the first secondary school and first newspaper west of the Rockies. Even more remarkably, after the missionaries introduced the alphabet in the mid-1800s, Hawaiians became the most literate population of the time, with 90% able to read and write! Hawaiian-language newspapers became the rage, spreading news from distant continents to the most remote Hawaiian valleys. It all started at this tiny print house, an off-the-beaten-track museum on the edge of Lahainaluna High School campus. Note the limited hours. ⏲ *25 min. 980 Lahainaluna Rd.* ☎ *808/662-0560. Free admission. Open Mon–Wed 10am to 4pm and by appointment.*

⓮ **Lahaina Jodo Mission.** An enormous Buddha statue (some 12-ft./3.7m high and weighing 3½ tons) beams over this temple garden. It came here from Japan in 1968, to commemorate the 100th anniversary of the Japanese arrival in Hawai'i. On the first weekend in July, this temple hosts a beautiful lantern ceremony and Obon dance—not to be missed. ⏲ *10–15 min. 12 Ala Moana St. (off Front St., near the Mala Wharf).* ☎ *808/661-4304. Free admission. Daily during daylight hours.*

The Lahaina Jodo Mission temple.

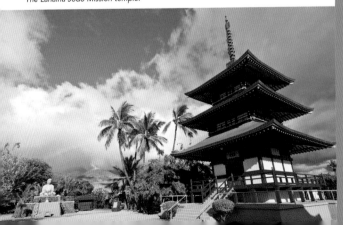

South Maui

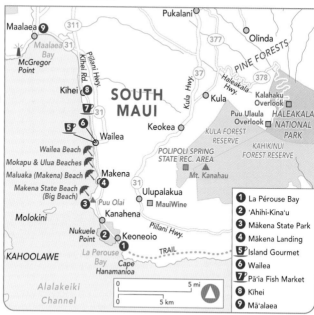

Pukalani

Maalaea ❾

(311)

Maalaea (31)
Bay

McGregor
Point

Piilani Hwy.
Kihei Rd.

Kihei ❽

**SOUTH
MAUI**

Olinda

(377)

PINE FORESTS

(37)

Haleakala
Hwy.

Kula Hwy.

(378)

Kalahaku
Overlook ☐

○ Kula

(31)

❼

❻

❺ ❻

Wailea

Wailea Beach

Mokapu & Ulua Beaches

Maluaka (Makena) Beach

*Makena State Beach
(Big Beach)*

❸

❹

Makena

Keokea ○

*Puu Ulalu
Overlook* ☐

**HALEAKALA
NATIONAL
PARK**

*KULA FOREST
RESERVE*

*KAHIKINUI
FOREST RESERVE*

*POLIPOLI SPRING
STATE REC. AREA*

☐ Mt. Kanahau

Ulupalakua
☐ MauiWine

(31)

Molokini

Puu Olai

Kanahena

❷

Piilani Hwy.

○ Keoneoio

❶

*La Perouse
Bay*

Cape
Hanamanioa

KAHOOLAWE

*Nukuele
Point*

TRAIL

❶	La Pérouse Bay
❷	'Ahihi-Kina'u
❸	Mākena State Park
❹	Mākena Landing
❺ 🅿	Island Gourmet
❻	Wailea
❼	Pā'ia Fish Market
❽	Kihei
❾	Mā'alaea

*Alalakeiki
Channel*

0	5 mi
0	5 km

To experience South Maui's treasures, you have to get wet: strap on a snorkel, climb into a kayak, or just dip in a toe. You won't appreciate this hot, dry coastline by merely looking out the window as you drive by. Once home to small Hawaiian fishing villages, the south shore now includes four distinct communities: windy Mā'alaea, traffic-swollen Kīhei, glitzy Wailea, and wild, serene Mākena—a paradise locals fight to keep pristine. START: 'Āhihi-Kīna'u Natural Area Reserve.

Travel Tip

Your south Maui adventure begins at the untamed end of the road, then wends its way back to civilization. Pack a swimsuit, towel, hat, hiking shoes, plenty of water, sunscreen, and (depending on what you want to do) snorkel gear and/or a kayak (see chapter 6 for rental recommendations). Get going early to avoid the hot sun; start off before 7am in the winter and 6am in the summer for the best weather conditions.

Drive south on Mākena Road, past Pu'u Olai to 'Āhihi Bay, where the road turns to gravel. Go another 2 miles (3.2km) along the coast to La Pérouse Bay.

❶ ★ **La Pérouse Bay & Monument.** At the road's end in South Maui, a pyramid of lava rocks marks the spot where the first Westerner to "discover" the island, French explorer Admiral Comte de La Pérouse, set foot on Maui in 1786. Park here, and if you're up for it, start hiking. Bring plenty of water and sun protection, and wear shoes that can withstand walking on loose, prickly lava rocks. From La Pérouse Bay, you can pick up **Hoa-pili Trail,** the old king's highway that once circled the island. The trail crosses a beach and shadeless lava plains, winding down to the lighthouse at the tip of Cape Hānamanioa, about a .75-mile (1.2km) round trip. Give yourself an hour or two to soak in the solitude of this wilderness.

Return north on Mākena Road 1.6 miles (2.6km) to park in gravel lot on left.

❷ ★ 'Āhihi-Kīna'u Natural Area Reserve. This stark, seemingly barren 1,238-acre preserve protects dynamic marine ecosystems, fragile anchialine ponds, and lava fields from Haleakalā's last eruption of 200-500 years ago. 'Āhihi Bay is a favorite snorkel spot for experienced waterfolk. Park at the gravel lot and walk 5 minutes north to enter at Kanahena Cove. Portions of the preserve are temporarily restricted, to allow fragile marine resources to recover from over-use. For current information on what's open and what's not, visit http://dlnr.hawaii.gov/ecosystems/nars/maui/ahihi-kinau-2 or call ☎ 808/984-8100.

Continue north on Mākena Road to Mākena State Park. Choose from three entrances: the southernmost is unpaved with street parking, while the other two have large paved lots and portable toilets.

❸ ★★★ Mākena State Park (Big Beach). This gorgeous stretch of sand is stunning at all hours of the day, particularly in the early morning when dolphins like to visit. See p 81.

Head north on Mākena Rd. (which becomes Mākena Alanui), turn left on Hono'iki St., and then right on Mākena Rd.

❹ ★ Mākena Landing. This beach park with boat-launching facilities, showers, toilets, and picnic tables has generally calm waters

A sunrise view from `Ahihi-Kina`u Natural Area Reserve.

The waters off Mākena Beach.

teeming with colorful tropical fish. It's the perfect place for beginner kayakers and snorkelers. **Mākena Kayak Tours** (p 106) specializes in teaching first-time kayakers. Or if history is more to your taste, go south on Mākena Road from the landing; on the right is **Keawalai Congregational Church ★** (☎ 808/879-5557), built in 1855. Surrounded by *tī* leaves (planted for spiritual protection) and built of 3-foot (.9m) thick lava rock with coral for mortar, this Protestant church sits on its own cove. On Sundays, voices soar in song during the 9:30am Hawaiian-language service.

Travel north on Mākena Alanui, which becomes Wailea Alanui. Turn into the parking lot past the Four Seasons Resort Wailea.

5 **Island Gourmet Market.** This well-stocked grocery and deli dishes out everything from eggs and hash-browns to French macaroons. Choose from ten types of poke (raw, seasoned fish). *Shops at Wailea, 3750 Wailea Alanui Dr., Wailea.* ☎ *808/874-5055.* $

6 ★ Wailea. From serene Mākena proceed into multimillion-dollar high-rise luxury. Wailea's resorts line the palm-fringed gold coast. For an up-close look, park in the public beach access lot between the **Four Seasons Resort Maui** and the **Grand Wailea** and walk the 3-mile (4.8km) round-trip beach path. It has terrific views of Kahoʻolawe and Molokini (plus whales in winter) and the ocean side of the path is planted with rare native coastal flowers and trees. The Four Seasons and the Grand Wailea both have **museum-quality art collections** and offer self-guided tours. Allow about an hour, longer if you want to linger with the art.

Go left on Wailea Alanui Road and left again at stop sign to Okolani Drive, which becomes Kīhei Road.

7 **kids** **Pāʻia Fish Market.** This north shore favorite opened a counter on the south shore. Get your mahi or opakapaka burger to go and eat it across the street at Kalama Beach Park. *1913 S. Kīhei Rd.* ☎ *808/874-8888.* $

Maui's Early History

The first Hawaiian settlers arrived by canoe. Unsurpassed navigators, early Polynesians used the stars, birds, and currents to guide them across thousands of miles. They packed their canoes with food, plants, medicine, tools, and animals: everything necessary for building a new life on a distant shore. No one is sure exactly when they arrived, but artifacts at the **Malu'uluo Lele Park** in Lahaina (see p 51) date back to between A.D. 700 and 900.

Over the ensuing centuries, a distinctly Hawaiian culture arose. Sailors became farmers and fishermen. They built highly productive fishponds, terraced *kalo lo'i* (taro patches), and massive rock *heiau* (temples). Farmers cultivated more than 400 varieties of *kalo*, their staple food; 300 types of sweet potato; and 40 different bananas. Hawaiian women fashioned intricately patterned *kapa* (barkcloth)—some of the finest in all of Polynesia.

Each of the Hawaiian Islands was its own kingdom, governed by *ali'i* (high-ranking chiefs) who drew their authority from an established *kapu* (taboo) and caste system. Those who broke the *kapu* could be sacrificed. In the early years, Maui was divided into three chiefdoms: Hāna, Wailuku, and Lahaina. Pi'ilani, a 15th-century ruler from Hāna, became the first to unite Maui. His rule was a time of peace; he built fishponds and began the highway that encircled the island.

The ancient Hawaiian creation chant, the *Kumulipō*, depicts a universe that began when heat and light emerged out of darkness, followed by the first life form: a coral polyp. The 2,000-line epic poem is a grand genealogy, describing how all species are interrelated, from gently waving seaweeds to mighty human warriors. It is the basis for the Hawaiian concept of *kuleana*, a word that simultaneously refers to privilege and responsibility. To this day, Native Hawaiians view the care of their natural resources as a filial duty and honor.

❽ Kīhei. Kīhei consists of unimaginative condos and mini-malls—crowded up against a string of golden beaches, every one near perfect. At the north end of town, the **Hawaiian Islands Humpback Whale National Marine Sanctuary** (725 Kīhei Rd.; www.hawaiihumpback whale.noaa.gov; ☎ 808/879-2818) offers some background on the mighty whales that visit Hawai'i from November to April. Next door, the **Ko'ie'ie Fishpond** is a prime example of ancient Hawaiian aquaculture. Continue north on Kīhei Road to **Kealia Pond National Wildlife Preserve** (☎ 808/875-1582), a 700-acre (283ha) U.S. Fish and Wildlife wetland preserve that's a fantastic place to see many endangered Hawaiian species, like the black-crowned herons and

Wildlife can be seen at Kealia Pond National Wildlife Preserve.

Hawaiian stilts, coots, and ducks. From July to December, hawksbill turtles come ashore here to lay

A touch pool at Maui Ocean Center.

eggs. Stroll along the preserve's boardwalk, dotted with interpretive signs and shade shelters, through sand dunes, and around ponds. The boardwalk starts at the outlet of Kealia Pond on the ocean side of North Kīhei Road (near MM 2 on Hwy. 31).

Continue north on Hwy. 31, then go left on Hwy. 30 to the Māʻalaea turn off. It's about 3 miles (4.8km).

9 ★★★ kids **Māʻalaea.** The star of this wind-blasted harborside village is the **Maui Ocean Center,** Hawaiʻi's largest aquarium. This 5-acre (2ha) facility houses numerous family-friendly exhibits, including a 100-foot-long (30m), 750,000-gallon tank featuring sharks, rays, and dazzling schools of fish. The aquarium is designed to usher you from the beach to the depths of the ocean. A see-through tunnel goes right through the tank,

Ocean Safety

The range of watersports available in Maui is astounding—this is a prime water playground with conditions for every age and ability. But the ocean is also an untamed wilderness; don't expect a calm swimming pool.

Many people who visit Hawai'i underestimate the power of the ocean. With just a few precautions, your Pacific experience can be a safe and happy one.

Before jumping in, **familiarize yourself with your equipment.** If you're snorkeling, make sure you feel at ease breathing and clearing water from the snorkel.

Take a moment to **watch where others are swimming.** Observe weather conditions, swells, and possible riptides. If you get caught in big surf, dive underneath each wave until the swell subsides. Never turn your back to the ocean; rogue waves catch even experienced water folk unaware.

Be realistic about your fitness—more than one visitor has ended his or her vacation with a heart attack in the water.

Don't go out alone, or during a storm.

Note that **sharks** are not a big problem in Hawai'i; in fact, local divers look forward to seeing them. Only 2 of the 40 shark species present in Hawaiian waters are known to bite humans, and then usually it's by accident. But here are the general rules for avoiding sharks: **Don't swim at dusk or in murky water**—sharks may mistake you for one of their usual meals. And, while it should be obvious, it bears repeating: **Don't swim where there are bloody fish** in the water, as sharks become aggressive around blood.

so you're surrounded by marine creatures on all sides. If you're a certified scuba diver, you can participate in the **Shark Dive Maui Program,** which allows you (for a fee of $199) to plunge into the aquarium and swim with the sharks, stingrays, and tropical fish. ⏲ *2 hr. or more.* Māʻalaea Harbor Village,

192 Māʻalaea Rd. (the triangle btw. Honoapiʻilani Hwy. and Māʻalaea Rd.). www.mauioceancenter.com. ☎ *808/270-7000. Buy tickets online to avoid long lines. Admission $28 adults, $25 seniors, $20 children 3–12. Daily 9am–5pm (until 6pm July–Aug).*

Central Maui

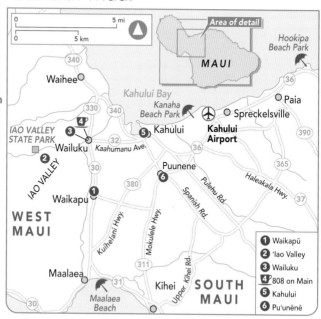

Hookipa Beach Park

MAUI

Area of detail

Waihee

Kahului Bay

Kanaha Beach Park

Paia

Spreckelsville

IAO VALLEY STATE PARK

Wailuku

Kaahumanu Ave.

Kahului

Kahului Airport

IAO VALLEY

Waikapu

Puunene

WEST MAUI

Kuihelani Hwy.

Mokulele Hwy.

Spanish Rd.

Pulehu Rd.

Haleakala Hwy.

Maalaea

Kihei

Upper Kihei Rd.

SOUTH MAUI

Maalaea Beach

1 Waikapū
2 'Iao Valley
3 Wailuku
4 808 on Main
5 Kahului
6 Pu'unēnē

The central plain between Maui's two volcanoes is the site of the main airport, where you'll probably arrive. Distinctly untouristy, it's home to the majority of the island's population, the heart of the business community, and the center of the local government. START: **Waikapū.**

① kids **Waikapū.** Tucked up against the verdant West Maui mountains, you'll find the **Maui Tropical Plantation** (p 27). Spend an hour here riding the 40-minute narrated tram ride through fields of pineapple, vegetables, and plumeria trees, or soaring overhead on a zipline. Check out the country store and farm stand before you leave.

Turn left on Honoapi'ilani Hwy #30 then left on Main Street. In .5 miles (.8km) take a slight right onto 'Īao Valley Road. Follow it to the end, about 2 miles (3.2km).

② ★★ kids **'Īao Valley.** This peaceful valley, full of tropical plants, rainbows, waterfalls, swimming holes, and hiking trails (two of them paved and easy), offers cool rejuvenation. The park and stream get their names from the **'Īao Needle,** a phallic rock that juts an impressive 2,250 feet (686m) above sea level. Pack a picnic, take your swimsuit, and spend a couple of hours in the shady rainforest. **Kepaniwai Park** has streamside picnic tables and charming memorial buildings that celebrate each of Hawai'i's diverse ethnic cultures: a

Hawaiian thatched hale (house), a Filipino farmer's hut, a Chinese pavilion, and a Portuguese villa. *Note:* At press time, the park was closed for repair after major flooding. *ʻĪao Valley State Park, 54 S. High St., Wailuku.* ☎ *808/984-8109. Open daily 10am–4pm.*

Return via Main Street into the town of Wailuku.

❸ ★ **Wailuku.** With its faded wooden storefronts, old plantation homes, and shops straight out of the 1940s, quaint little Wailuku is worth exploring. Stop at the **Bailey House Museum,** then continue northeast of the town center to see the ancient sites of the **Halekiʻi-Pihana Heiau State Monument.** See p 71.

🍴 **808 on Main.** Pop into this bustling restaurant for hearty sandwiches, soups, and salads. The lamb lettuce cups and "Squealer" (pulled pork and coleslaw on a hoagie) are both tasty. *2051 Main St., Wailuku* ☎ *808/242-1111.$$*

Head east on Main St., which becomes Kaʻahumanu Ave., leading into the town of Kahului.

❺ **Kahului.** Aside from picking up supplies at Costco or Whole Foods, this industrial town is not the place to spend your vacation. There are few attractions worth noting, however. The first is **Maui Nui Botanical Gardens** (150 Kanaloa Ave; www.mnbg.org; ☎ 808/249-2798). Once the site of a sad little zoo, the gardens are now a rich, living library of rare native Hawaiian plants. Ask to see the *hapai* (pregnant) banana trees that produce fruit inside their trunk. Then head to the **Maui Arts & Cultural Center** (1 Cameron Way; www.mauiarts.org; ☎ 808/242-7469) where the Schaefer International Gallery hosts top-quality art exhibits. From here, head over to **Kanahā Beach Park,** where kiters and windsurfers catch air and twirl above the surf like fluorescent butterflies. Across the street, peek into the **Kanahā Wildlife Sanctuary** (Haleakalā Hwy. Ext. and Hāna Hwy; ☎ 808/984-8100). See if you can spot an endangered Hawaiian stilt—a tuxedoed bird with skinny pink legs.

From Kaʻahumanu Ave., turn south on Puʻunēnē Ave. Follow it through town to Hansen Rd. Turn left and the Sugar Museum is on your left.

❻ **Puʻunēnē.** Soak up a little more colorful history in this central Maui ghost town. Once a thriving sugar-plantation town, Puʻunēnē today consists of a post office, a shuttered sugar mill, and the **Alexander & Baldwin Sugar Museum** (p 45).

A black-necked Hawaiian stilt at the Kanahā Wildlife Sanctuary.

Kalaupapa, Moloka'i

A visit to remote Kalaupapa on the island of Moloka'i is a once-in-a-lifetime experience. This isolated peninsula at the base of the world's tallest sea cliffs is a simply stunning locale. You must travel here on foot, by mule, or by plane—there's no road, and access by water is not allowed—but the trek is well worth the effort. Kalaupapa's lush valleys once supported several Native Hawaiian communities. But residents were evicted in 1865 when King Kamehameha V signed the Act to Prevent the Spread of Leprosy, which ultimately sent some 8,000 people with the disease (now called Hansen's Disease) to this natural prison. The exiles' suffering was eased somewhat by the arrival of Father Damien, a Belgian priest who worked tirelessly on their behalf. Patients were finally freed to come and go in the 1960s, but a handful of elderly folks still live here. To protect their privacy, visitation is restricted to 100 people a day, age 16 and older, with permits. START: **Kahului Airport on Maui.**

Travel Tip

One alternative to the mule ride is to hike down the Kalaupapa Trail. To do this, you'll need to book the first flight to Ho'olehua Airport, arrange airport transfer to the trailhead in Kualapu'u, and plan to start hiking by 7:30am in order to meet Damien Tours at the base of the sea cliffs by 9am. The descent takes 60 to 90 minutes to hike; it's 90 to 120 minutes back up.

① Kahului Airport, Maui. Plan to fly out *early*—it's only a half-hour flight to Molokai, but you must get there in time to meet your mule tour by 7:30am, so you can meet the bus tour by 9am. If you're worried about logistics, consider flying to Moloka'i the day before your tour and spending the night. See "Travel Tip," below.

② Moloka'i Airport. If you've signed up for the mule ride (see **③**), fly into Ho'olehua airport, where **Kalaupapa Mule Tour** guides will meet you to transport you to the mule barn. A quicker, equally scenic option is to fly directly into Kalaupapa by booking a tour package with **Makani Air** (www.makani air.com; ☎ **808/834-1111**).

③ ★★★ Kalaupapa Mule Tour. Get to the Sproat family's mule barn no later than 7:30am. The guides will select the perfect animal for you to ride. The surefooted animals step down the narrow, muddy trail daily, rain or shine, pausing often to calculate their next move—and always, it seems to me, veering a little too close to the edge. The first switchback may make you gasp, but the mules have safely tromped up and down the trail for years. ⏱ *7.5 hr. round trip. 100 Kalae Hwy., Ste. 104, on Hwy. 470, 5 mi (8km) north of Hwy. 460. www.muleride.com. ☎ 800/567-7550. $209 per person. Riders must be at least 16 years old and physically fit.*

④ ★★★ Kalaupapa Trail. The trail is only 3 miles long, but it zigzags down a knuckle-whitening 1,700-foot cliff, via a series of 26 switchbacks. Whether you ride it or hike it, take time to savor the views.

⑤ ★★★ Damien Tours. To explore this beautiful and haunting place, you must join **Damien Tours** (www.damientoursllc.com; ☎ **808/ 567-6171**) for a 3-hour tour of the peninsula's most fascinating sites.

Tours cost $50. Whether you arrive by foot, mule or plane, you'll be met by a friendly guide driving an old school bus around 9–9:30am. Climb aboard for a journey along the steep, craggy cliffs to **Father Damien's grave.** Born to wealth in Belgium in 1840, Father Damien arrived on Moloka'i in 1873 and devoted his life to caring for the sufferers of Hansen's Disease. He himself died of the disease in 1889 and was canonized in 2009. Other tour stops include **St. Philomena Church,** built by patients in 1872, and **Kalaupapa** Book Store, filled with a wealth of information on the history and people of this place, and their remarkable resilience.

Travel Tip

If the simplicity of Moloka'i appeals to you, consider spending the night and taking a day or two to explore the island. There is only one hotel on the island, **Hotel Molokai,** Kamehameha V Hwy., Kaunakakai (www.hotelmolokai.com; ☎ **877/ 553-5347** or 808/660-3408). Rates here start at $169. If you'd prefer a condo or vacation rental, contact **Molokai Vacation Properties** (www. molokai-vacation-rental.com; ☎ **800/367-2984** or 808/553-8334). The agents represent an assortment of fantastic rentals, most of them oceanfront and all guaranteed to be clean and fully equipped. You can book online, but it's best to contact the office directly. Their customer service is excellent.

Molokai Mule Ride.

Upcountry Maui

A 10,023-foot tall volcano lords over Maui. The fertile slopes of Haleakalā, or House of the Sun, are home to cowboys, farmers, and easygoing folk. Crisp air, rolling green pastures, and flower farms are the highlights of the area known as "upcountry." Bring a jacket; as locals like to joke, "It's cooler in Kula." START: **Makawao.**

1 ★ Makawao. Maui has a long-standing tradition of ranchers and rodeo masters, and this cool, misty upcountry town is its epicenter. Modern-day *paniolo* (cowboys) come here to fuel up on cream puffs and stick donuts from **Komoda Store & Bakery,** 3674 Baldwin Ave. (☎ **808/572-7261**), a 100-year-old family grocery that seems frozen in time. The neighboring businesses offer chic clothing, fine art, and decent snacks. Five minutes down Baldwin Avenue, you'll find the gracious **Hui No'eau Visual Arts Center** (p 116).

Take Makawao Avenue to the light at Kula Hwy #37, turn left. Turn left at Ke St., then right onto Lower Kula Rd.

2 La Provence. Every item in this French bakery is exquisite. Arrive before noon or risk watching the mango blueberry scone walk out the door without you. *Enjoy an addictively good crepe in the garden.* 3158 Lower Kula Hwy. ☎ *808/878-1313.* $$.

Wares for sale at Hui No'eau Visual Arts Center.

Return to Kula Hwy. #37. It's a 20-minute detour down 'Ōmaopio Rd. to Surfing Goat Dairy and about a 20-minute detour up Waipoli Rd. to Ali'i Kula Lavender Farm. (You can also hit Surfing Goat Dairy at the end, on your way back down the mountain.)

❸ ★ **Kula.** Continue south through the bucolic rolling hills of this upland community, past old flower farms, humble cottages, and new suburban ranch houses with million-dollar views that take in the ocean, isthmus, West Maui Mountains, Lāna'i, and Kaho'olawe in the distance. Kula sits at a cool 3,000 feet (914m), just below the cloud line, and from here a winding road snakes its way up to **Haleakalā National Park** (see p 89). Everyone in this area grows something—Maui onions, carnations, orchids, and proteas, those strange-looking blossoms that look like "Star Trek" props. Must stops: **Surfing Goat Dairy** (p 39) and **Ali'i Kula Lavender Farm** (p 40).

Continue on Hwy. 37 for 11 miles (17.7km).

❹ ★ **Kēōkea.** Fill up your gas tank in this charming blink-and-you'll-miss-it town. Peruse the whimsical artwork at **Keokea Gallery** (9230 Kula Hwy., ☎ **808/878-3555**) and sip a cup of Joe at **Grandma's Coffee House** (p 16).

Continue on Hwy. 37 for 17 miles (27km).

❺ ★ **'Ulupalakua.** The final stop on the upcountry tour is **'Ulupalakua Ranch,** a 20,000-acre (8,094ha) spread once owned by legendary sea captain James Makee. The ranch is now home to Maui's only **winery,** established in 1974 by Napa vintner Emil Tedeschi. Stop in the tasting room and sample a few vintages, which have truly improved with age. Across from the winery are the remains of the three smoke-stacks of the **Makee Sugar Mill,** built in 1878. This is home to Maui artist Reems Mitchell, who carved the mannequins on the front porch of the **'Ulupalakua Ranch Store**: a Filipino with his fighting cock, a cowboy, a farmhand, and a sea captain, each representing a piece of Maui history. *MauiWine, 14815 Pi'ilani Hwy. www.mauiwine.com.* ☎ *808/878-6058. Daily 10am–5:30pm. Free tastings; free tours given 10:30am and 1:30pm.*

The Road to Hāna

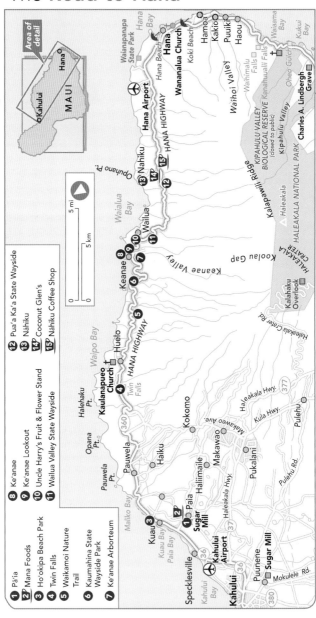

1 Pā'ia
2 Mana Foods
3 Ho'okipa Beach Park
4 Twin Falls
5 Waikamoi Nature Trail
6 Kaumahina State Wayside Park
7 Ke'anae Arboreteum
8 Ke'anae
9 Ke'anae Lookout
10 Uncle Harry's Fruit & Flower Stand
11 Wailua Valley State Wayside
12 Pua'a Ka'a State Wayside
13 Nāhiku
14 Coconut Glen's
15 Nāhiku Coffee Shop

Top down, sunscreen on, swimsuit handy, and radio tuned to a Hawaiian music station: It's time to explore the Hāna Highway (Hwy. 36). This wiggle of a road winds for 45 miles (72km) along Maui's northeastern shore, passing taro patches, magnificent seascapes, waterfall pools, botanical gardens, and verdant rainforests. Bring water, snacks, beach towels, and a fully charged camera. The drive itself should take only about 2 hours, but plan to spend a full day to enjoy all the sights along the way. START: **Pā'ia.**

The Road to Hāna.

1 Pā'ia. Fuel up on gas and groceries. There are several options for breakfast, if you'd like a hearty meal before you go. See p 123 for more details.

2 Mana Foods. Stock up on sandwiches, drinks, and ginger candies to stave off potential road sickness. *49 Baldwin Ave., Pā'ia.* ☎ *808/579-8078. $*

Drive east on the Hāna Highway (Hwy. 36) until just before MM 9.

3 ★ kids Ho'okipa Beach Park. See p 78.

After MM 16, the road is still called the Hāna Highway, but the number changes from Hwy. 36 to Hwy. 360, and the mile markers go back to 0. Stop at MM 2.

4 Twin Falls. Pull over on the mountainside and park; the waterfall and pool are a 3- to 5-minute walk. The mountain stream water is a bit chilly when you first get in, but it's good for swimming. If it's crowded, keep going; plenty of other waterfalls are coming up on this next stretch of the road, which gets narrower and extra-curvy from here on. Try counting every fern-draped bridge you cross—at least 59 of them before you get to Hanā, including many beautiful, one-lane arches built 100 years ago.

Continue to MM 9.

5 kids Waikamoi Nature Trail. Stretch your legs here with an easy .75-mile (1.2km) loop-trail hike. Look for the QUIET TREES AT WORK sign and follow the path.

Just past MM 12, you'll find:

6 kids Kaumahina State Wayside Park. This is a good pit stop, with actual restrooms and a great view of the rugged coastline all the way down to the jutting Ke'anae Peninsula.

Ke'anae Congregational Church.

Between MM 16 and MM 17, take right-hand turn-off to reach:

7 ★★ **kids** **Ke'anae Arboretum.** Maui's botany is represented here in three parts: native forest; introduced forest; and traditional Hawaiian food and medicine plants. You can swim in the refreshing pools of Pi'ina'au Stream or walk a mile-long (1.6km) trail into Ke'anae Valley's lush tropical rainforest.

Return to Hāna Hwy. Just past MM 17, turn left (north) onto Ke'anae Rd., which leads down to the Ke'anae Peninsula.

8 ★★★ **kids** **Ke'anae Peninsula.** The old Hawaiian village of **Ke'anae** stands out against the Pacific like a place time forgot. For untold generations, Native Hawaiians have lived off the land here, diverting fresh stream water into their *kalo lo'i* (taro patches). Take a reverent stroll through the **Ke'anae**

An overview of the Ke'anae Peninsula.

Congregational Church (☎ 808/ 248-8040), built in 1860 of lava rocks and coral mortar; it stands in stark contrast to the surrounding green fields. Stop by **Aunty Sandy's** (210 Ke'anae Rd., ☎ 808/ 248-7448) for warm banana bread.

Return to Hāna Highway and continue east for about ¼ mile. Look for a turnout on your left (ocean side).

9 **Ke'anae Lookout.** Stop here to take in a postcard-worthy panorama of the entire Ke'anae Peninsula, from its checkerboard pattern of green taro fields to its salt-kissed coast etched in black lava.

Around MM 18 look for:

10 **Uncle Harry's Fruit & Flower Stand.** On this stretch of the road, you'll start to see numerous small stands selling fruit or flowers. Uncle Harry sells a variety of fruits and juices Monday through Saturday.

Just before MM 19.

11 ★★ **Wailua Valley State Wayside.** Climb the stairs beneath an archway of *hau* (tree hibiscus) for jaw-dropping views in both directions: the taro patches of Wailua village on side and the waterfalls of Ko'olau Gap on the other. Imagine the massive erosional forces that carved this valley.

Coconut Glen's ice cream stand.

Between MM 22 and MM 23.

⑫ Puaʻa Kaʻa State Wayside.
Waterfalls provide background
music for this small park area with a
shaded picnic area and restrooms.
Cross the stream to take a quick
dip in the falls. Ginger plants are
everywhere: Pick some and stash
them in your car so that you can
travel with their sweet smell.

Just after MM 25, turn left onto
narrow Nāhiku Rd., which leads 3
miles (4.8km) from the highway, at
about 1,000 feet (305m) elevation,
down to sea level.

⑬ Nāhiku. This remote, wildly
beautiful area was once a thriving
village of thousands; today the
population has dwindled to fewer
than a hundred—including a few
Hawaiian families, but mostly
extremely wealthy mainland residents who jet in for a few weeks at
a time. At the end of the road, you
can see the remains of the old
wharf from the town's rubber-
plantation days. There's a small picnic area off to the side. Dolphins
are frequently seen in the bay.

Continue south on Hwy. 360.
You'll have your choice of
refreshment stops, one at MM
27.5, the other just past MM 28.

⑭ Coconut Glen's. When you
see Coconut Glen's rainbow-
splashed sign, pull over and
indulge in some truly splendid ice
cream—dairy-free and made with
coconut milk. Scoops of chocolate
chili, lilikoi, and honey macadamia
nut ice cream are served in coconut
bowls, with coconut chips as spoons.
This whimsical stand oozes aloha.
From here, you're only 20 minutes
away from Hāna town. *Hāna Hwy.,
at MM 27.5 www.coconutglens.
com;* ☎ *808/248-4876.*

⑮ Nāhiku Coffee Shop. What a
delight to stumble across this small
coffee shop with locally made baked
goods, Maui-grown coffee, banana
bread, organic tropical-fruit smoothies, and my favorite, the Original
and Best Coconut Candy. It's part
of a cluster of a half dozen food
stands selling hot dishes—though
you can never be sure which will be
open when. My favorite is the Thai
place at the end. *Hāna Hwy. ½
mile past MM 28. No phone. $.*

Hāna

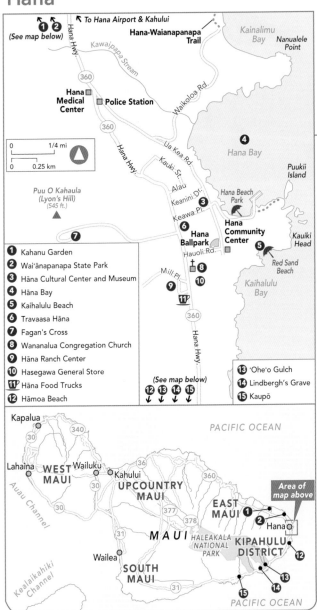

To Hana Airport & Kahului

Hana-Waianapanapa Trail

(See map below)

Kawaipapa Stream

Kainalimu Bay

Nanualele Point

(360)

Hana Medical Center

Police Station

(360)

Waikoloa Rd.

Hana Bay ❹

Puukii Island

Ua Kea Rd.

Kauki St.

Alau

Keanini Dr. ❸

Keawa Pl.

Hana Beach Park

0   1/4 mi

0   0.25 km

Puu O Kahaula (Lyon's Hill) (545 ft.)

❼

❻

Hana Ballpark

Hauoli Rd.

Hana Community Center

Kauiki Head

❺ Red Sand Beach

Kaihalulu Bay

Mill Pl. ❽

❾   ⑩

⑪

(360)

Hana Hwy

❶ Kahanu Garden
❷ Wai'ānapanapa State Park
❸ Hāna Cultural Center and Museum
❹ Hāna Bay
❺ Kaihalulu Beach
❻ Travaasa Hāna
❼ Fagan's Cross
❽ Wananalua Congregation Church
❾ Hāna Ranch Center
⑩ Hasegawa General Store
⑪ Hāna Food Trucks
⑫ Hāmoa Beach

(See map below)

⑫ ⑬ ⑭ ⑮

⑬ 'Ohe'o Gulch
⑭ Lindbergh's Grave
⑮ Kaupō

Kapalua

(340)

PACIFIC OCEAN

(30)

Lahaina   **WEST MAUI**   Wailuku

(30)

Kahului

(36)

UPCOUNTRY MAUI

(360)

Auau Channel

Area of map above

(30)

EAST MAUI ❶

❷

Hana

(377)   (378)

M A U I

HALEAKALA NATIONAL PARK

(31)

KIPAHULU DISTRICT

⑫

⑬

Wailea   (31)

SOUTH MAUI

⑭

⑮

Kealaikahiki Channel

PACIFIC OCEAN

Hāna is where islanders come for vacation. After the long journey to get here, take a deep breath. Inhale the scent of sea salt, white ginger, and ripe guava. Ahhhh . . . *this* is probably what you came to Maui in search of. Hāna enjoys more than 90 inches of rain a year, more than enough to keep the scenery lush. Banyans, bamboo, breadfruit trees—everything seems larger than life in this rainforested coastal town. Explore the magical landscape: red and black sand beaches, valleys threaded with silver waterfalls, and sparkling blue pools. Be extra kind to the locals; remember, you're only one of hundreds of visitors who breeze through their humble community every day. START: **Hāna.**

Travel Tip

Wake early to see the sun rise out of the sea. In the morning hours you'll have Hāna's waterfalls and beaches all to yourself. Day-trippers arrive in town around 11am and stay until about 4pm; during that window, the area is overrun with hundreds of people, all in a hurry. By staying here overnight, you can avoid them and soak up the extra solitude.

From Hwy. 360 turn toward the ocean on Ula'ino Road, just past MM 31.

❶ ★★ kids Kahanu Garden. Plan to arrive when the gate opens at 10am to have plenty of time to explore this 472-acre (191ha) garden, including the world's largest collection of breadfruit trees. Across the wide lawn, you'll see the imposing **Pi'ilanihale Heiau,** a massive temple built by a lineage of powerful Maui chiefs. The structure's mammoth proportions are humbling: 3 acres (1.2 ha) with stacked rock walls 50 feet (15m) tall and 8-to-10 feet (2.4m–3m) thick. Historians believe it was built in several stages, beginning as early as the 13th century, with basalt rocks hand-carried from Hāna Bay, some 5 miles (8km) away. The breadfruit trees at the base of the back wall are likely descendants of those planted in ancient times.

Take plenty of time to roam Kahanu Garden's 472 acres.

🕐 *1 hr. Ula'ino Rd. www.ntbg.org.* ☎ *808/248-8912. Guided tours $25; self-guided tours $10; children 12 and under free. Mon–Sat 9am–2pm.*

Continuing east on Hwy. 360, just past MM 32, turn left and take Honokulani Rd. to the ocean.

❷ ★★★ kids Wai'ānapanapa State Park. Get up early to see shiny black-sand Wai'ānapanapa Beach and hike the coastal trail. Plan to spend at least a couple of hours at this 120-acre (49ha) park that appears like a vivid dream, with bright-green jungle foliage on three sides and cobalt-blue water lapping at its shore. Swimming in the ocean is not the best here (rough seas, strong currents), but you can plunge into a freshwater cave pool just above the beach. Warm up by walking the coastal trail past blowholes, sea arches, and *lauhala* groves. *End of Honokalani Rd., off Hāna Hwy. (Hwy. 360), Hāna.* ☎ *808/248-4843. Open daily 24 hours.*

Continue on Hwy. 360. As you enter Hāna, the road splits about ½ mile (.8km) past MM 33, at the police station. Both roads will take you to Hāna, but Uakea Road is more scenic.

❸ ★★ kids Hāna Cultural Center and Museum. With the sun starting to reach its zenith, take a cooling break while touring this small museum's excellent collection of Hawaiian quilts, artifacts, books, and photos. Kids will love the thatched *hale* (houses) for cooking and canoe storage. 🕐 *30 min. 4974 Uakea Rd. www.hanaculturalcenter. org.* ☎ *808/248-8622. Mon–Fri 10am–4pm; $3 donation.*

From Uakea Rd., turn left on Keawa Pl. to the bay.

The black sands of Wai'ānapanapa Beach.

❹ ★ kids Hāna Bay. Come here to watch the activities in the bay—fishermen throwing net, paddlers pulling their canoes into the water, and local kids belly-flopping off the pier. You'll find restrooms, showers, picnic tables, barbecues, and a snack bar here. The red cinder cone looming over the southeast side of the bay is **Kau'iki Hill,** the birthplace in 1768 of Queen Ka'ahumanu, who played a huge role in Hawai'i's history by encouraging her people to convert from the old religion to Christianity.

Go to the south end of Uakea Rd. and park.

❺ Kaihalulu Beach. See p 79 for directions to, and a description of, this stunning "hidden" red-sand beach.

Return to Hāna Hwy. 360. Park across the street from the hotel.

❻ Travaasa Hāna. If you can afford it, this is THE place to stay in Hāna (and one of the state's top resorts). If they aren't too busy, the staff generally is amenable to taking you on a tour in their speedy golf carts. Ask to see the sausage tree, and the dogtooth anklet in the lobby. They have an excellent spa here, too. Plan on half-hour to see this elegant resort, longer if you want to get a meal or a drink at one of the restaurants here. See p 150.

❼ kids Fagan's Cross. Across the street from the Travaasa Hāna, find the trailhead for an uphill hike to the 30-foot-high (9m) white cross (made of lava rock), erected in memory of Paul Fagan, who founded Hāna Ranch as well as the hotel formerly known as Hotel Hāna-Maui. The 3-mile (4.8km) round-trip hike provides a gorgeous view of the Hāna coast,

store, and **Hāna Ranch Restaurant**.
Mill Place, off of Hāna Hwy. 360.

⑩ ★ Hasegawa General Store.
This legendary general store,
established in 1910 and immortalized in song since 1961, is a good
place to find picnic items (chips,
fruit, cookies, soda, bread, lunch
fixings) and Hāna-specific souvenirs.
There's also an ATM if you're low
on cash for fruit stands. *5165 Hāna
Hwy.* ☎ *808/248-8231.*

⑪ Hāna Food Trucks. A caravan
of food trucks has rushed to fill
the void of culinary options in this
remote outpost. A minute down
the road from Hasegawa's, Ono
Organic Farm has a stand selling
gorgeous, ripe tropical fruit. The
trucks behind the stand have a
decent selection of plate lunches
and fish tacos, but the best meal is
to be found a little further on at
Hāna Burger (5670 Hāna *Hwy. 360).*
www.hanaranch.com/hana-burger.
☎ *808/268-2820).* Hāna Ranch supplies this food truck with grass-fed
beef and beautiful tomatoes. The
gourmet burgers taste great pared
with the bucolic view. The only
downside: it's often closed.

Fagan's Cross.

especially at sunset. The uphill trail
starts across Hāna Highway from
the Travassa Hāna. (Enter the pastures at your own risk; they're often
occupied by glaring bulls and cows
with new calves.) Watch your step
as you ascend this steep hill. The
hike can take 1 to 2 hours, depending on how fast you hike and how
long you linger at the top admiring
the breathtaking view.

South on Hwy. 360, just past
Hauoli Rd., the next 4 sites are in
close proximity.

**⑧ Wananalua Congregation
Church.** Stop for photos of this
historic church, built from coral
stones from 1838 to 1842 during
the missionary rush to convert the
natives. ⏱ *15 min. Hwy. 360, just
past Hauoli Rd.*

⑨ Hāna Ranch Center. This
small cluster of buildings comprises
Hāna's entire commercial center,
with a post office, bank, general

Head south on Hwy. 360 and turn
left on Haneo'o Rd.

⑫ ★★ Hāmoa Beach. See p 78.
En route to Hāmoa, look also for
red-sand **Koki Beach,** which is visible from Haneo'o Road.

Haneo'o Rd. rejoins Hana Hwy.
360. Continue south another
7 miles (11km).

⑬ ★★★ kids 'Ohe'o Gulch.
Time to hit the water again, in the
Kīpahulu section **of Haleakalā
National Park** (see p 89). For years
people called this series of

Waimoku Falls.

stair-step waterfalls "Seven Sacred Pools." It's a misnomer; there are more than 7 pools—and all water in Hawai'i is considered sacred. Park rangers offer safety information, exhibits, books, and a variety of walks and hikes year-round; check at the station for current activities. Don't miss the magnificent 400-foot (122m) **Waimoku Falls,** reachable via an often-muddy, but rewarding, hour-long uphill hike through a magical bamboo forest. Expect showers on the Kīpahulu coast. *www.nps.gov/hale.* ☎ *808/248-7375. Admission $25 per car.*

Continue 1 mile (1.6km) past 'Ohe'o Gulch on the ocean side of Hwy. 360.

⓮ **Lindbergh's Grave.** Aviation fans make the trek to honor renowned pilot Charles A. Lindbergh (1902–1974), who was the first to fly solo across the Atlantic. He settled in Kīpahulu, where he died of cancer in 1974, and was buried under river stones in a seaside graveyard behind the 1857 **Palapala Ho'omau Congregational Church.** You'll have no trouble finding his tombstone, which is engraved with his favorite words from the 139th Psalm: "If I take the wings of the morning and dwell in the uttermost parts of the sea."

Drive about 6 miles (9.6km) farther on Hwy. 360, which becomes Pi'ilani Hwy 31.

⓯ **Kaupō.** If you still have daylight, continue on (or wait until the next day) to remote, rural Kaupō. The road turns to gravel at times, but isn't too bad—despite what your rental car agent might claim. Kaupō highlights include the lovingly restored 1859 **Huialoha Church** (www.huialohachurchkaupo. org) with its old schoolhouse ruins and lovely pebble beach; and farther down the road, the **Kaupo Store,** an eclectic old country store that carries a range of bizarre goods and doesn't keep any of its posted hours, but is a fun place to "talk story" with the staff about this area, which at one time supported a substantial population. *Store:* ☎ *808/248-8054. Mon–Sat 10am–5pm.* ●

'Ohe'o Gulch.

Beaches Best Bets

Best **Black Sand**
★ Wai'ānapanapa State Park, *MM 32, Hāna Highway (Hwy. 360), Hāna* (p 82)

Best for **Body Surfing**
★ Kama'ole III Beach Park, *South Kīhei Road, Kīhei* (p 80) and ★★ Hāmoa Beach, *Haneo'o Road, Hāna* (p 78)

Best for **Families**
★ Kama'ole III Beach Park, *S. Kihei Road, Kihei* (p 80)

Longest **White-Sand Beach**
★★★ Mākena State Beach Park (Big Beach), *South Mākena Road, Mākena* (p 81)

Best for **Kayaking**
★★★ Maluaka Beach (Mākena Beach), *Mākena Road, Mākena* (p 81)

Best for **Picnicking**
Wahikuli County Wayside Park, *MM 23, Honoapi'ilani Highway (Hwy. 30), Lahaina* (p 81)

Most **Romantic**
★★ Wailea Beach, *Wailea Alanui Road, Wailea* (p 82)

Best for **People-Watching**
★★ Ka'anapali Beach, *Kaanapali* (p 79)

Safest for **Kids**
★★ H. P. Baldwin Park ("Baby Beach" at far west end), *MM 6, Hāna Highway (Hwy. 360), between Spreckelsville and Pā'ia* (p 78); and Launiupoko County Wayside Park, *MM 18, Honoapi'ilani Highway (Hwy. 30), Lahaina* (p 81)

Safest for **Swimming**
★ Kama'ole III Beach Park, *South Kīhei Road, Kīhei* (p 80)

Best for **Snorkeling**
★★★ Kahekili Beach Park, *Ka'anapali* (p 79)

Best **View**
★★ Maluaka Beach, *Mākena Road, Mākena (p 81)* and Kaihalulu (Red Sand) Beach, *Off Uakea Road, Hāna* (p 79)

Best for **Surfing & Windsurfing**
★★★ Ho'okipa Beach Park, *just before MM 9, Hāna Highway (Hwy. 36), Paia* (p 78)

Best for **Sunbathing**
★★ Hāmoa Beach, *Haneo'o Road, Hāna* (p 78)

Previous page: The black lava sands of Wai'ānapanapa Beach.
Below: The gray sands of Hāmoa Beach are a mix of coral and lava.

Maui Beaches A to Z

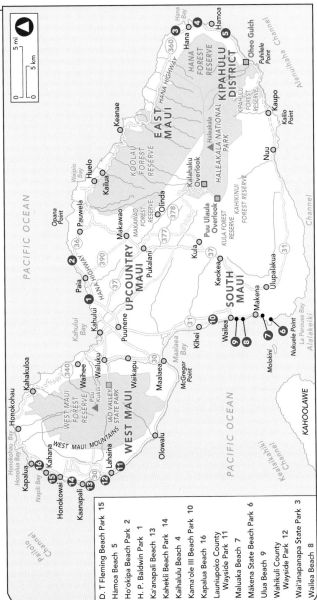

D. T Fleming Beach Park 15
Hämoa Beach 5
Hoʻokipa Beach Park 2
H. P. Baldwin Park 1
Kaʻanapali Beach 13
Kahekili Beach Park 14
Kaihalulu Beach 4
Kamaʻole III Beach Park 10
Kapalua Beach 16
Launiupoko County Wayside Park 11
Maluaka Beach 7
Mäkena State Beach Park 6
Ulua Beach 9
Wahikuli County Wayside Park 12
Waiʻanapanapa State Park 3
Wailea Beach 8

Maui Beaches A to Z

★ D. T. Fleming Beach Park.
This wide, quiet, out-of-the-way beach cove is good for families. Immediately north of the Ritz-Carlton Hotel, it's bordered by ironwood trees, which provide plenty of shade, and the water is generally good for swimming and snorkeling. Facilities include restrooms, showers, picnic tables, barbecue grills, lifeguards, and a paved parking lot. *Past MM 30, Honoapi'ilani Hwy. (Hwy. 30), Kapalua.*

★★ Hāmoa Beach. Viewed from above, this half-moon-shaped, gray-sand beach is a vision of paradise. The wide stretch of sand (a mix of coral and lava) is three football fields long and sits below 30-foot black-lava sea cliffs. Swells on this unprotected beach break offshore and roll in, making it a popular surfing and bodysurfing area. Hāmoa is often swept by powerful rip currents, so take care. The calm left side is best for snorkeling in summer. Travaasa Hāna resort has numerous facilities for guests, plus outdoor showers and restrooms for nonguests. Parking is limited. *Haneo'o Rd., off Hāna Hwy. (Hwy. 360), Hāna.*

★★★ Ho'okipa Beach Park.
Ho'okipa means "hospitality," and this sandy beach on Maui's north shore certainly rolls out the red carpet for wave-riders–it's among the world's top spots for windsurfing and kiting. Daring watermen and -women paddle out to carve waves up to 25 feet tall on the reef's multiple surf breaks. Spectators are welcome as well; head to the cliff-top parking lot for a bird's-eye view of the action. On flat days, you can snorkel over the reef's trove of marine life. Check out the sea turtles napping on the sand below the cliff (but give the resting reptiles at least 15 feet leeway). Facilities include restrooms, showers, pavilions, picnic tables, barbecue grills, and parking. *2 miles past Pā'ia on the Hāna Hwy. (Hwy. 36).*

★★ H. P. Baldwin Park. This beach park draws lots of locals: dog walkers, yoga enthusiasts, boogie boarders, fishermen, and young families. The far ends of the beach are safest for swimming: "the cove" in the lee of the rocks at the north end, and "baby beach" at the south end, where an exposed reef creates a natural sandy swimming pool. Facilities include a pavilion with picnic tables, barbecue grills, restrooms, showers, a semipaved

Maui's Beaches—Open to All

Maui has more than 80 accessible beaches of every conceivable description, from rocky black-sand beauties to powdery golden ones. The ones I list in this chapter represent my personal favorites, carefully chosen to suit a variety of needs, tastes, and interests. All beaches, even those in front of exclusive resorts, are public property; Hawai'i state law requires resorts and hotels to offer public right-of-way access to the beach, as well as public parking. So don't be shy—just because a beach fronts a hotel doesn't mean you can't enjoy it.

parking area, a soccer field, and lifeguards. *At MM 6, Hāna Hwy. (Hwy. 360), btw. Sprecklesville and Pā 'ia, turn left on Alawai Rd., follow to the ocean.*

★★ **Ka'anapali Beach.** Four-mile-long (6.4km) Ka'anapali is one of Maui's best beaches, with grainy gold sand as far as the eye can see. Because Ka'anapali is so long, and because most hotels have adjacent swimming pools, the beach is crowded only in pockets—you'll find plenty of spots to be alone. There's decent snorkeling around **Black Rock,** in front of the Shera-ton. The water is clear, calm, and populated with clouds of tropical fish. Facilities consist of outdoor showers. Parking is a problem, though. *Look for* PUBLIC BEACH ACCESS *signs off Ka'anapali Pkwy., off Honoapi'ilani Hwy. (Hwy. 30), at the Ka'anapali Resort.*

★★★ **Kahekili Beach Park** This beach gets top marks for everything: a grassy park with pavilion and palm trees, plenty of soft golden sand, and a vibrant coral reef only a few fin-kicks from shore. Herbivo-rous fish (such as surgeonfish and rainbow-colored parrotfish) are

Kama'ole III Beach Park.

off-limits to fishermen here, so the snorkeling is truly excellent. Facili-ties include picnic tables, barbe-cues, showers, restrooms, and paved parking—a real bonus on a stretch of coast where parking is often a problem. *From Honoapi'ilani Hwy. (Hwy. 30) just north of Ka'anapali Resort, follow Pu'ukoli'i Road to its end.*

Kaihalulu (Red Sand) Beach. This beach on the hidden side of Kau'iki Hill, just south of Hāna Bay, is a stunner. Originally a volcanic cinder cone that lost its seaward wall to erosion, spilling red cinders everywhere, its coarse red sand is

Kaihalulu (Red Sand) Beach.

fringed with black lava rocks and glacier-blue water. Three things to know about this beach: You have to trespass to get here; the path can be extremely dangerous due to heavy rains (there have been several serious injuries on the muddy, slippery terrain); and nudity (illegal in Hawai'i) is common here. If you are determined to go, inquire about conditions on the trail, which drops several stories down to the ocean rocks. To reach the beach, walk south on Uakea Road, past Hau'oli Street and the Travassa Hotel, to the gated parking lot for the hotel's cottages. Turn left and cross the open field next to the Hāna Community Center. Look for a dirt trail and follow it past a huge ironwood tree down to the shoreline. (Avoid the cinder trail on the hill; it's prone to erosion). Follow the coast to a rocky point, then climb up to meet the cinder trail. As the trail turns a corner, the burnt-red beach comes into view. A lava outcropping protecting the bay makes it safe for swimming; snorkeling is fun here, and there's a natural whirlpool area on the Hāna Bay side of the cove. Stay away from the surge area where the ocean enters the cove.

★ **Kama'ole III Beach Park.** On weekends this beach is jampacked with picnickers, swimmers, and snorkelers, but during the week, "Kam-3" (as locals call it), is often empty. There's a playground for children and a grassy lawn that meets the sand; swimming is safe, although scattered lava rocks are toe stubbers at the water line, and parents should watch to make sure kids don't venture too far out—the bottom slopes off quickly. Both the north and south shores are rocky fingers with a surge big enough to attract fish (and snorkelers that watch them), while winter waves attract bodysurfers. Facilities include restrooms, showers, picnic tables, barbecue grills, swing set, and lifeguards. *S. Kīhei Rd., across from Keonekai Rd., Kīhei.*

★★★ **Kapalua Beach.** This is a postcard-perfect beach: a golden crescent bordered by two palm-studded points. Protected from strong winds and currents by lava-rock promontories, Kapalua's calm waters are great for snorkelers and swimmers of all ages and abilities, and the bay is big enough to paddle a kayak around without getting into the more challenging channel that separates Maui from Moloka'i. Facilities include outdoor showers, restrooms, lifeguards, a rental shack, and plenty of shade. Parking is limited to about 30 spaces in a

Kapalua Beach.

Mākena State Beach Park's Big Beach.

small lot. *Past MM 30, by Napali Kai Beach Resort, Honoapiʻilani Rd., Kapalua.*

kids Launiupoko County Wayside Park. Families with children will love this small, shady park with a large wading pool for kids and a small sandy beach with good swimming when conditions are right. The view from the park is one of the best, with the islands of Kahoʻolawe, Lānaʻi, and Molokaʻi in the distance. Facilities include a paved parking lot, restrooms, showers, picnic tables, and barbecue grills. It's crowded on weekends. *MM 18, Honoapiʻilani Hwy. (Hwy. 30), Lahaina.*

★★★ Mākena State Beach Park (Big Beach). One of the most popular beaches on Maui, Mākena is so vast it never feels crowded. Locals call it **"Big Beach"**—more than 100 feet wide, it stretches out 3,300 feet from Puʻu ʻOlai, the tall cinder cone on its north end, to its southern rocky point. The golden sand is luxuriant, deep, and soft, but the shorebreak is steep and powerful—many a visitor has broken an arm in the surf here. If you're an inexperienced swimmer, better to watch the pros shred waves on skimboards. Facilities are limited to portable toilets, but there's plenty of parking and lifeguards at the first two entrances. Dolphins often frequent these

waters, and nearly every afternoon a heavy cloud rolls in, providing welcome relief from the sun. Clamber up the Puʻu ʻOlai to find **Little Beach** on the other side, a small crescent of sand where assorted nudists defy the law to work on their all-over tans. *Three entrances off of South Mākena Rd., Mākena.*

★★★ Maluaka Beach. Talk about views: With Molokini Crater and Kahoʻolawe both visible in the distance, this short, wide, palm-fringed crescent of golden sand is set between two black-lava points and bounded by big dunes topped by a grassy knoll. Swimming and kayaking in the mostly calm bay are first-rate. Facilities include restrooms, showers, grass park, and paved parking. *From Mākena Alanui, turn left on Mākena Keonoio.*

★ Ulua Beach. One of the most popular beaches in Wailea, Ulua is a long, wide crescent of gold sand between two rocky points. When the ocean is calm, Ulua offers Wailea's best snorkeling; when it's rough, the waves are excellent for bodysurfers. Crowded conditions make it perfect for meeting people. Facilities include showers and restrooms. *Look for the blue shoreline access sign, on Wailea Alanui Dr., Wailea.*

Wahikuli County Wayside Park. One of Lahaina's most popular beach parks, Wahikuli is packed

Wailea Beach.

on weekends, but during the week it's a prime spot for swimming, snorkeling, sunbathing, and picnicking. Facilities include paved parking, restrooms, showers, and small pavilions with picnic tables and barbecue grills. *MM 23, Honoapi'ilani Hwy. (Hwy. 30), btw. Lahaina and Ka'anapali.*

★★★ Wai'ānapanapa State Park.

This 120-acre (49ha) beach park is wonderful for shoreline hikes and picnicking, although swimming is generally unsafe (powerful rip currents, strong waves breaking offshore). The black-sand beach gets crowded on weekends; weekdays are generally a better bet. Facilities include 12 cabins, a beach park, picnic tables, barbecue grills, restrooms, showers, and a parking lot. *MM 32, Hāna Hwy. (Hwy. 360), Hāna. See p 89.*

★ Wailea Beach.

From this beach, the view out to sea is magnificent, framed by neighboring Kaho'olawe and Lāna'i and the tiny crescent of Molokini. Grab your sweetie at sunset and watch the clear waters tumble to shore; this is as romantic as it gets. Facilities include restrooms, outdoor showers, and limited free parking. *Look for blue shoreline access sign, on Wailea Alanui Dr., Wailea.* ●

The Legend of Wai'ānapanapa

Wai'ānapanapa Park gets its name from the legend of the Wai'ānapanapa Cave. Chief Ka'akea, a jealous and cruel man, suspected his wife, Popoalaea, of having an affair. Popoalaea left her husband and hid herself in a chamber of the Wai'ānapanapa Cave. A few days later, when Ka'akea was passing by the cave, the shadow of a servant gave away Popoalaea's hiding place, and Ka'akea killed her. During certain times of the year, the water in the tide pool turns red as a tribute to Popoalaea, commemorating her death. (Killjoy scientists claim, however, that the change in color is due to the presence of small red shrimp.

6 The Great **Outdoors**

Haleakalā National Park

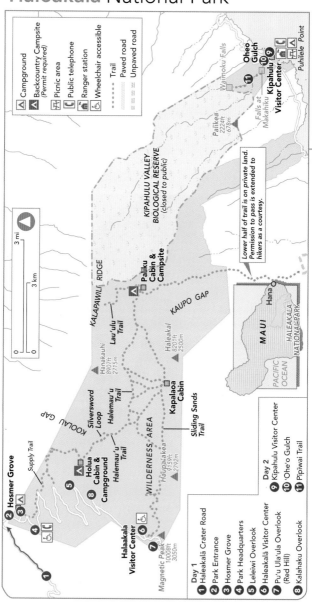

Campground
Backcountry Campsite *(Permit required)*
Picnic area
Public telephone
Ranger station
Wheelchair accessible
Trail
Paved road
Unpaved road

Waimoku Falls

Oheo Gulch

Kipahulu Visitor Center

Puhilele Point

Palikea 2224ft 678m

KIPAHULU VALLEY BIOLOGICAL RESERVE *(closed to public)*

Falls at Makahiku

KALAPAWILI RIDGE

Paliku Cabin & Campsite

KAUPO GAP

Lau'ulu Trail

Supply Trail

3 mi

3 km

Lower half of trail is on private land. Permission to pass is extended to hikers as a courtesy.

MAUI

Hana

PACIFIC OCEAN

HALEAKALA NATIONAL PARK

2 Hosmer Grove

Hanakauhi 8907ft 2715m

Haleakal 8201ft 2500m

Kapalaoa Cabin

Silversword Loop

Halemau'u Trail

KOOLAU GAP

Sliding Sands Trail

WILDERNESS AREA

Hāupaakea 9157ft 2792m

Holua Cabin & Campground

Halemau'u Trail

Haleakala Visitor Center

Magnetic Peak 10008ft 3050m

Previous page: A surfer drops to the curl of Hawaii's big surf.

The summit of Haleakalā, the House of the Sun, is a spectacular natural phenomenon. More than 1.3 million people a year ascend the 10,023-foot-high mountain to peer into the world's largest dormant volcano. (Haleakalā has not rumbled for at least 100 years, but it's still officially considered active.) Haleakalā National Park's lunar-like landscape is home to numerous rare and endangered plants, birds, and insects. There are actually two parts: **Haleakalā Summit** and **Kīpahulu** (p. 86), in the dense rainforest on Maui's east coast. No roads link the two sections; you'll visit them separately, taking at least a day to explore each place. Whichever you visit first, save your park receipt to get free entry at the other section. START: Kahului.

Travel Tips

The town of Pukalani is the last stop for food and gas (there are no facilities within the national park). On the way back down the mountain, put your car in low gear so you won't destroy your brakes on the descent.

Day One
From Kahului, take Hwy. 37 to Hwy. 377 to Hwy. 378.

❶ ★★★ Haleakalā Crater Road. Just driving up the mountain is an experience. On Haleakalā Crater Road (Hwy. 378), 33 switchbacks travel through numerous climate zones, passing in and out of clouds, fog, and rain, to finally deliver a view that extends for more than 100 miles (161km). Be on the lookout for downhill bicyclists, stray cattle, and naïve nēnē, the native Hawaiian geese.

❷ Park Entrance. A ranger will collect an entrance fee of $25 per car (or $20 per motorcycle), good for a week of unlimited entry at both the summit and Kīpahulu districts.

❸ ★★★ Hosmer Grove. Birders should make a beeline to this small campground and forest. In Hawai'i's territorial days, forester Ralph Hosmer tried to launch a timber industry. It failed, but a few of his sweet-smelling cedars and pines remain. A half-mile loop trail snakes from the parking lot through the evergreens to a picturesque gulch, where rare **Hawaiian honeycreepers** flit above native 'ōhi'a and sandalwood trees.

❹ ★★ Park Headquarters. Stop here to pick up park information and camping permits, use the restroom, fill your water bottle, and purchase park swag. Keep an eye out for the native Hawaiian goose, the gray-brown **nēnē** with its black face, buff cheeks, and partially webbed feet. Nēnē once flourished throughout Hawai'i, but habitat destruction and non-native predators (rats, cats dogs, mongooses) nearly caused their extinction. By

A view from atop Haleakalā.

Hawaii's endangered nēnē, or Hawaiian goose.

1951 there were only 30 left. Boy Scouts helped to re-introduce them into Haleakalā. The species remains endangered, but is now protected as Hawai'i's state bird. *www.nps.gov/hale.* ☎ *808/572-4400. Daily 7am–3:45pm.*

❺ ★★ Leleiwi Overlook. Just beyond MM 17, pull into the parking area. From here a short trail leads you to a stellar view of the crater. When the clouds are low and the sun is in the right place—usually around sunset—you might experience a phenomenon known as the "Specter of the Brocken": You'll can see a reflection of your shadow, ringed by a rainbow, in the clouds below. This optical illusion occurs only three places on the planet: Haleakalā, Scotland, and Germany.

❻ ★★★ Haleakalā Visitor Center. Just before the summit, this small building offers a panoramic view of the volcanic landscape, with photos identifying the various features and exhibits that explain its history, ecology, geology, and volcanology. (Restrooms and water are available here, too.) Rangers offer excellent free **naturalist talks** daily in the summit building and lead guided hikes from here (check website for times). *www.nps.gov/hale.* ☎ *808/572-4400. Daily sunrise–3pm.*

❼ ★★★ Pu'u 'Ula'ula Overlook (Red Hill). Here, at the volcano's highest point, a glass-enclosed windbreak makes a prime viewing spot, crowded with shivering folks at sunrise. (You'll also notice a mysterious cluster of buildings: Haleakalā Observatories, unofficially dubbed **Science City.**) This is also the best place to see a rare **silversword,** a botanical wonder that's like a spacey artichoke with attitude. Silverswords grow only in Hawai'i, take from 4 to 30 years to bloom, and then, usually between May and October, send up a 1- to 6-foot stalk covered in reddish, sunflower-like blooms. Don't walk too close to silversword plants—footfalls can damage their roots.

❽ ★★ Kalahaku Overlook. On your way back down the summit, stop here to gaze into the distance. On a clear day you can see all the way across Alenuihaha Channel to the often-snowcapped summit of Mauna Kea on the Big Island.

Day Two
❶ Kīpahulu Visitor Center. Eleven wiggly miles (18km) past Hāna on Hwy. 360, the Kīpahulu center offers information, books, exhibits, and ranger-led walks year-round. The entry fee is $25 per car or $20 per motorcycle (also good

for entry at Haleakalā summit district). Restrooms and drinking water are available. *www.nps.gov/hale.* ☎ *808/248-7375. Daily 8:30–5pm.*

② ★★★ **'Ohe'o Gulch.** A one-lane stone bridge passes over this charismatic stream, which breaks into multiple waterfalls cascading down to the tumultuous ocean. Often called the Seven Sacred Pools (a misnomer—there are more than seven pools, and in Hawai'i *all* water is sacred), the famous pools are gorgeous, though often packed with visitors (note that it's not a good idea to swim in the pools in the winter rainy season). Take time to explore the surrounding forest, which includes native coastal species such as *hala* (screwpine) and *hau* (tree hibiscus).

③ ★★★ **Pīpīwai Trail.** A short hike above 'Ohe'o Gulch will take you to two spectacular **waterfalls.** The trail begins across the street from the ranger station's central

The overlook for Makahiku Falls.

parking area. Follow the trail ½ mile to the overlook for **Makahiku Falls,** a 200-foot-tall beauty. Continue another 1.5 miles, across two bridges and through a bamboo forest, to the dazzling 400-foot-tall **Waimoku Falls.** It's a hard uphill hike, but worth every step. Beware of falling rocks; never stand beneath the falls.

Going to the Summit

You need reservations to view sunrise from the summit. The National Park Service now limits how many cars can access the summit between 3am and 7am. Book your spot up to 60 days in advance at www.recreation.gov. A fee of $1.50 (on top of park entrance fees) applies. You'll need to show your reservation receipt and photo I.D. to enter the park. Watching the sun's first golden rays break through the clouds is indeed spectacular, although I recommend sunset instead: It's equally beautiful—and warmer! Full-moon nights can be ethereal, too.

Whenever you go, know that weather at the summit is extreme, ranging from blazing sun to sudden snow flurries. Glorious views aren't guaranteed; the summit may be misty or overcast at any time of day. As you ascend the slopes, the temperature drops about 3 degrees every 1,000 feet (305m), so the top can be 30 degrees cooler than sea level—and the alpine wind can really sting. Come prepared with warm layers and rain gear. Before you head up the mountain, get current weather conditions from the park (☎ **808/572-4400**) or the **National Weather Service** (☎ **866/944-5025**, option 4).

Maui's Best Hiking & Camping

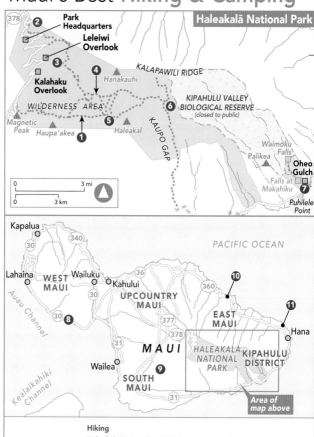

Haleakalā National Park

Park Headquarters
Leleiwi Overlook
Kalahaku Overlook
WILDERNESS AREA
Magnetic Peak
Haupa'akea
Hanakauhi
KALAPAWILI RIDGE
KIPAHULU VALLEY BIOLOGICAL RESERVE
(closed to public)
Haleakalā
KAUPO GAP
Waimoku Falls
Palikea
Oheo Gulch
Falls at Makahiku
Puhilele Point

0 — 3 mi
0 — 3 km

Kapalua
PACIFIC OCEAN
Lahaina
WEST MAUI
Wailuku
Kahului
UPCOUNTRY MAUI
Au'au Channel
EAST MAUI
Hana
MAUI
HALEAKALĀ NATIONAL PARK
KIPAHULU DISTRICT
Wailea
SOUTH MAUI
Kealaikahiki Channel
Area of map above

Hiking

Haleakalā National Park: Halemau'u Trail 4
Haleakalā National Park: Sliding Sands Trail 1
Ke'anae Arboretum 10
Polipoli State Park 9
Wai'ānapanapa State Park 11

Camping

Haleakalā National Park: Hōlua 3
Haleakalā National Park: Hosmer Grove 2
Haleakalā National Park: Kapalaoa 5
Haleakalā National Park: Kīpahulu 7
Haleakalā National Park: Palikū 6
Olowalu Campground 8
Wai'ānapanapa 11

Over a few brief decades, Maui has transformed from a rural island to a fast-paced resort destination, but its natural beauty largely remains; many pristine places can be explored only on foot. Bring your own gear, as there are no places to rent camping equipment on Maui.

Haleakalā National Park

★★★ **Hiking.** Hiking into Maui's dormant volcano is an experience like no other. The terrain inside the wilderness area of the volcano, which ranges from burnt-red cinder cones to ebony-black lava flows, is astonishing. Inside the crater are some 27 miles (43km) of hiking trails, two camping sites, and three cabins. The best route takes in two trails: Descend into the crater along **Sliding Sands Trail,** which begins on the rim at 9,800 feet (2,987m) and descends to the valley floor at 6,600 feet (2,012m), and back out along **Halemau'u Trail.** The 11-mile (18km) one-way descent takes 9 hours. (Plus you'll need to catch a ride back to your starting point.) Some shorter options include the .5-mile **Hosmer Grove Nature Trail,** or just the first mile or two of **Sliding Sands Trail** (even this short hike can be exhausting at the high altitude). A good day hike is **Halemau'u Trail** to Hōlua Cabin and back, an 8-mile, half-day trip. For more information on Haleakalā, see p 85. *To get to the summit from Kahului, take Hwy. 37 to Hwy. 377 to Hwy. 378.* www.nps.gov/hale. ☎ 808/572-4400.

Camping. Hosmer Grove Campground, at 6,800 feet (2,073m), is a small grassy lawn surrounded by forest near the entrance to Haleakalā National Park. This is the best place to spend the night if you want to see the Haleakalā sunrise or catch sight of native Honeycreeper birds. Note that you must make a reservation if you plan to visit the summit between 3am and 7am (see p 87). Nights here are chilly, and can drop below freezing. In the park's coastal section, the popular **Kīpahulu Campground** is a large grass field just past the Kīpahulu Visitor Center, a peaceful spot with picnic tables, grills, and pit toilets. The most idyllic spots are away from the parking, under the *hala* trees facing the ocean. Expect rain and mosquitoes. Drinking water is only available at the Visitor Center. No permits are needed for either of these campgrounds (you do have to pay the park entrance fee); tent sites are first come, first served, and campers can stay for only 3 nights during a 30-day period.

Wilderness Camping. Three campgrounds inside the crater are

Hiking trails traverse the red cinder-cone terrain of the Haleakalā crater.

spaced so that each is a day's walk from the previous one: **Hōlua** is just off Halemau'u Trail at 6,920 feet (2,109m), **Kapala'oa** is on the Sliding Sands Trail in the center of the crater, and **Palikū** is on the eastern end by **Kaupō Gap.** Each campground features a cozy cabin with 12 padded bunks (bring your own bedding), cooking utensils, a propane stove, and a wood-burning stove with firewood. Cabins can be reserved up to 180 days in advance at www.recreation.gov or call ☎ **877/444-6777**; a flat rate of $75 is charged for the entire cabin. You will need a valid credit card to reserve by phone. The person who made the reservation must pick up the permit at the Haleakalā Visitor Center. **Hōlua** and **Palikū** also offer tent camping, with pit toilets and nonpotable catchment water. Permits are issued daily at park headquarters (first-come, first-serve); campers are limited to 2 nights in one cabin and 3 nights total in the wilderness per month.

Ke'anae Arboretum
Hiking. An easy, family-friendly 2-mile (3.2km) walk through the Ke'anae Arboretum explores a forest with both native and introduced plants. Allow 45 minutes, longer if you want to swim. Bring rain gear and mosquito repellent. *47 miles (76km) from Kahului, along the Hāna Hwy.*

Olowalu
★ **Camping.** Halfway to Lahaina, this campground abuts one of the island's best coral reefs. It's perfect for snorkeling and (during winter) whale watching; kayak rentals are available. Tent sites are $20 with access to porta-potties and outdoor showers. There are also "tentalows" with twin or king beds with linens, as well as private outdoor showers; they're close to the highway, but still cheap-ish at $80 per night ($95 in holiday season). Large groups can rent a set of six A-frame cabins (each sleeps 6) with bathrooms, showers, and a kitchen. *800 Olowalu Village Rd., off of Honoapi'ilani Hwy.* www.campolowalu.com. ☎ *808/661-4303.*

Polipoli State Park
★ **Hiking.** Halfway up the slope of Haleakalā, this state recreation area doesn't feel like typical Hawai'i (it's

Go With a Guide

Maui's oldest hiking company is **Hike Maui ★★** (www.hikemaui.com; ☎ **866/324-6284** or 808/879-5270), headed by Ken Schmitt, who pioneered guided treks on the Valley Isle. Hike Maui offers numerous treks island-wide, ranging from an easy 1-mile, 3-hour hike to a waterfall ($85) to a strenuous full-day hike in Haleakalā Crater ($179). On Hike Maui's popular East Maui waterfall trips ($124), you can swim and jump from the rocks into rainforest pools. Guides share cultural and botanical knowledge along the trail. All prices include equipment and transportation. Hotel pickup costs an extra $25 per person.

The Maui chapter of the **Sierra Club ★★** offers the best deal by far: guided hikes for a $5 donation. Volunteer naturalists lead small groups along historic coastlines and up into forest waterfalls. Go to www.mauisierraclub.org or call ☎ **808/573-4147.**

Safe Hiking & Camping

Most of the dangers to avoid while out adventuring involve water. **Flash floods** in Hawai'i happen suddenly, as downpours up the mountain cause streams to rise 4 feet in less than 10 minutes. People have been swept away, trapped, or forced to spend the night wet and shivering on the mountain. Don't let this happen to you. Watch the weather while hiking and never cross a flooding stream (even in a car). **Don't drink** stream water and don't swim if you have open wounds—feral pigs and deer spread *leptospirosis*, a bacterium that produces flulike symptoms and can be fatal. Don't jump into a fresh or saltwater pool without checking for **submerged rocks,** and don't ever approach **blowholes**—they can suck you in. At the shoreline, be aware that **rogue waves** can knock you over. Don't turn your back to the ocean.

Other do's and don'ts: Do carry your trash out and head back before sundown. Twilight near the equator is short-lived; it gets dark quickly! Finally, Maui is not crime free: Don't leave valuables unprotected. Carry a day pack if you're camping, and avoid camping alone.

downright cold at 6,200 ft./1,890m). But there's great hiking on the Polipoli Loop, an easy 5-mile (8km) hike that takes about 3 hours and branches out to a variety of longer trails. Dress warmly to meander through groves of eucalyptus, swamp mahogany, and hybrid cypress. *Take Hwy. 37 to Keokea and turn right on Hwy. 337; after less*

Towering trees shade the hiking trails in Polipoli State Park.

than ½ mile (.8km) turn on Waipoli Rd. and continue for 10 miles (16km) to the park.

Wai'ānapanapa State Park
★★★ **Hiking & Camping.**
Tucked in a tropical rainforest on the outskirts of Hāna, dreamy Wai'ānapanapa State Park features a black-sand beach set in an emerald forest, with camping and hiking. The coastal trail is an easy, 6-mile (9.7km) hike that parallels the sea, traveling past lava cliffs and a forest of *hala* trees. The park has 12 cabins and a tent campground. (Go for the cabins; it rains torrentially here). Tent sites are $18 per night for up to 6 people. Cabins ($90 per night, 2-night minimum) sleep six and have minimally stocked kitchens and covered lānai; reserve online at https://camping.ehawaii.gov/camping or call ☎ 808/984-8109. *Just after MM 32 on the Hāna Hwy (Hwy.360), turn off at* WAI'ĀNAPANAPA STATE PARK *sign. Follow Wai'ānapanapa Rd. to end.*

Maui's Best Golf Courses

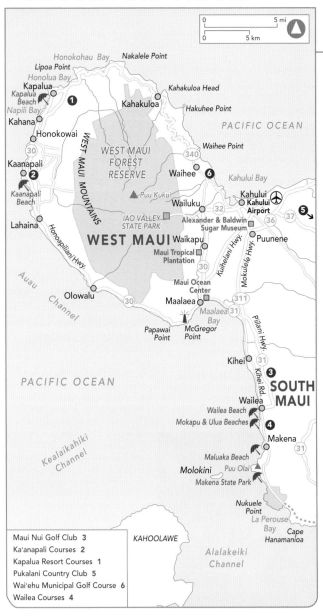

Maui Nui Golf Club	**3**
Ka'anapali Courses	**2**
Kapalua Resort Courses	**1**
Pukalani Country Club	**5**
Wai'ehu Municipal Golf Course	**6**
Wailea Courses	**4**

In some circles, Maui is synonymous with golf. Golfers have many outstanding layouts to choose from, from world championship courses to municipal parks with oceanfront views. Greens fees are pricey, but twilight tee times can be a giant deal. Be forewarned; the trade winds in the afternoon and can seriously alter your game.

Renting Golf Gear

Stand-by Golf (www.hawaiistandbygolf.com; ☎ 888/645-2665) rents clubs and offers savings off greens fees at Ka'anapali, Wailea Gold and Emerald, and Pukalani golf courses.

Golf Club Rentals (www.mauiclubrentals.com; ☎ 808/665-0800) has custom-built clubs for men, women, and juniors (right- and left-handed), which can be delivered islandwide; rates start at $25 a day.

Maui Nui Golf Club (formerly Elleair). Unspooling across the foothills of Haleakalā, this playground is just high enough to afford spectacular ocean vistas from every hole. It's beautiful and forgiving. *Just one caveat:* Go in the morning. Not only is it cooler, but more important, it's less windy. In the afternoon the winds bluster down Haleakalā with great gusto. Facilities include a clubhouse, driving range, putting green, pro shop, and lessons. *470 Līpoa Pkwy., Kīhei. www.mauinuigolfclub.com.*

☎ *808/874-0777. Greens fees $119; twilight rate $54–$89.*

★ **Ka'anapali Courses.** The courses at Kaanapali offer a challenge to all golfers, from high handicappers to near pros. The par-72, 6,305-yard **Royal Ka'anapali Course** is a true Robert Trent Jones, Sr., design, with lots of wide bunkers, long stretched-out tees, and the largest, most-contoured greens on Maui. The par-72, 6,250-yard **Ka'anapali Kai,** an Arthur Jack Snyder design, is shorter than the Royal course, but its narrow, hilly fairways require more accuracy. Facilities include a driving range, putting course, and clubhouse with dining. Weekdays are your best bet for tee times. *Off Hwy. 30, Ka'anapali. www.kaanapaligolfcourses.com.* ☎ *808/661-3691. Greens fees Royal Ka'anapali Course $255 ($179 resort guests), twilight rate $149, super twilight $109; Ka'anapali Kai Course $205 ($139 resort guests), twilight rate $99, super twilight $79. At first*

There are spectacular views from the Mākena courses.

Golf Tips

If you're trying to get a tee time at a public course, weekdays are always better than weekends. You'll have better luck teeing off after 9am, and afternoons generally are wide open. And, of course, book in advance, as soon as you have your travel dates. Bring extra balls: The rough is thick, water hazards are everywhere, and the wind wreaks havoc with your game. Trade winds of 10 to 30 mph (16–48kph) are not unusual between 10am and 2pm; you may have to play two to three clubs up or down to compensate. On the greens, your putt will *always* break toward the ocean. Hit deeper and more aggressively in the sand—the sand used on most Hawai'i courses is firmer and more compact than on mainland courses. And bring a camera for the spectacular views.

stoplight in Ka'anapali, turn onto Ka'anapali Pkwy. Clubhouse is the first building on your right.

★★★ Kapalua Resort Courses.
The views from these two championship courses are worth the greens fees alone. The par-72, 6,761-yard **Bay Course,** designed by Arnold Palmer and Ed Seay, is relatively forgiving, with wide fairways, but the greens are tricky to read. The par-73, 6,547-yard **Plantation Course,** site of the Hyundai Tournament of Champions, is a Ben Crenshaw and Bill Coore design set on a rolling hillside, which rewards low shots and precise chipping. Facilities include locker rooms, a driving range, and a good restaurant. Weekdays are your best bet for tee times. *Off Hwy. 30, Kapalua. www.golfatkapalua.com.* ☎ *808/669-8877). Greens fees: Bay Course $225 ($205 resort guests), twilight rates (1pm on) $165, super twilight $125; Plantation Course $325 ($265 resort guests), twilight rates $225, super twilight $185.*

Pukalani Country Club. This cool par-72, 6,962-yard course offers a break from the resorts' high greens

fees, and it's really fun to play. High handicappers will love this course; more experienced players can increase the challenge by playing from the back tees. Facilities include club and shoe rentals, practice areas, lockers, a pro shop, and a restaurant. *360 Pukalani St., Pukalani. www.pukalanigolf.com.* ☎ *808/572-1314. Greens fees (including cart) $89, $63 noon–2:30pm, $53 after 2:30pm. Take Hāna Hwy. (Hwy. 36) to Haleakalā Hwy. (Hwy. 37) to the Pukalani exit; turn right onto Pukalani St. and go 2 blocks.*

Wai'ehu Municipal Golf Course
This par-72 links course is like two courses in one: The first 9 holes, built in 1930, are set along the dramatic coastline, while the back 9 holes, added in 1966, head toward the mountains. It's a fun course that probably won't challenge your handicap. The only hazard is the wind, which can rip off the ocean and play havoc with your ball. Facilities include a snack bar, driving range, practice greens, golf-club rental, and clubhouse. It's a public course, so greens fees are low—but getting a tee time is tough. *2199*

The Emerald Course in Wailea.

Kaho'okele St., Wailuku, HI 96793. www.mauicounty.gov/facilities/Facility/Details/157. ☎ 808/240-7400. Greens fees $55; cart $20. From Kahului Airport, turn right on the Hāna Hwy. (Hwy. 36), which becomes Ka'ahumanu Ave. (Hwy. 32). Turn right at stoplight onto Waiehu Beach Rd. (Hwy. 340). Go another 1½ miles (2.4km) to entrance on your right.

★★ **Wailea Courses.** You can choose among three courses at Wailea. The **Blue Course,** a par-72, 6,758-yard course designed by Arthur Jack Snyder and dotted with bunkers and water hazards, is for duffers and pros alike. A little more difficult is the par-72, 7,078-yard championship **Gold Course,** designed by Robert Trent Jones, Jr., with narrow fairways, several tricky dogleg holes, and natural hazards like lava-rock walls. Wailea's newest is the **Emerald Course,** also by Jones, Jr., with tropical landscaping and a player-friendly design. With 3 courses, getting a weekend tee time is slightly easier here than at other resorts, but weekdays are still best (the Emerald Course is usually toughest to book). Facilities include 2 pro shops, restaurants, locker rooms, and a golf training facility. Wailea Alanui Dr. (off Wailea Iki Dr.), Wailea. www.waileagolf.com. ☎ 888/328-MAUI (6284) or 808/875-7450. Greens fees $199-$250 ($140–$190 resort guests), twilight rates $119-$165.

Golfing on a Budget

If your heart is set on playing on a resort course, book at least a week in advance. Ardent golfers on a budget should play in the afternoon, when discounted twilight rates are in effect. There's no guarantee you'll get 18 holes in, especially in winter when it's dark by 6pm, but you'll have an opportunity to experience these world-famous courses at half the usual fee.

For discount tee times, call **Stand-by Golf** (www.hawaiistandbygolf.com; ☎ **888/645-BOOK** [2665] or 808/665-0800) between 7am and 10pm. Stand-by offers discounted (up to 50% off) greens fees and guaranteed tee times for same-day or future golfing.

The Great Outdoors

Maui's Best Snorkeling

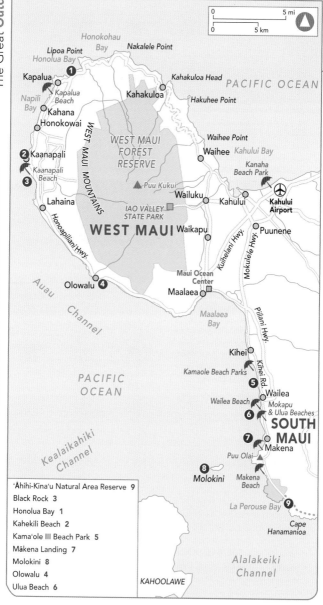

| 0 | | 5 mi |
| 0 | | 5 km |

PACIFIC OCEAN

Honokohau Bay
Nakalele Point
Lipoa Point
Honolua Bay
Kapalua ●1
Kahakuloa Head
Kapalua Beach
Kahakuloa
Hakuhee Point
Napili Bay
Kahana
Honokowai
Waihee Point
WEST MAUI FOREST RESERVE
Waihee Kahului Bay
●2 Kaanapali
Kanaha Beach Park
Kaanapali Beach
●3
▲ Puu Kukui
Wailuku Kahului
Kahului Airport
Lahaina
IAO VALLEY STATE PARK
WEST MAUI
Honoapiilani Hwy.
Waikapu
Puunene
Kuihelani Hwy.
Mokulele Hwy.
Auau Channel
Olowalu ●4
Maui Ocean Center
Maalaea
Maalaea Bay
Piilani Hwy.
Kihei
Kihei Rd.
Kamaole Beach Parks
●5
Wailea
PACIFIC OCEAN
Wailea Beach
●6
Mokapu & Ulua Beaches
SOUTH MAUI
●7 ● Makena
Kealaikahiki Channel
Puu Olai ▲
●8 Molokini
Makena Beach
La Perouse Bay
●9
Cape Hanamanioa
Alalakeiki Channel
KAHOOLAWE

'Āhihi-Kina'u Natural Area Reserve 9
Black Rock 3
Honolua Bay 1
Kahekili Beach 2
Kama'ole III Beach Park 5
Mākena Landing 7
Molokini 8
Olowalu 4
Ulua Beach 6

Snorkeling is the main attraction in Maui—and almost anyone can do it. All you need are a mask, a snorkel, fins, and some basic swimming skills. If you've never snorkeled before, most resorts and excursion boats offer instruction, but it's plenty easy to figure it out for yourself: In many places all you have to do is wade into the water and look down. Below are my favorite snorkeling spots in Maui.

★★ 'Āhihi-Kina'u Natural Area Reserve.

'Āhihi Bay is a 2,000-acre (809ha) state natural area reserve in the lee of Cape Kīna'u, on Maui's rugged south coast, where Haleakalā's red-hot lava ran to the sea in 1790. Fishing is strictly *kapu* (forbidden) here, and the fish know it; they're everywhere in this series of rocky coves and black-lava tide pools. After you snorkel, check out La Pérouse Bay on the south side of Cape Kīna'u, where French admiral La Pérouse became the first European to set foot on Maui. Note: the Hawai'i State Department of Land and Natural Resources has temporarily restricted access to portions of the reserve; go to http://hawaii.gov/dlnr/dofaw/nars/reserves/maui/ahihikinau for updated information on the closure or call ☎ 808/984-8800. *Drive south on Mākena on Mākena Alanui Rd.*

★ Black Rock.

At the north edge of Ka'anapali Beach, in front of the Sheraton, Black Rock has an easy entry and is populated with clouds of tropical fish. You might even spot a turtle or two. *Look for* PUBLIC BEACH ACCESS *signs off Ka'anapali Pkwy. (off Honoapi'ilani Hwy./Hwy.30), in the Ka'anapali Resort.*

★★★ Honolua Bay.

Spectacular coral formations glitter beneath the surface of this gemlike bay, a Marine Life Conservation District, at the upper northwest tip of the island. You'll have to swim a fair distance to reach the coral, though. Walk through a thick grove (take care with the boat ramp entry; it's slippery);

once you're in the water, head to the right. Turtles, rays, and a variety of snappers and goatfish will cruise along beside you. In the crevices are eels, lobster, and an array of rainbow-hued fish. Dolphins sometimes come here to rest. No facilities. *MM 32 on Honoapi'ilani Hwy.*

★★★ Kahekili Beach.

The north side of Ka'anapali Beach happens to be A+ for snorkeling, thanks to active marine management. Herbivorous species (surgeon fish and colorful parrotfish) are off-limits to fishermen here. A vibrant, healthy reef beckons just a few fin-kicks from shore. Count the different types of coral you see and look for eels poking out of holes. *End of Pu'ukoli'i Rd., off of Honoapi'ilani Hwy. in Ka'anapali.*

kids Kama'ole III Beach Park.

Locals love this beach: Not only does it have wide pockets of golden sand, but it's also the only one with a playground for children and a grassy lawn. For snorkeling, look

One of the creatures you may encounter while snorkeling in Maui.

Where to Get Snorkel Gear

You'll find rental gear and ocean toys all over the island. Most seaside resorts are stocked with watersports equipment (complimentary or rentals). **Snorkel Bob's** (www.snorkelbob.com) rents snorkel gear, boogie boards, wetsuits, and more at numerous locations: At Nāpili Bay, 5425 C Lower Honoapi'ilani Hwy., Lahaina (☎ **808/669-9603**); 1217 Front St., Lahaina (☎ **808/661-4421**); 3350 Lower Honoapi'ilani Hwy. #201, Honokowai (☎ **808/667-9999**); in Azeka's II Shopping Center, 1279 S. Kīhei Rd., Kīhei (☎ **808/875-6188**); 2411 S. Kīhei Rd., Kīhei (☎ **808/879-7449**); and 100 Wailea Ike Dr., Wailea (☎ **808/874-0011**). All are open daily 8am–5pm.

   Boss Frog's Dive, Surf, and Bike Shops (www.bossfrog.com) offers snorkel, boogie board, longboard, and stand-up paddleboard rentals and other gear; locations include: 150 Lahainaluna Rd., in Lahaina (☎ **808/661-3333**); 3636 Lower Honoapi'ilani Rd. in Ka'anapali (☎ **808/665-1200**); Nāpili Plaza, 5095 Nāpilihau St. in Nāpili (☎ **808/669-4949**); and 1215 S. Kīhei Rd. (☎ **808/891-0077**), 1770 S. Kīhei Rd. (☎ **808/874-5225**), and Dolphin Plaza, 2395 S. Kīhei Rd. (☎ **808/875-4477**) in Kīhei.

Snorkeling with butterflyfish.

toward the rocky fingers extending out in the north and south shores; they are fish magnets. *S. Kīhei Rd., across from Keonekai Rd., Kīhei.*

★★ **Mākena Landing.** If you're a confident swimmer, head to Mākena Landing, hug the north end of the bay, and round the point. You'll be treated to diverse corals and fish, turtles and caves. Look closely and you might spy a shy white-tip shark hiding in a cavern. A great place to dive or launch kayaks. *On Mākena Rd., just north of juncture with Honoiki St.*

★★★ **Molokini.** Like a crescent moon fallen from the sky, the crater of Molokini sits almost midway between Maui and the uninhabited island of Kaho'olawe. The 100-foot-deep bowl serves as a natural sanctuary for tropical fish and snorkelers, who arrive daily in a fleet of dive boats to this marine-life preserve. Note that in high season, Molokini can be crowded. See "Sail-Snorkel Trips," p 99, for information on getting to Molokini.

★★ **Olowalu.** Great snorkeling around MM 14, where, about 150 to 225 feet (46–69m) from shore, turtles line up to have cleaner wrasses pick off small parasites. Manta rays congregate here as well. *MM 14, Honoapi'ilani Hwy. 5 miles (8km) south of Lahaina.*

Sail-Snorkel Trips

Trilogy ★★★ (www.sailtrilogy.com; ☎ **888/MAUI-800** [628-4800] or 808/TRILOGY [874-5649]) offers my favorite snorkel-sail trips, on a fleet of custom-built catamarans. Their full-day **Maui-to-Lāna'i sail** from Lahaina Harbor to Hulopo'e Marine Preserve is the only cruise that includes a ground tour of the island and Hulopo'e Beach. The trip costs $205 for adults, $153 for ages 13 to 18, $100 for children 3 to 12. Trilogy's half-day **snorkel-sail trips to Molokini,** leaving from Mā'alaea Harbor; cost $135 for adults, $101 for teens, $68 for kids 3 to 12. All trips include breakfast (Mom's homemade cinnamon buns) and a barbecue lunch. In winter, 2-hour **whale watches** depart Ka'anapali Beach ($59 adults, $44 teens, $30 children).

Maui Classic Charters ★★ (Mā'alaea Harbor, slip 55 and slip 80; www.mauicharters.com; ☎ 800/736-5740 or 808/879-8188) offers morning and afternoon **snorkel cruises to Molokini** on *Four Winds II,* a 55-foot glass-bottom catamaran. Rates for the morning sail are $105 for adults and $75 for children 3 to 12, with continental breakfast and barbecue lunch to buy on board. The afternoon sail is a steal at $49, though the captain usually only visits Coral Gardens, which is accessible from shore. Hoping to catch sight of dolphins? Try the 5-hour **snorkel journey to Molokini and Mākena** on the catamaran *Maui Magic* (cost $120 adults, $90 children 5 to 12). All Maui Classic trips include beer, wine, and soda, plus snorkeling gear and instruction; the 5-hour *Maui Magic* trip also includes continental breakfast and barbecue lunch. In whale season (Dec 22–Apr 22), the *Four Winds* runs a 3½-hour **whale-watching trip** for $45 adults, $33 ages 3 to 12.

The **Pacific Whale Foundation ★★** (101 N. Kīhei Rd., Kīhei; www.pacificwhale.org; ☎ **800/249-5311** or 808/249-8811) supports its whale research and conservation programs by offering **whale-watch cruises, dolphin encounters,** and **snorkel tours** out of both Lahaina and Mā'alaea harbors. Options include a fun **Island Rhythms Sunset Cruise** with Marty Dread (a local entertainer who woos whales with rollicking tunes) and **full moon cruises** with astronomer-storyteller Harriet Witt. Snorkel trips start at $93, whale watches at $33.

For an action-packed experience, the 65-foot powerboat *Pride of Maui* (Mā'alaea Harbor; www.prideofmaui.com; ☎ **877/TO-PRIDE** [867-7433] or 808/242-0955) offers 5-hour snorkel cruises that visit Molokini and Turtle Town or Mākena. The cost is $124 for ages 13 and up ($99 if you book online) and $93 for ages 3 to 12. Continental breakfast, barbecue lunch, open bar, gear, and instruction are included.

Ulua Beach. Come here in the morning when the waters are calm, before trade winds kick up, to look for camouflaged frogfish. *Look for blue shoreline access sign on Wailea Alanui Dr., Wailea.*

Adventures on Land

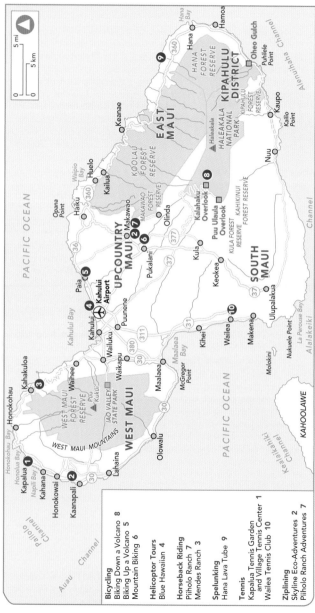

PACIFIC OCEAN

Auau Channel

Pailolo Channel

Honokohau Bay
Honokohau
Kahana
Honokowai
Kaanapali

1 Kapalua
2
3 Kahakuloa

Napili Bay
Kapalua
Honolua Bay

Waihee

WEST MAUI FOREST RESERVE

Puu Kukui ▲

IAO VALLEY STATE PARK

WEST MAUI MOUNTAINS

WEST MAUI

Lahaina
Olowalu

Waikapu

Wailuku

Maalaea

Maalaea Bay
McGregor Point

(30)
(380)
(311)

Kahului Bay

Kahului
4 ✈ Kahului Airport
5 Paia
Puunene

Opana Point

Haiku

Kailua
Huelo
(360)
(36)

Waipio Bay

KOOLAU FOREST RESERVE

UPCOUNTRY MAUI
6 Makawao
7 **2**
Olinda
(377)

Pukalani

Kula

Keokea

Ulupalakua
(37)

Keanae

EAST MAUI

MAKAWAO FOREST RESERVE

8 ■ Kalahaku Overlook
■ Puu Ulaula Overlook

▲ Haleakala

HALEAKALA NATIONAL PARK

KULA FOREST RESERVE
KAHIKINUI FOREST RESERVE

SOUTH MAUI

Kihei
10 Wailea
Makena

Nukele Point
La Perouse Bay
Molokini

PACIFIC OCEAN

Kealaikahiki Channel
Alalakeiki Channel

KAHOOLAWE

HANA FOREST RESERVE

Hana Bay
Hana
9
(360)
Hamoa

KIPAHULU DISTRICT

■ Oheo Gulch
Puhilele Point

KIPAHULU FOREST RESERVE

Kailio Point
Kaupo
Nuu

Alenuihaha Channel
Channel

0 ___ 5 mi
0 ___ 5 km

PACIFIC OCEAN

Maui is known for its inviting waters, but you'll also discover plenty of land-based adventures to enjoy. Haleakalā is perfect for bicycling and horseback riding; the warm, sunny days are terrific for tennis, and real daredevils can try ziplining.

Bicycling
Biking Down a Volcano. Several companies offer the opportunity to coast down Haleakalā, from near the summit to the shore, on basic cruiser bikes. It can be a thrilling experience—but be careful if you aren't a seasoned cyclist; serious accidents are not uncommon. Bike tours aren't allowed in Haleakalā National Park, so your van will take you to the summit first, then drop you off just outside of the park. You'll descend through multiple climates and ecosystems, past eucalyptus groves and flower-filled gulches. Bear in mind: The roads are steep and curvy, with no designated bike lanes and little-to-no shoulder. In winter and the rainy season, conditions can be particularly harsh; temperatures at the summit can drop below freezing and 40-mph winds howl. Wear warm layers whatever the season. Maui's oldest downhill company, **Maui Downhill,** offers a sunrise safari bike tour, including continental breakfast and brunch stop (not hosted). All rates include hotel pickup, transport to the top, bicycle, safety equipment, and breakfast. *199 Dairy Rd., Kahului. www. mauidownhill.com.* ☎ *800/535-BIKE*

(2453) or 808/871-2155. From $155 (check website for discounts).

Biking Up a Volcano. If you've got the chops to pedal *up* Haleakalā, the pros at **Maui Cyclery ★★★** can outfit you and provide a support vehicle. Tour de France athletes launch their Maui training sessions from this full-service Pā'ia bike shop, which rents top-of-the-line equipment and offers a range of guided tours and cycling camps. *99 Hāna Hwy., Pā'ia; www.gocycling maui.com.* ☎ *808/579-9009.*

Mountain Biking. If muddy trails are more your style, hit up Moose at **Krank Cycles ★★★** for a tricked-out bike and directions to the Makawao Forest trails. *1120 Makawao Ave., Makawao; www. krankmaui.com.* ☎ *808/572-2299.*

Helicopter Flights
Maui from the Air. Only a helicopter can bring you face-to-face with remote sites like Maui's little-known Wall of Tears, near the summit of Pu'u Kukui in the West Maui Mountains. You'll glide through canyons etched with 1,000-foot (305m) waterfalls and over dense rainforests; you'll climb high enough to glimpse the summit of Haleakalā,

Coasting down Haleakalā.

and fly by the dramatic vistas at Moloka'i. **Blue Hawaiian's ★★★** pilots are part Hawaiian historian, part DJ, part tour guide, and part amusement-ride operator. As you soar through the clouds, you'll learn about the island's flora, fauna, history, and culture. Blue Hawaiian is the only helicopter company in the state using high-tech, environmentally friendly (and quiet) Eco-Star helicopters. *Kahului Airport. www.bluehawaiian.com.* ☎ *800/745-2583 or 808/871-8844. Flights vary 30–90 min. for $153–$510 per person.*

Horseback Riding

Makawao. Maui has spectacular adventure rides through rugged ranch lands, into tropical forests, and to remote swimming holes. My favorite is **Pi'iholo Ranch ★★**, in Makawao, a working cattle ranch owned by the *kama'āina* (long-time resident) Baldwin family, where a variety of 2- to 3-hour private rides meander across the misty slopes of Haleakalā with picnic stops (starting at $229). You can play "Cowboy for a Day" and learn how to round up cattle ($349); on the "Heli Ranch Experience" ($3,823 for 2 people), a limo takes you to the Kahului heliport to board an A-Star helicopter and fly to a private ranch cabin for breakfast and a 2-hour horseback ride. *Waiahiwi Rd., Makawao. www.piiholo.com.* ☎ *808/270-8750. Rides start at $229.*

Kahakuloa. For an "out west" type of adventure, I like **Mendes Ranch & Trail Rides ★★.** The 300-acre (121ha) spread is a real-life working cowboy ranch with a full array of natural wonders: waterfalls, palm trees, coral-sand beaches, lagoons, tide pools, a rainforest, and its own volcanic peak (more than a mile high). Wrangler guides will take you from the edge of the rainforest out to the sea and even teach you to lasso. They'll field questions and

Stairs descend into the Hāna Lava Tube, an ancient cave formed by lava flows.

point out native flora, but generally just let you soak up Maui's natural splendor. A 1½-hour morning or afternoon ride costs $110; add a barbecue lunch at the corral for an additional $30. *3530 Kahekili Hwy., 5 miles (8km) past Wailuku. www.mendesranch.com.* ☎ *808/244-7320. Morning or afternoon ride $110; barbeque lunch additional $15.*

Spelunking

★ Hāna Lava Tube. When you're out in Hāna, you can descend into darkness to explore a million-year-old underground lava tube/cave. See for yourself how the Hawaiian Islands were made. Wander through the subterranean world and take a spin through the red *tī*-leaf maze as well. The self-guided tours take 30 to 45 minutes. *205 Ulaino Rd. just north of Hāna. www.mauicave.com.* ☎ *808/248-7308. Daily 10:30am–4pm. Admission $12 ages 6 and up.*

Tennis

★★★ Kapalua Tennis Garden and Village Tennis Center. Opened in 1979, the Tennis Garden

Ziplining the Haleakalā course.

has 10 Plexi-Pave courts paired in tiered clusters, with four lit for night play and surrounded by lush tropical foliage. Each set of courts is secluded in landscaped privacy with its own viewing lanai. Also available: private lessons, stroke-of-the-day clinics, drop-in clinics, and tournaments. The staff can match you up with a partner if you need one. *Kapalua Resort. www.golfatkapalua. com/tennis.* ☎ *808/662-7730. Courts $20 per person. Passes available.*

★★ **Wailea Tennis Club.** One of Maui's best tennis facilities, this resort club features 11 Plexi-Pave courts (3 nighttime courts), backboard or wall, pro shop, lessons, and doubles clinics. *131 Wailea Iki Place, Wailea. www.waileatennis.com.* ☎ *808/879-1958. Courts $20 per person.*

Ziplining

★ **Pi'iholo Ranch Adventures.** Explore this family ranch (see p 102) in the Makawao forest from above—flying through the eucalyptus canopy on one of six ziplines. Tour packages include access to the aerial bridge, tree platforms, ziplines (including side-by-side lines that you can ride with friends), and a trip to nearby waterfalls where you can take a refreshing dip. *799 Pi'iholo Rd., Makawao. www.piiholo zipline.com.* ☎ *808/572-1717. Tours: $99–$229.*

★ **Skyline EcoAdventures.** Go on, let out a wild holler as you soar above a rainforested gulch or down the slope of a mountain. Pioneers of this internationally popular activity, the Skyline owners brought the first ziplines to the U.S. and launched them from their home, here on Maui. Eco-conscious and carbon-neutral, the company donates thousands of dollars to local environmental agencies. Skyline has two courses, one on the west side and the other halfway up Haleakalā. Both are fast and fun, the guides are savvy and safety-conscious, and the scenery is breathtaking. In Ka'anapali, you can even "zip and dip": drop off your line into a mountain pool. Tours operate daily and take riders ages 12 and up, weighing between 80 and 300 pounds. *2½ miles up Haleakalā Hwy., Makawao. www. zipline.com.* ☎ *808/878-8400. Skyline EcoAdventures Ka'anapali: 2580 Keka'a Dr. #122 (meet at Fairway Shops), Lahaina (*☎ *808/662-1500). Tours: $107–$249.*

Adventures in the Ocean

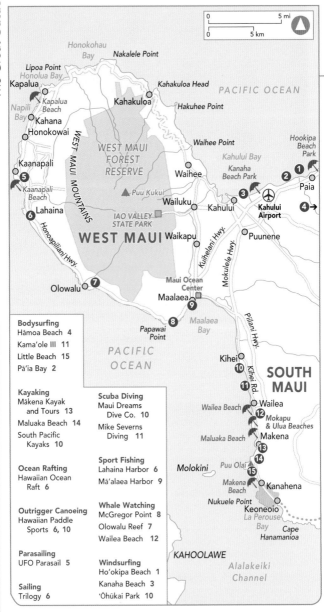

0   5 mi
0   5 km

Honokohau Bay
Nakalele Point
Lipoa Point
Honolua Bay
Kapalua
Napili Bay
Kapalua Beach
Kahana
Honokowai
Kaanapali
Kaanapali Beach
Lahaina
WEST MAUI MOUNTAINS
WEST MAUI FOREST RESERVE
Puu Kukui
IAO VALLEY STATE PARK
WEST MAUI
Honoapiilani Hwy.
Olowalu
Kahakuloa Head
Hakuhee Point
Kahakuloa
PACIFIC OCEAN
Waihee Point
Kahului Bay
Kanaha Beach Park
Waihee
Wailuku
Kahului
Waikapu
Kuihelani Hwy.
Mokulele Hwy.
Puunene
Kahului Airport
Hookipa Beach Park
Paia
Maui Ocean Center
Maalaea
Papawai Point
Maalaea Bay
PACIFIC OCEAN
Piilani Hwy.
Kihei
Kihei Rd.
SOUTH MAUI
Wailea Beach
Wailea
Mokapu & Ulua Beaches
Maluaka Beach
Makena
Molokini
Puu Olai
Makena Beach
Nukuele Point
La Perouse Bay
Keoneoio
Kanahena
Cape Hanamanioa
KAHOOLAWE
Alalakeiki Channel

Bodysurfing
Hāmoa Beach 4
Kamaʻole III 11
Little Beach 15
Pāʻia Bay 2

Kayaking
Mākena Kayak and Tours 13
Maluaka Beach 14
South Pacific Kayaks 10

Ocean Rafting
Hawaiian Ocean Raft 6

Outrigger Canoeing
Hawaiian Paddle Sports 6, 10

Parasailing
UFO Parasail 5

Sailing
Trilogy 6

Scuba Diving
Maui Dreams Dive Co. 10
Mike Severns Diving 11

Sport Fishing
Lahaina Harbor 6
Māʻalaea Harbor 9

Whale Watching
McGregor Point 8
Olowalu Reef 7
Wailea Beach 12

Windsurfing
Hoʻokipa Beach 1
Kanaha Beach 3
ʻŌhūkai Park 10

To really appreciate Maui, you need to get off the land and into the sea. Trade winds off the Lahaina coast and the strong wind that rips through Maui's isthmus make sailing around the island exciting. Or you can go head-to-head with a 1,000-pound marlin in a big game fishing battle; slowly glide over the water in a kayak; hover high above it in a parasail; or get into the water and scuba dive, bodysurf, board surf, or windsurf.

Bodysurfing

Riding the waves without a board, becoming one with the rolling water, is an exquisite art. Some bodysurfers just rely on their hands to ride the waves; others use a pair of open-heeled swim fins to help propel them through the water. The best bodysurfing beach for beginners is **Kama'ole III** in Kīhei. Secluded **Hāmoa Beach** in Hāna offers up steady swells, and in winter **Pā'ia Bay,** just outside of Pā'ia town, has great waves. If you don't mind nudity (illegal, but still practiced here), clamber over the Pu'u 'Olai cinder cone at **Mākena State Beach Park (Big Beach)** to find **Little Beach,** probably the best bodysurfing cove on the island.

Kayaking

Gliding silently over the water, propelled by a paddle, seeing Maui from the sea the way the early Hawaiians did—that's what ocean kayaking is all about. One of Maui's best kayak routes is south along the coast from **Maluaka Beach** in Mākena, where there's easy access, calm water, and sensational views. Go out in the early mornings; the wind comes up around 11am, making seas choppy and paddling difficult.

Ocean Rafting

If you're semiadventurous and looking for a more intimate experience with the sea, try ocean rafting, cruising along the coast on inflatable rafts that hold 6 to 24 passengers. One of the best (and most

Ocean kayaking lets you see Maui as the early Hawaiians did.

reasonable) outfitters is **Hawaiian Ocean Raft;** its 5-hour tour includes three stops for snorkeling and stops to search for dolphins, plus continental breakfast and midmorning snacks. *Lahaina Harbor. www.hawaii oceanrafting.com.* ☎ *888/677-RAFT (7238) or 808/661-7238. From $77 for adults, from $68 for children 5–12.*

Outrigger Canoe

Learn how to paddle a six-person canoe in sync with family or friends, just as the ancient Polynesians did when colonizing these islands. Several hotels (Fairmont Kea Lani Maui and the Andaz Maui) have their own boats and offer wonderful cultural trips right off the beach. Otherwise, book with **Hawaiian Paddle Sports ★★★**. The guides share knowledge about Maui's culture, history, and marine life. When turtles, whales, manta rays, or monk seals surface alongside your canoe,

Kayak Tours

For beginners, **Mākena Kayak and Tours ★** (www.makenakayak. com; ☎ 808/879-8426) is an excellent choice. Professional guide Dino Ventura leads a 2½-hour trip from Mākena Landing and loves taking first-timers over the secluded coral reefs and into remote coves. His $65 tour includes snorkel and kayak equipment; the 4-hour tour costs $95. If Dino is booked, try **South Pacific Kayaks,** 95 Halekauai St., Kīhei (www.southpacifickayaks.com; ☎ **800/776-2326** or 808/875-4848). Maui's oldest kayak-tour company leads trips that run from 3 to 5 hours and range in price from $74 to $225. The company rents equipment, too, and will meet you at Mākena Landing with kayaks ready to go.

you'll feel like a *National Geographic* explorer. *www.hawaiian paddlesports.com.* ☎ *808/442-6436. From $149 per person.*

Parasailing
Soar high above the crowds (at around 800 ft./244m) for a bird's-eye view of Maui. This adventure sport, a cross between skydiving and water-skiing, involves sailing through the air, suspended under a large parachute attached by towline to a speedboat. Keep in mind that parasailing tours don't run during whale season (roughly mid-May through mid-December). My favorite time is 8am, when the light is

fantastic. Book with **UFO Parasail,** which picks you up at Ka'anapali Beach. *www.ufoparasail.net.* ☎ 800/FLY-4-UFO (359-4836) or 808/661-7-UFO (661-7836). $79 for 800 ft.(244m) or $89 for 1200 ft. (366m).

Sailing
Trilogy ★★★ (see box p. 99) offers my favorite snorkel-sail trips.

Scuba Diving
Maui offers plenty of undersea attractions worth strapping on a tank for. Most divers start with **Molokini,** which can only be reached by boat. The sunken crater

You might encounter a shark while diving.

Whale-Watching

Maui is a favorite destination for Hawaiian humpback whales, who make the 3,000-mile (4,828km) swim from the chilly waters of Alaska to bask in Maui's warmth. The massive marine mammals get downright frisky from about November to May (though January and February are the peak months). Seeing whales leap out of the sea or perfect their tail slap is mesmerizing. You can hear them sing underwater, too! Just duck your head a foot below the surface and listen for creaks, groans, and otherworldly serenades. Bring binoculars to one of the following spots: **McGregor Point,** on the way to Lahaina, scenic lookout at MM 9; **Olowalu Reef,** along the straight part of Honoapi'ilani Highway, between McGregor Point and Olowalu; or **Wailea Beach Marriott Resort & Spa** (3700 Wailea Alanui Dr., Wailea), on the Wailea coastal walk, with a telescope installed for whale-watching.

For a closer look, I recommend jumping aboard a maneuverable high-speed raft. **Capt. Steve's Rafting Excursions** (www.captainsteves.com; ☎ 808/667-5565) offers 2-hour whale-watches out of Lahaina Harbor (from $55 adults, $45 children 5–12).

Maui's warm waters are prime habitat for humpback whales.

offers astounding visibility (you can often peer down 100 ft.) and an abundance of marine life, from clouds of yellow butterflyfish to manta rays. Experienced divers can explore Molokini's dramatic **back wall ★★★**, which plunges 350 feet and is frequented by larger marine animals. Other top sites include **Māla Wharf,** the **St. Anthony** (a sunken longliner), and **Five Graves** at Mākena Landing. Don't be scared off by the latter's ominous name—it's a magical spot with sea caves and arches. Most operators offer no-experience-necessary dives, ranging from $100 for one tank to $150 for two tanks. Visit the scuba gurus at **Maui Dreams Dive Company** (www.mauidreamsdiveco.com; ☎ 808/879-3584), for advice, equipment, and to book an intro beach dive ($69) or guided scooter dives ($99-$129) to WWII wrecks and frogfish hideouts. **Mike Severns Diving** (www.mikeseverns diving.com; ☎ 808/879-6596), is also great, offering two-tank dives for $145 ($130 with your own equipment).

Maui has Hawaii's best windsurfing beaches.

Sport Fishing

Marlin (as big as 1,200 lb.), tuna, *ono*, and mahimahi swim in Maui's coastal and channel waters. No license is required; just book a sport-fishing vessel out of **Lahaina** or **Māʻalaea** harbors. Most charter boats carry a maximum of 6 passengers; you can walk the docks, inspect boats, and talk to captains and crews; or book through **Sportfish Hawaii** (www.sportfishhawaii.com; ☎ **877/388-1376**). A shared boat for a half-day of bottom-fishing starts at $149. A half-day exclusive (you get the entire boat) starts at $699; a full-day exclusive starts at $1,095. Many captains tag and release marlin or keep the fish for themselves (sorry, that's Hawaiʻi style). If you want to eat your mahimahi for dinner or have your marlin mounted, tell the captain before you go.

Surfing

If you'd like to try out the ancient Hawaiian sport of *heʻe nalu* (wave sliding), call **Tide and Kiva Rivers,** two local boys (actually twins), who have been surfing since they could walk. Lessons are 1½-hours long and include equipment and instruction. They decide where the lesson will take place, based on their client's ability and where the surf is on that day. Tide claims he has beginners standing up in their first lesson. *www.riverstothesea.com.*

☎ *855/6284-7873 or 808/280-8795. 1½-hr. group lesson $124, 1½-hr. private instruction $225.*

Windsurfing

Maui has Hawaiʻi's best windsurfing beaches. In winter, windsurfers from around the world flock to the town of **Pāʻia** to ride the waves. **Hoʻokipa Beach,** internationally known for its brisk winds and excellent waves, is the site of several world-championship contests. **Kanaha,** west of Kahului Airport, also has dependable winds. When the winds turn northerly, the northern end of **Kīhei** is the spot to be, especially **ʻŌhūkai Park,** the first beach as you enter South Kīhei Road from the northern end; it has good winds, easy access, parking, and a long strip of grass to assemble your gear. **Hawaiian Sailboarding Techniques,** 425 Koloa St., Kahului (www.hstwindsurfing.com; ☎ **800/968-5423** or 808/871-5423), offers rentals and 2½-hour lessons from $99 at Kanahā Beach early in the morning before the breeze gets too strong for beginners. **Maui Windsurf Company,** 22 Hāna Hwy., Kahului (www.mauiwindsurfcompany.com; ☎ **808/877-4816**), rents top quality equipment (Goya boards, sails, and roof racks) from $59, and offers 2½-hour group lessons from $99. ●

Shopping Best Bets

Best Alohawear
★★ Moonbow Tropics, 36 Baldwin Ave. (p 115)

Best Antiques
★★ Bird of Paradise Unique Antiques, 56 N. Market St. (p 115)

Best Art
★★★ Hui Noe 'au, 2841 Baldwin Ave. (p 116) and ★★★ Village Galleries, 120 and 180 Dickenson St. (p 117).

Best Bookstore
★★★ Maui Friends of the Library, In Queen Ka'ahumanu Center 275 Ka'ahumanu Ave. (p 117)

Best Flower Lei
Pukalani Superette, 15 Makawao Ave., Pukalani (p 118) and ★★★ Native Intelligence, 1980 Market St., Wailuku (p 118)

Best Gifts for Kids
★★ Maui Ocean Center, 192 Mā'alaea Rd. (p 119)

Best Handblown Glass
★★ Hot Island Glassblowing Studio & Gallery, 3620 Baldwin Ave. (p 116)

Best Hawaiian Art & Gifts
★★★ Hāna Coast Gallery, At Travaasa Hāna (p 115) and ★★★ Native Intelligence, 1980 Market St. #2, Wailuku (p 118)

Best Local Fashion
★★★ Tamara Catz, 83 Hāna Hwy., Pā'ia (p 118) and ★★ Maggie Coulombe, Whalers Village, 2535 Ka'anapali Pkwy. (p 117)

Best Shoes
★★★ Sandal Tree, multiple locations (p 119)

Best Souvenir to Ship Home
★★ Proteas of Hawai'i, 15200 Haleakalā Hwy., next to Kula Lodge (p 118)

Best Swimwear
★★★ Letarte, 24 Baldwin Ave., Pā'ia (p. 120) and ★★★ Maui Girl, 12 Baldwin Ave., Pā'ia (p. 120).

Best T-Shirt Selection
★ Crazy Shirts, multiple locations (p 120)

Previous page: A colorful rack of aloha shirts at Moonbow Tropics.

Maui Shopping

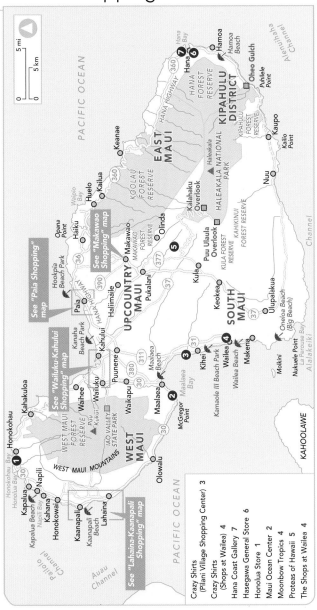

Crazy Shirts (Pilani Village Shopping Center) **3**
Crazy Shirts (Shops at Wailea) **4**
Hana Coast Gallery **7**
Hasegawa General Store **6**
Honolua Store **1**
Maui Ocean Center **2**
Moonbow Tropics **5**
Proteas of Hawaii **5**
The Shops at Wailea **4**

Lahaina & Ka'anapali Shopping

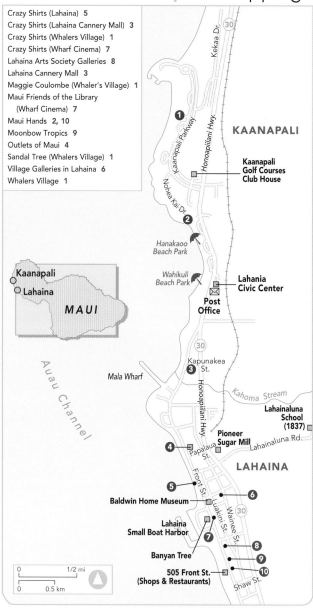

KAANAPALI

Kaanapali
Golf Courses
Club House

Hanakaoo
Beach Park

Wahikuli
Beach Park

Lahania
Civic Center

Post
Office

Kaanapali

Lahaina

MAUI

A u a u   C h a n n e l

Mala Wharf

Kapunakea
St.

Kahoma Stream

Lahainaluna
School
(1837)

Pioneer
Sugar Mill

Lahainaluna Rd.

LAHAINA

Baldwin Home Museum

Lahaina
Small Boat Harbor

Banyan Tree

505 Front St.
(Shops & Restaurants)

| 0 | | 1/2 mi |
| 0 | 0.5 km | |

Pa'ia Shopping

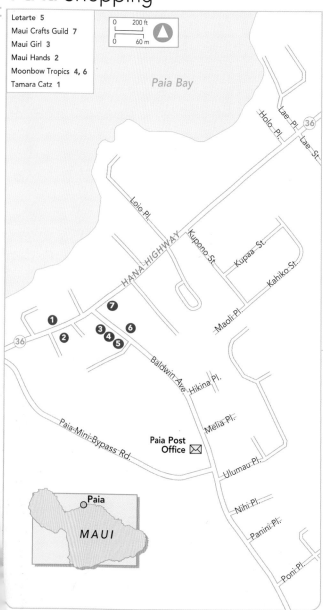

Letarte 5
Maui Crafts Guild 7
Maui Girl 3
Maui Hands 2
Moonbow Tropics 4, 6
Tamara Catz 1

0   200 ft
0   60 m

Paia Bay

Holo Pl.

Lae Pl.

Lae St.

36

Loio Pl.

HANA HIGHWAY

Kupono St.

Kupaa St.

Kahiko St.

Maoli Pl.

36

❶

❷

❸ ❹ ❺

❻

❼

Baldwin Ave.

Hikina Pl.

Melia Pl.

Paia-Mini-Bypass Rd.

Paia Post
Office ✉

Ulumau Pl.

Nihi Pl.

Panini Pl.

Poni Pl.

Paia

MAUI

Wailuku & Kahului Shopping

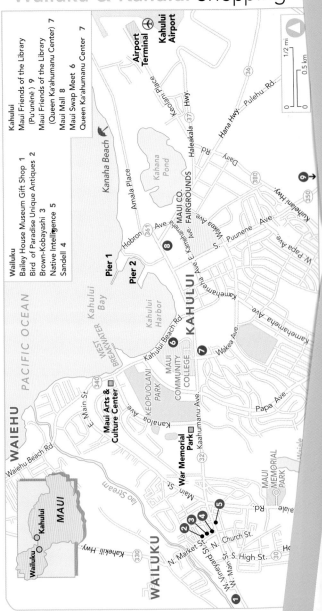

Wailuku
Bailey House Museum Gift Shop **1**
Bird of Paradise Unique Antiques **2**
Brown-Kobayashi **3**
Native Intelligence **5**
Sandell **4**

Kahului
Maui Friends of the Library
(Pu'unēnē) **9**
Maui Friends of the Library
(Queen Ka'ahumanu Center) **7**
Maui Mall **8**
Maui Swap Meet **6**
Queen Ka'ahumanu Center **7**

Makawao Shopping

0 — 1/10 mile
0 — 100 meters

Makawao ○

MAUI

Collections 4
Holiday & Co. 5
Hot Island Glassblowing
 Studio & Gallery 2
Hui No'eau Visual Arts
 Center 1
Maui Hands 6
Pukulani Superette 7
Sherri Reeve Gallery
 and Gifts 3

Maui Shopping A to Z

Alohawear
★★ Moonbow Tropics
LAHAINA, PĀ'IA, WAILEA   Find classy aloha shirts and colorful Rainbow Jo sundresses here. *612 Front St., Lahaina. www.moonbowtropics. com.* ☎ *808/667-7998. Also at 20 & 27 Baldwin Ave., Pā'ia,* ☎ *808/579-8775; and Shops at Wailea, 3750 Wailea Alanui Dr., Wailea,* ☎ *808/874-1170. AE, DISC, MC, V. Map p 114.*

Antiques & Collectibles
★★ Bird of Paradise Unique Antiques WAILUKU   I love wandering through the nostalgic Hawaiiana here. Items range from 1940s rattan furniture to vintage aloha shirts and classic Hawaiian music on cassettes. *56 N. Market St.* ☎ *808/242-7699. AE, MC, V. Map p 113.*

★ Brown-Kobayashi WAILUKU
The focus is gracious living with Asian antiques. You'll find Japanese kimonos and obi, exotic Chinese woods, and more. *38 N. Market St.* ☎ *808/242-0804. AE, MC, V. Map p 113.*

Art
★★★ Hāna Coast Gallery
HĀNA   If you only go to one gallery, make it this award-winning one devoted entirely to Hawai'i's top artists. It has Maui's best selection under one roof (sculptures, paintings, prints, feather work, stonework, and carvings). *Travaasa Hāna hotel, 5031 Hāna Hwy. www.hanacoast.com.* ☎ *808/248-8636. AE, MC, V. Map p 111.*

You'll find classic Hawaiian music for sale at Bird of Paradise Unique Antiques.

★★ **Hot Island Glassblowing Studio & Gallery** MAKAWAO Watch artists transform molten glass into works of art in this Makawao Courtyard studio, where an award-winning family of glass blowers built its own furnaces. The colorful works displayed range from small jellyfish paperweights to large museum-quality vessels. *3620 Baldwin Ave. www.hotislandglass.com.* ☎ *808/572-4527. AE, DISC, MC, V. Map p 115.*

★★★ **Hui No'eau Visual Arts Center** MAKAWAO Visit this wonderful gallery and then browse the gift shop, which features local

Intriguing sculptures at the Hui No'eau Visual Arts Center.

artists' ceramics, jewelry, and screenprints. *2841 Baldwin Ave. www.huinoeau.com.* ☎ *808/572-6560. AE, DISC, MC, V. Map p 115.*

★ **Lahaina Arts Society Galleries** LAHAINA Changing monthly exhibits of the Maui artist-members range from paintings to fiber art, to ceramics, sculpture, prints, jewelry, and more. Art in the Park fairs are every second and fourth weekend of the month. *648 Wharf St. www.lahaina-arts.com.* ☎ *808/661-3228. MC, V. Map p 112.*

★★ **Maui Crafts Guild** PĀ'IA The high quality and unique artwork at this artist-owned and -operated guild encompasses everything from pit-fired raku to hand-painted fabrics, jewelry, beadwork, traditional Hawaiian stonework, and even banana bark paintings. *120 Hāna Hwy. www.mauicraftsguild.com.* ☎ *808/579-9697. AE, MC, V. Map p 114.*

★★ **Maui Hands** KA'ANAPALI, MAKAWAO, PĀ'IA Great Hawaiian gifts can be found at here, where 90% of the items are made by Maui artists and sold at prices that aren't inflated. *1169 Makawao Ave. www.mauihands.com.* ☎ *808/572-2008. Also in the Hyatt Regency, 210 Nohea Kai Dr., Ka'anapali* ☎ *808/667-7997; and at 84 Hāna Hwy., Pā'ia* ☎ *808/579-9245. AE, MC, V. Map p 112.*

★ **Sherri Reeve Gallery and Gifts** MAKAWAO   Want to take a bit of the vibrant color and feel of the islands home with you? This open-air gallery sells everything from inexpensive cards, hand-painted tiles, and T-shirts to original works and limited editions. *3669 Baldwin Ave. www.sreeve.com.* ☎ *808/572-8931. AE, DISC, MC, V. Map p 115.*

★★★ **Village Galleries in Lahaina** LAHAINA   The oldest continuously operated gallery on Maui is known among art collectors as a showcase for regional artists. *120 and 180 Dickenson St. www.villagegalleriesmaui.com.* ☎ *808/661-4402 or 808/661-5559. Map. p 112. Also at the Ritz-Carlton Kapalua, 1 Ritz-Carlton Dr.* ☎ *808/669-1800. Map p 143.*

Books

★★★ **kids Maui Friends of the Library** KAHULUI, LAHAINA, PU'UNÊNÊ   This non-profit all-volunteer organization collects cast-off books and sells them for a song. You'll discover Hawaiian titles, kids' books, mysteries, and even board games on the well-curated shelves. Proceeds fund public libraries and the island's brand-new bookmobile. Finding the Pu'unênê location is a worthwhile adventure—books there cost only 25 cents! *In the Queen Ka'ahumanu Center, 275 Ka'ahumanu Ave., Kahului. www.mfol.org.* ☎ *808/877-2509. Also in*

A painting at the Sherri Reeve Gallery.

the Wharf Center, Lahaina, ☎ *808/667-2696; and in Pu'unênê, ½ mile past HC&S sugar mill, behind Pu'unê nê School (follow the "BOOKS" signs),* ☎ *808/871-6563. Map p 112.*

Fashion

★ **Collections** MAKAWAO   This eclectic shop is filled with spirited clothing reflecting the ease and color of island living. *3677 Baldwin Ave. www.collectionsmauiinc.com.* ☎ *808/572-0781. MC, V. Map p 115.*

★★ **Holiday & Co.** MAKAWAO   This chic boutique offers a luxurious collection of cashmere sweaters, leather handbags, lace lingerie, and irresistible jewelry. *3681 Baldwin Ave. www.holidayandcomaui.com.* ☎ *808/572-1470. AE, DC, DISC, MC, V. Map p 115.*

★★ **Maggie Coulombe** KA'ANAPALI   Maggie Coulombe makes high fashion in comfortable

Island couture at Maggie Coulombe.

wrap-around styles in jersey, silk and linen, plus jewelry and a few surprises. *Whalers Village, 2535 Ka'anapali Pkwy. www.maggie coulombe.com.* ☎ *808/283-7414. AE, DC, DISC, MC, V. Map p 112.*

★★★ **Tamara Catz** PĀ'IA Designed on Maui, Catz's filmy cotton slips, maxi-dresses, and pantsuits embroidered with birds and flowers capture the relaxed elegance and heat of the tropics. *83 Hāna Hwy., Pā'ia. www.tamara catz.com.* ☎ *808/579-9184 AE, DISC, MC, V. Map p 114.*

Flowers
★★ **Proteas of Hawai'i** KULA Send these other-worldly flowers back home to your friends—not only will they survive shipping anywhere in the world, but your pals will also be astounded and amazed. *15200 Haleakalā Hwy. next to Kula Lodge. www.proteasofhawaii.com.* ☎ *808/878-2533. AE, DISC, MC, V. Map p 111.*

General Stores
★★ **Hasegawa General Store** HĀNA I love this century-old family-run store, its aisles crammed with groceries and tee-shirts and necessities of every sort. Check out the wall full of machetes above the office

window. *5165 Hāna Hwy.* ☎ *808/ 248-8231. AE, MC, V. Map p 111.*

★ **Honolua Store** KAPALUA In pricey Kapalua, this is my favorite place for everyday essentials, clothing, even budget-priced deli items. *502 Office Rd. www.kapalua.com/ shopping/honolua-store.* ☎ *808/ 665-9105. AE, DC, DISC, MC, V. Map p 111.*

★ **Pukalani Superette** PUKALANI This small, family-owned grocery has decent-priced produce and some of the most outstanding lei on Maui at very moderate prices. Ask for the heavenly scented puak-enikeni. *15 Makawao Ave.,* ☎ *808/572-7616. MC, V. Map p 115.*

Hawaiian Art & Gifts
★★★ **Bailey House Museum Gift Shop** WAILUKU For made-in-Hawaii items, this small shop is a must stop, for everything from exquisite woods, Hawaiian music, books, and traditional Hawaiian games to pareus, *lauhala* hats, hand-sewn pheasant hatbands, jams and jellies, and an occasional Hawaiian quilt. *2375-A Main St. www.mauimuseum.org.* ☎ *808/244-3326. MC, V. Map p 113.*

★★★ **Native Intelligence** WAILUKU It's like a museum, only

Polynesian artifacts for sale at Native Intelligence.

A fish plate at the Maui Ocean Center's gift shop.

you can take these marvelous Polynesian artifacts home. Stock up on locally made clothing, finely woven *lauhala* hats, carved shell jewelry, and fresh flower lei. *1980 Market St. #2. www.native-intel.com. ☎ 808/242-2421. MC, V. Map p 113.*

Kids

★★ kids Maui Ocean Center MAALAEA Stop here for plush stuffed marine animals, nature books, T-shirts, and an array of fine artwork, jewelry, and Hawaiian art created by some of the island's most prominent artists. *Mā'alaea Harbor Village, 192 Mā'alaea Rd. (the triangle btw. Honoapi'ilani Hwy. and Mā'alaea Rd.). www.mauioceancenter. com. ☎ 808/270-7000. AE, DISC, MC, V. Map p 111.*

Shoes

★★ Sandal Tree KA'ANAPALI The best store for sandals, with a range of shoes from OluKai "slippers" to athletic shoes and dressy pumps, plus hats, handbags and more. Prices are reasonable. *Whalers Village, 2435 Ka'anapali Pkwy.*

www.sandaltree.com. ☎ 808/667-5330. AE, MC, V. Map p 112.

Shopping Centers

Lahaina Cannery Mall LAHAINA A former pineapple cannery is now a maze of shops and restaurants, including Long's Drugs and Starbucks. *1221 Honoapi'ilani Hwy. www.lahainacannerymall.com. ☎ 808/661-5304. Map p 112.*

Maui Mall KAHULUI This is a place for daily shopping with stores like Whole Foods and Longs Drugs. Don't miss **Tasaka Guri Guri**, a decades-old purveyor of icy treats. *70 E. Ka'ahumanu Ave. www.mauimall. com. ☎ 808/877-8952. Map p 113.*

★ Outlets of Maui LAHAINA This Front Street outlet mall features designer brands, two restaurants, a magic show, and a movie-theater multiplex. *900 Front St. www.outlets ofmaui.com. ☎ 808/661-8277. Map p 112.*

kids Queen Ka'ahumanu Center KAHULUI With more than 100 shops, restaurants, and theaters, Ka'ahumanu covers the basics, from **Victoria's Secret** to **Macy's,** plus local novelties like **Camellia Seed Shop,** where you can sample lip-puckering "crack seed" (preserved fruits dusted in *li hing mui* powder). *275 Ka'ahumanu Ave. www.queen kaahumanucenter.com. ☎ 808/877-3369. Map p 113.*

★ The Shops at Wailea WAILEA This classy open-air mall sells high-end gifts, clothing, and accessories. My faves include **Kī'i Gallery,** one of Hawai'i's most comprehensive collections of fine art, and **The Enchantress,** *the* place for tiaras, glitter gel, and other such essentials. *3750 Wailea Alanui. www. theshopsatwailea.com. ☎ 808/891-6770. Map p. 111.*

The Shops at Wailea.

★ kids Whalers Village

Ka'anapali   Find upscale brands such as Tommy Bahama's and Kate Spade here, plus several good restaurants. It's fun to stroll around, gawk at the giant whale skeleton, and check out the free 'ukulele lessons. *2435 Ka'anapali Pkwy.* www.whalersvillage.com. ☎ 808/661-4567. Map p 112.

★ Maui Swap Meet KAHULUI

Some 300 vendors and plenty of parking, every Saturday from 7am to 1pm, make this a bargain shopper's paradise; from fresh vegetables to original artwork and funky antiques, there's something for everyone. *At Maui Community College, in an area bounded by Kahului Beach Rd. and Wahine Pio Ave. (access via Wahine Pio Ave.).*

☎ 808/244-3100. Admission: 50¢. No credit cards. Map p 113.

★★★ Letarte PĀ'IA   Sisters Lisa

Letarte Cabrinha and Michele Letarte Ross are the designers behind this luxe collection of high-end swimwear and cover-ups. *24 Baldwin Ave.* www.letarteswimwear.com. ☎ 808/579-6022. AE, MC, V. Map p. 114.

★★★ Maui Girl PĀ'IA   This

locally owned beach shack sells mix-and-match bikinis in every color, and must-have beach sheets. *12 Baldwin Ave.* www.maui-girl.com. ☎ 808/579-9266. AE, MC, V. Map p. 114.

★ Crazy Shirts VARIOUS LOCA-

TIONS   These 100% cotton T-shirts not only last for years, but they also make perfect souvenirs and gifts. *Whalers Village,* ☎ 808/661-0117, *map p 112; 865 Front St.,* ☎ 808/661-4775, *map p 112; Wharf Cinema,* ☎ 808/661-4712, *map p 112; Piilani Village Shopping Center,* ☎ 808/875-6440, *map p 111; Lahaina Cannery Mall,* ☎ 808/661-4788, *map p 112; Shops at Wailea,* ☎ 808/875-6435, *map p 111.* AE, DISC, MC, V.

Sandell WAILUKU   For the inside

scoop on Maui politics and a bit of social commentary, stop by to chat with artist-illustrator-cartoonist David Sandell, who has provided insight on Maui since the early 1970s through his artwork. Also check out his inexpensive T-shirts. *133 Market St.* www.sandellmaui.com. ☎ 808/249-0234. Map p 113. ●

Dining Best Bets

Best on the Beach
★★★ Mama's Fish House $$$$
799 Poho Place, Kū'au (p 129)

Best Breakfast
★★ Nalu's South Shore Grill $$
*Azeka I Shopping Center, 1280 S.
Kīhei Rd., Kīhei (p 130)*

Best Brunch
★★★ Mala Ocean Tavern $$
*Azeka I Shopping Center, 1280 S.
Kīhei Rd., Kīhei (p 129)*

Best on a Budget
★ CJ's Deli & Diner $ *Ka'anapali
Fairway Shops (p 126)*

Best for Families
★★ Nalu's South Shore Grill $$
*Azeka I Shopping Center, 1280 S.
Kīhei Rd., Kīhei (p 130)*

Best Fish Sandwich
★★ Pā'ia Fish Market $ *110 Hāna
Highway & Baldwin Ave., Pā'ia
(p 130)*

Best Lū'au
★★★ Old Lahaina Lū'au $$$$
1251 Front St., Lahaina (p 127)

Best Pizza
★★ Flatbread & Company $$
89 Hāna Hwy., Pā'ia (p 126)

Most Romantic
★★★ Gerard's $$$$
174 Lahainaluna Rd., Lahaina (p 126)

Best Splurge
★★★ Ka'ana Kitchen $$$$ *Andaz
Resort, Wailea (p 128)*

Best Sushi
★★ Sansei Seafood Restaurant
and Sushi Bar $$$ *Locations in
Kapalua & Kīhei (p 131)* and
★★★ Morimoto Maui $$$$
Andaz Resort, Wailea (p 129)

Best Local Cuisine
★★★ Tin Roof $ *360 Papa Pl.,
Kahului. (p 132)*

Best Healthy Choice
Joy's Place $ *1993 S. Kīhei Rd.,
Kīhei (p 128)*

Best View
★★★ Mala Ocean Tavern *1307
Front St., Lahaina* $$$ *(p 129)* and
★ Kula Lodge $$ *Haleakalā
Highway, Kula (p 128)*

Previous page: The signature Tahitian Pearl dessert at Mama's Fish House.

Maui & Pā'ia Dining

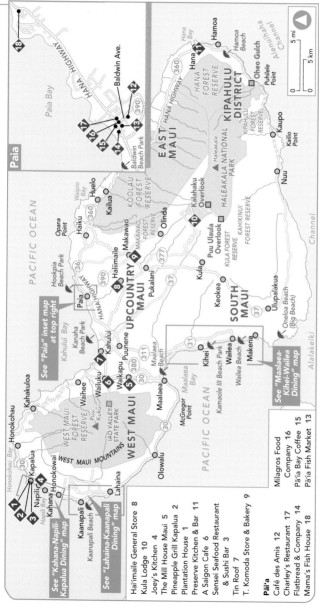

Hā'imaile General Store 8
Kula Lodge 10
Joey's Kitchen 4
The Mill House Maui 5
Pineapple Grill Kapalua 2
Plantation House 1
Preserve Kitchen & Bar 11
A Saigon Cafe 6
Sensei Seafood Restaurant
& Sushi Bar 3
Tin Roof 7
T. Komoda Store & Bakery 9

Milagros Food
Company 16
Pā'ia Bay Coffee 15
Pā'ia Fish Market 13

Pā'ia
Café des Amis 12
Charley's Restaurant 17
Flatbread & Company 14
Mama's Fish House 18

Lahaina & Ka'anapali Dining

CJ's Deli and Diner **1**
The Feast at Lele **11**
Gerard's **7**
Hula Grill **2**
Joey's Kitchen **2**
Lahaina Coolers **9**
Lahaina Grill **6**
Mala Ocean Tavern **4**
Pāia Fish Market **10**
Old Lahaina Lūʻau **5**
Roy's Ka'anapali **3**
Uluani's Shave Ice **8**

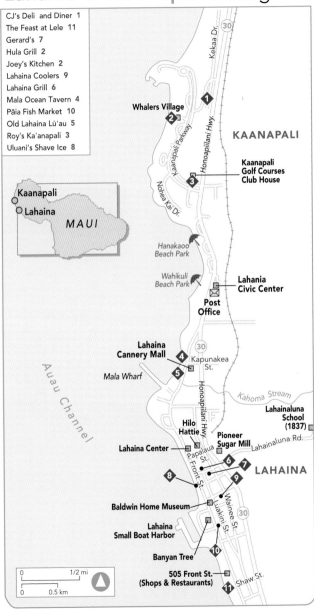

Kīhei & Wailea Dining

Cafe O Lei 6
Joy's Place 5
Ka'ana Kitchen 8
Ko 11
Longhi's 9
Morimoto Maui 7
Nalu's South Shore Grill 2
Pa'ia Fish Market 4
Peggy Sue's 1
Sansei Seafood Restaurant
   and Sushi Bar 3
Spago Maui 10

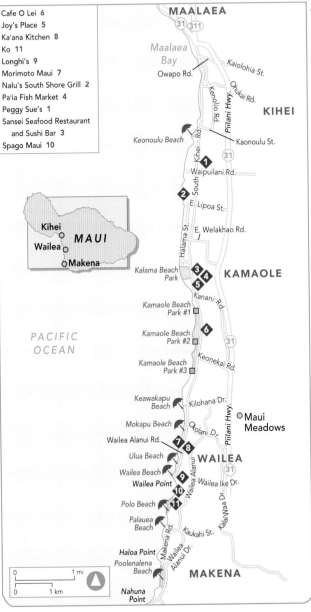

MAALAEA

31 311

Maalaea
Bay

Owapo Rd.

Kaiolohia St.

Kenolio Rd.

Ohukai Rd.

Piilani Hwy.

KIHEI

Keonoulu Beach

South Kihei Rd.

Kaonoulu St.

31

Waipuilani Rd.

E. Lipoa St.

Halama St.

E. Welakhao Rd.

Kalama Beach
Park

KAMAOLE

Kanani Rd.

Kamaole Beach
Park #1

Kamaole Beach
Park #2

31

Keonekai Rd.

Kamaole Beach
Park #3

PACIFIC
OCEAN

Keawakapu
Beach

Kilohana Dr.

Maui
Meadows

Mokapu Beach

Okolani Dr.

Piilani Hwy.

Wailea Alanui Rd.

Ulua Beach

WAILEA

Wailea Beach

Wailea Alanui

31

Wailea Point

Wailea Ike Dr.

Polo Beach

Kilani Waa Dr.

Palauea
Beach

Kaukahi St.

Makena Rd.

Wailea
Alanui Dr.

Haloa Point

Poolenalena
Beach

MAKENA

Nahuna
Point

Kihei
MAUI
Wailea
Makena

0   1 mi
0   1 km

Maui Restaurants A to Z

★★ Café des Amis PĀ'IA
CREPES/MEDITERRANEAN/INDIAN Savory and sweet crepes are the stars here, along with delicious Indian curries. The outdoor seating features live music in the evenings. *42 Baldwin Ave. www.cdamaui.com.* ☎ *808/579-6323. Entrees $10–$20. MC, V. Breakfast, lunch & dinner daily. Map p 123.*

★ kids Café o Lei KĪHEI
AMERICAN/SUSHII There's something for everyone here, from brick-oven flatbreads to sushi to juicy prime rib. The Maui onion soup is a favorite. *2439 S. Kīhei Rd. www.cafeoleirestaurants.com.* ☎ *808/891-1368. Entrees $5–$27. AE, MC, V. Lunch & dinner daily. Map p 125.*

★ kids Charley's Restaurant
PĀ'IA *AMERICAN* This north shore landmark is a mix of a 1960s hippie hangout, a windsurfers' power-breakfast spot, and a honky-tonk bar that gets going after dark. *142 Hāna Hwy. www.charleysmaui.com.* ☎ *808/579-9453. Entrees $10–$27. AE, DISC, MC, V. Breakfast, lunch & dinner daily. Map p 123.*

The Feast at Lele features traditional South Seas dancing.

★ kids CJ's Deli & Diner
KA'ANAPALI *AMERICAN/DELI* Colorful and slightly chaotic, this fun, affordable deli sports a huge billboard menu that spans the back wall and a . . . basketball hoop? Practice your free throws while ordering French toast made with Hawaiian sweet bread. *Ka'anapali Fairway Shops, 2580 Keka'a Dr. (just off the Honoapi'ilani Hwy./Hwy. 30). www.cjsmaui.com.* ☎ *808/667-0968. Entrees $5–$19. AE, MC, V. Breakfast, lunch & dinner daily. Map p 124.*

★★ The Feast at Lele LAHAINA
POLYNESIAN Taking lū'au cuisine to a new level, the owners of Old Lahaina Lū'au (p 127) provide the food and dances from Hawai'i, Tonga, Tahiti, Cook, New Zealand, and Samoa in an outdoor setting. Entrees from each island are served at white-clothed, candlelit tables set on the sand. *505 Front St. www.feastatlele.com.* ☎ *886/244-5353 or 808/667-5353. Set 5-course menu $115 adults, $85 children 2–12; gratuity not included. AE, MC, V. Dinner daily. Map p 124.*

★★ kids Flatbread & Company
PĀ'IA *PIZZA* Hand-tossed organic flatbreads are sprinkled with delectable toppings: Maui goat cheese, macadamia-nut pesto, and slow-roasted pork. This fun restaurant is regularly packed; call ahead. *71 Baldwin Ave. www.flatbreadcompany.com.* ☎ *808/579-9999. Entrees $15–$28. Lunch & dinner daily. MC, V. Map p 123.*

★★★ Gerard's LAHAINA
FRENCH Chef Gerard Reversade turns out exceptional French cuisine in this elegant Victorian house. The chilled cucumber soup is transcendent, its delicacy amplified by goat cheese and fresh dill. The

Old Lahaina Lū'au

Maui's best lū'au features terrific food and entertainment in a peerless oceanfront setting. The lū'au begins at sunset and features Tahitian and Hawaiian entertainment, including all versions of hula dancing—ancient hula, hula from the missionary era, modern hula. The entertainment is riveting, even for jaded locals. The high-quality food, served from an open-air thatched structure, is as much Pacific Rim as authentically Hawaiian: imu-roasted kalua pig, baked mahimahi in Maui-onion cream sauce, guava chicken, teriyaki sirloin steak, lomi salmon, poi, dried fish, *poke*, Hawaiian sweet potato, sautéed vegetables, seafood salad, and the ultimate treat, taro leaves with coconut milk. **Old Lahaina Lū'au** (1251 Front St., Lahaina; www.oldlahainaluau.com; ☎ **800/248-5828** or 808/667-1998). $103 for adults, $72 for kids 12 and under.

dessert menu has a half-dozen excellent offerings, including a marvelous *millefeuille. In the Plantation Inn, 174 Lahainaluna Rd. www.gerardsmaui.com.* ☎ *808/661-8939. Entrees $36–$56. AE, DC, DISC, MC, V. Dinner daily. Map p 124.*

★★★ kids **Hali'imaile General Store** HALI'IMAILE *AMERICAN* Chef Bev Gannon, one of the 12 original Hawaii Regional Cuisine chefs, heads up this foodie haven

Hali'imaile General Store puts a Texas spin on Hawaiian favorites.

amid the pineapple fields with her innovative spin on good ol' American cuisine, bringing Hawaiian and Texas flavors together. *Hali'imaile Rd. www.bevgannonrestaurants.com.* ☎ *808/572-2666. Entrees $16–$46. AE, DC, DISC, MC, V. Lunch Mon–Fri; dinner daily. Map p 123.*

★ kids **Hula Grill** KA'ANAPALI *HAWAI'I REGIONAL/SEAFOOD* Skip the main dining room and dig your toes in the sand at the Barefoot Bar on the beach, where you can nosh on burgers, fish, pizza, and salad. *Whalers Village, 2435 Ka'anapali Pkwy. www.hulagrill.com.* ☎ *808/667-6636. Entrees $10–$20 in Barefoot Bar, $20–$40 in dining room. AE, DC, DISC, MC, V. Lunch & dinner daily. Map p 124.*

★★ **Joey's Kitchen** KA'ANAPALI, NĀPILI, *HAWAI'I REGIONAL/FILIPINO* Chef Joey Macadang-dang of Roy's (see p 131) opened two restaurants of his own: a to-go place in Whaler's Village and a slightly fancier eatery in Nāpili. Explore upscale Filipino dishes like seafood *sinigang* or stick to tried-and-true spare ribs. *Whalers Village,*

2435 Ka'anapali Pkwy. www.joeys kitchenhimaui.com. ☎ *808/868-4474. Open daily 8am–3pm. Also at 5095 Nāpilihau St., Nāpili.* ☎ *808/214-5590. Open Tues–Sun 10am–2pm and 4–10pm. Entrees $9–$39. MC, V. Mon–Sat. Map p 124.*

Joy's Place KĪHEI *HEALTHY DELI/SANDWICHES* If you are craving a healthy, delicious lunch, it's worth hunting for this tiny hole in the wall with humongous sandwiches, fresh salads, hot soups, and smoothies. *Island Surf Bldg., 1993 S. Kīhei Rd. (entrance to the restaurant is on Auhana St.).* ☎ *808/879-9258. All items under $16. MC, V. Mon–Sat 8am–3pm. Map p 125.*

★★★ Ka'ana Kitchen WAILEA *HAWAI'I REGIONAL CUISINE* Foodies, don't miss dining here. Sit ringside where you can watch chef Isaac Bancaco in action. Start off with a hand-mixed cocktail and the grilled octopus: fat chunks of tender meat tossed with frisée, watercress, and goat cheese. If the menu is a bingo card, every choice is a winner. *At the Andaz Maui, 3550 Wailea Alanui Dr. www.maui.andaz. hyatt.com.* ☎ *808/573-1234; Entrees $21–$56. AE, DC, DISC, MC, V. Breakfast, dinner daily 6:30–11am and 5:30–9pm. Map p 125.*

★★ Kō WAILEA *GOURMET PLANTATION CUISINE* The word *kō* means "cane," as in sugar cane, back to the old plantation days when the sugar-cane plantations had "camp" housing for each ethnic group and each had its own cuisine. There are wonderful taste treats you are only going to find here—don't miss them. *Fairmont Kea Lani, 4100 Wailea Alanui Dr., Wailea. www.fairmont.com/kealani.* ☎ *808/875-4100. Entrees $21–$50. AE, DC, DISC, MC, V. Lunch & dinner daily. Map p 125.*

Awe-inspiring upcountry views at Kula Lodge.

★ kids Kula Lodge KULA *HAWAI'I REGIONAL/AMERICAN* With huge breakfasts and awe-inspiring views, this upcountry lodge is a cozy stop for visitors going up (or down) Haleakalā. *15200 Haleakalā Hwy. (Hwy. 377). www.kulalodge. com.* ☎ *808/878-1535. Entrees $10–$35. AE, DC, DISC, MC, V. Breakfast, lunch & dinner daily. Map p 123.*

★ kids Lahaina Coolers LAHAINA *AMERICAN/INTERNATIONAL* This ultracasual indoor/outdoor restaurant is a hangout for hungry surfers on a tight budget. *180 Dickensen St. www.Lahainacoolers.com.* ☎ *808/661-7082. Entrees $8–$28. AE, DC, DISC, MC, V. Breakfast, lunch & dinner daily. Map p 124.*

★★★ Lahaina Grill LAHAINA *NEW AMERICAN* This classy restaurant serves award-winning dishes: the zesty "toy box" heirloom-tomato salad served in a martini glass, the aromatic Kona coffee–roasted rack of lamb, and the divinely rich seared ahi with foie gras, truffle oil, and fig compote. *127 Lahainaluna Rd. www.lahainagrill. com.* ☎ *808/667-5117. Entrees $40–$60. AE, DC, DISC, MC, V. Dinner daily. Map p 124.*

★ Longhi's WAILEA *ITALIAN* The open-air room, black-and-white checkered floor, and yummy Italian cuisine (plus terrific breakfasts) make this a fine Wailea stop. *Shops at Wailea, 3750 Wailea Alanui Dr. www.longhis.com.* ☎ *808/891-8883. Entrees $12–$85. AE, DC, MC, V. Breakfast, lunch & dinner daily. Map p 125.*

★★★ Mala Ocean Tavern

LAHAINA *AMERICAN* Everything about this tiny tavern overlooking Mala Wharf is perfect: a view of surfing sea turtles, an epic brunch menu, and dinner options ranging from healthy Indonesian *gado gado* to hedonistic mac and cheese. *1307 Front St. www.malaoceantavern.com.* ☎ *808/667-9394. Reservations recommended. Entrees $18–$42. AE, DC, DISC, MC, V. Lunch & dinner daily, weekend brunch. Map p 124*

★★★ Mama's Fish House

KŪ'AU *SEAFOOD* This beachfront institution is the realization of a South Pacific fantasy. Though pricey, a meal at Mama's is a complete experience from the moment you arrive. The menu lists the names of the anglers who reeled in the day's catch and the Tahitian Pearl dessert is almost too stunning to eat. *799 Poho Place, just off the Hāna Hwy. www.mamasfishhouse. com* ☎ *808/579-8488.. Entrees $26–$58. DC, DISC, MC, V. Lunch & dinner daily. Map p 123.*

★ Milagros Food Company PĀIA

SOUTHWESTERN/MEXICAN Sit outdoors and watch the parade of surfers, yogis, and tourists while enjoying fish tacos at this casual eatery. The tequila bar is on point. *Hāna Hwy. and Baldwin Ave. www. milagrosfoodcompany.com.* ☎ *808/ 579-8755. Lunch items $10–$13; dinner entrees $14–$19. DC, MC, V. Lunch & dinner daily. Map p 123.*

★★ Mill House WAIKAPŪ NEW

AMERICAN Chef Jeff Scheer's inventive menu includes beautiful hand-cut pasta, coffee-roasted beet salad, and Cornish hen with parsnip puree. Lunch is best; it's less pricey and you can see into stunning Waikapū valley. *At Maui Tropical Plantation, 1607 Honoapi'ilani Hwy. www.millhousemaui.com.* ☎ *808/ 270-0333. Lunch entrees $12–$28. Dinner entrees $18–$55. MC, V. Lunch and dinner daily. Map p 123.*

★★★ Morimoto Maui WAILEA

JAPANESE/PERUVIAN The immaculate kitchen houses a space-age freezer full of fish bought at auction, and a rice polisher that ensures that every grain is perfect. The tasting menu starts with Morimoto-san's signature appetizer, the toro tartare. Balanced on ice, it's edible artwork. *Andaz Maui, 3550 Wailea Alanui Dr. www.maui.andaz.hyatt. com.* ☎ *808/573-1234; Entrees*

Star chef Masaharu Morimoto's sleek restaurant in the Andaz Maui hotel.

Al fresco dining at the Pineapple Grill.

$16–$150. AE, DC, DISC, MC, V. Lunch, dinner daily. Map p 125.

★★ kids Nalu's South Shore Grill KĪHEI AMERICAN Acai bowls for breakfast, cubano sandwiches for lunch, burgers on brioche buns for dinner, and malasadas for dessert—this cheerful eatery indoor/outdoor has something delicious for everyone. Azeka I Shopping Center, 1280 S. Kīhei Rd. ☎ 808/891-8650. Entrees $6–$13 breakfast, $9–$20 lunch, $19–$28 dinner. Breakfast, lunch & dinner daily. AE, DISC, MC, V. Map p 125.

★★ kids Pā'ia Fish Market KĪHEI, LAHAINA, PĀ'IA SEAFOOD There's only one thing to order here: a fish sandwich. A giant slab of perfectly grilled 'ahi, opah, or 'opakapaka laid out on a bun with coleslaw and grated cheese is extra satisfying after a briny day at the beach. www.paiafishmarket.com. 1913 S. Kīhei Rd., Kīhei, ☎ 808/874-8888; 632 Front St., Lahaina, ☎ 808/662-3456; 110 Hāna Hwy., Pā'ia, ☎ 808/579-8030. Entrees $9–$22. AE, DISC, MC, V. Lunch & dinner daily. Map p 125.

★★ Pā'ia Bay Coffee PĀ'IA COFFEE SHOP Tucked behind a swimsuit shop, this courtyard café is Pā'ia's best-kept secret. Pop in for an expertly brewed espresso, fresh-baked croissant, or bagel sandwich. 115 Hāna Hwy. www.paiabaycoffee.com. ☎ 808/579-3111. Entrees

$5–$11. MC, V. Breakfast & lunch daily. Map p 123.

kids Peggy Sue's KĪHEI AMERICAN This 1950s-style diner has oodles of charm, with old-fashioned soda-shop stools and jukeboxes on every Formica table. You'll find shakes and floats, along with burgers, fries, and kids' meals for just $6.50. Azeka Place II, 1279 S. Kīhei Rd. ☎ 808/875-8944. Entrees $7–$12. AE, DISC, MC, V. Lunch & dinner daily. Map p 125.

★★ Pineapple Grill Kapalua KAPALUA HAWAI'I REGIONAL/AMERICAN This gracious dining room offers views of the Pacific and the misty West Maui Mountains. The menu ranges from sophisticated brunch and pub food to exquisite nightly specials. Wine is half-price on Wednesdays. 200 Kapalua Dr. www.pineapplekapalua.com. ☎ 808/669-9600. Entrees $10–$46. AE, MC, V. Breakfast, lunch & dinner daily. Map p 123.

★★ Plantation House KAPALUA HAWAI'I REGIONAL/AMERICAN Chef Jojo Vasquez's menu features simple yet sophisticated preparations that draw on an international culinary vocabulary. His kampachi tartare, lightly dressed in dashi soy and decorated with a spicy nasturtium flower, is bright and fresh. 2000 Plantation Club Dr. www.cohnrestaurants.com/plantationhouse. ☎ 808/669-6299. Entrees

$9–$19 breakfast, $11–$20 lunch, $29–$47 dinner. AE, MC, V. Daily 8am–9pm. Map p 123.

★ The Preserve Kitchen & Bar

HĀNA *HAWAI'I REGIONAL/ AMERICAN* This ingredient-driven menu (fresh fish caught by local fishermen, produce grown by nearby farmers, and fruits in season) is served in large dining room with a view of Kau'iki Hill. *Hāna Hwy.* ☎ *808/248-8212. Entrees $12–$40. AE, DISC, MC, V. Breakfast, lunch & dinner daily. Map p 123.*

★★ Roy's Ka'anapali LAHAINA

HAWAI'I REGIONAL There's no ocean view here, but the food makes up for it. The short ribs are stellar and the "canoe for two" appetizer is fun to share. For dessert, two words: chocolate soufflé. This signature dessert takes 20 minutes to prepare, so order it in advance. When it arrives, wait a moment for it to cool—don't burn your tongue on the hot lava chocolate! *Ka'anapali Golf Course, 2290 Ka'anapali Pkwy. www.royshawaii. com.* ☎ *808/669-6999. Entrees $14–$47. AE, DC, DISC, MC, V. Lunch & dinner daily. Map p 124.*

Sushi and sake at Sansei.

An entree at Roy's, a foodie favorite.

★★ A Saigon Café WAILUKU

VIETNAMESE Whatever you order—the steamed 'opakapaka with ginger and garlic, one of a dozen soups, the catfish simmering in a clay pot, or the fragrant lemongrass curry—you'll notice the freshness of the flavors. *1792 Main St.* ☎ *808/243-9560. $10–$28. MC, V. Lunch & dinner daily. Map p 123.*

★★ Sansei Seafood Restaurant and Sushi Bar KAPALUA &

KĪHEI *SUSHI, PACIFIC RIM* With its creative take on sushi (foie gras

Shave Ice: Sweet Hawaiian Snow

David and Ululani Yamashiro are near-religious about shave ice. At multiple shops around Maui under the name **Ululani's Hawaiian Shave Ice,** these wizards take the uniquely Hawaiian dessert to new heights. Ice is shaved to feather lightness and doused with your choice of syrup—any three flavors from calamansi lime to lychee to red velvet cake. David makes his own gourmet syrups with local fruit purees and a dash of cane sugar. Add a "snowcap" of sweetened condensed milk, and the resulting confection tastes like the fluffiest, most flavorful ice cream ever. Locals order theirs with chewy mochi morsels, sweet adzuki beans at the bottom, or tart *li hing mui* powder sprinkled on top. (Lahaina: 819 Front St. and 790 Front St.; Ka'anapali: 200 Nohea Kai Dr. [in Hyatt Regency]; Wailuku: 58 Maui Lani Pkwy Ste. 5000 [in Safeway center]; Kahului: 333 Dairy Rd.; and Kīhei: 61 S. Kīhei Rd.; www.ululanisshaveice. com; ☎ **360/606-2745;** All locations daily 10:30am–6:30pm [10:30am–10pm in Lahaina])

nigiri and "Pink Cadillac" rolls wrapped in pink rice paper), Sansei's menu scores higher with adventurous diners than with purists. The Dungeness crab ramen is outstanding, as are the early bird specials—50 percent off before 6pm. *Two Maui locations: 600 Office Rd., Kapalua.* ☎ *808/669-6286. Map p 123. Kīhei Town Center, Kīhei.* ☎ *808/879-0004. Map p 125. www. sanseihawaii.com. Entrees $16–$48. AE, DISC, MC, V. Dinner daily.*

★★★ **Spago** WAILEA *HAWAI'I REGIONAL/AMERICAN* Slide into the chic bar or snag an ocean-view table and enjoy an order of scrumptious 'ahi sesame-miso cones before moving on to the Chinois lamb chops. Fragrant truffle shavings can be added to your dish when in season. *Four Seasons Resort Maui, 3900 Wailea Alanui Dr. www. fourseasons.com/maui.* ☎ *808/879-2999. Entrees $39–$135. AE, DC, DISC, MC, V. Dinner daily 6–11pm. Map p 125.*

★★★ **Tin Roof** KAHULUI *HAWAI'I REGIONAL/FILIPINO Top Chef* star Sheldon Simeon serves top-quality, extra-flavorful local dishes at this hole-in-the-wall lunch spot. Try the addictive mochiko chicken with a side of rice, noodles, or kale salad. Sprinkle a "dime bag" of furikake on top to send your taste buds to heaven. No seating. *360 Papa Pl. www.tinroof maui.com.* ☎ *808/868-0753. Entrees $6–9. AE, DC, DISC, MC, V. Lunch daily. Map p 123.*

★★ kids **T. Komoda Store and Bakery** MAKAWAO *BAKERY* The Komoda family has been keeping Maui sweet for 100 years. This institution offers a glimpse back into the island's plantation-era past. Get here early before their famous stick donuts and cream puffs sell out; also check out the delicious pies, butter rolls, and chocolate cake. *3674 Baldwin Ave.* ☎ *808/572-7261. No credit cards. Map p 123. Closed Wed & Sun.* ●

Nightlife & Performing Arts
Best Bets

Best **Cocktails**
★ Monkeypod Kitchen, *10 Wailea Gateway Pl., Wailea (p 137)*

Best **Concerts**
★★★ Maui Arts and Cultural Center, *1 Cameron Way (p 138)*

Best **Dance Floor**
★★ Casanova, *1188 Makawao Ave. (p 137)*

Best Place to **Drink with Locals**
★ Kahului Ale House, *355 E. Kamehameha Ave. (p 137)*

Best **Karaoke**
★★ Sansei Seafood Restaurant & Sushi Bar, *1881 S. Kīhei Rd., Kīhei, and 600 Office Rd., Kapalua (p 139)*

Best **Hawaiian Music**
★★★ Masters of Hawaiian Slack-Key Guitar Series, *Nāpili Kai Beach Resort (p 139)*

Best **Hotel Lounge**
★ Four Seasons Lobby Lounge, *Four Seasons Wailea (p 137)*

Best **Local Brews**
★★ Maui Brewing Company, *605 Līpoa Pkwy., Kīhei and 4405 Honoapiʻilani Hwy., Kahana (p 137)*

Best **Lūʻau**
★★★ Old Lahaina Lūʻau, *1251 Front St. (p 140)*

Best **Movies Under the Stars**
★★★ Maui Film Festival, *Wailea Golf Course (p 138)*

Best **Show**
★★★ ʻUlalena, *Maui Theatre, 878 Front St. (p 138)*

Previous page: The Old Lahaina Luʻau.

Sunset Cocktails

For a rocking good time, climb aboard the Pacific Whale Foundation's **Island Rhythms Sunset Cocktail Cruise** ★★★ (www.pacificwhale.org; ☎ **808/249-8811**). Local reggae star Marty Dread gets everybody up and dancing on the deck of the boat. During whale season, even the Hawaiian humpbacks swim over to show their appreciation for his sweet serenades. Enjoy hearty appetizers and mixed cocktails while watching the sun sink into the liquid horizon. Book online for 10 percent discount, and board at Māʻalaea Harbor.

Landlubbers can head to the rooftop at **Fleetwood's on Front Street,** 744 Front St., Lahaina (www.fleetwoodsonfrontstreet.com; ☎ **808/669-6425**), where you can catch local rock stars jamming with superstar Mick Fleetwood and his friends. If you're looking for a swank cocktail with sultry entertainment, visit the **Four Seasons Lobby Lounge,** 3900 Wailea Alanui Dr., Wailea (www.fourseasons.com/maui.com; ☎ **808/874-8000**) or the **Luana Lounge at the Fairmont Kea Lani**, 4100 Wailea Alanui Dr., Wailea (www.fairmont.com/kea-lani-maui/dining/luana; ☎ **808/875-4100**).

Central & South Maui Nightlife

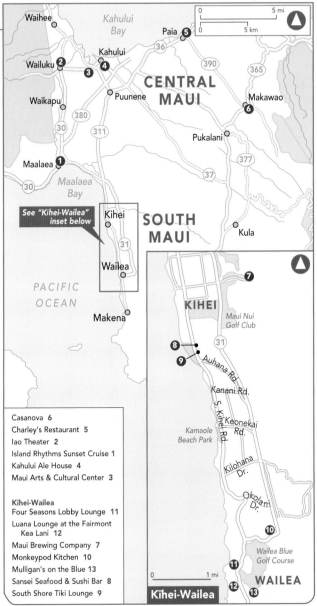

Casanova **6**
Charley's Restaurant **5**
Iao Theater **2**
Island Rhythms Sunset Cruise **1**
Kahului Ale House **4**
Maui Arts & Cultural Center **3**

Kīhei-Wailea
Four Seasons Lobby Lounge **11**
Luana Lounge at the Fairmont
Kea Lani **12**
Maui Brewing Company **7**
Monkeypod Kitchen **10**
Mulligan's on the Blue **13**
Sansei Seafood & Sushi Bar **8**
South Shore Tiki Lounge **9**

Kīhei-Wailea

Lahaina & Ka'anapali Nightlife

Feast at Lele 11
Fleetwood's on Front Street 10
Hula Grill 4
Kimo's 9
Longhi's 7
Masters of Hawaiian Slack-Key
    Guitar Series 2
Maui Brewing Company 3
Old Lahaina Lūaʻu 5
Sansei Seafood & Sushi Bar 1
ʻUlalena 8
Warren & Annabelle's 6

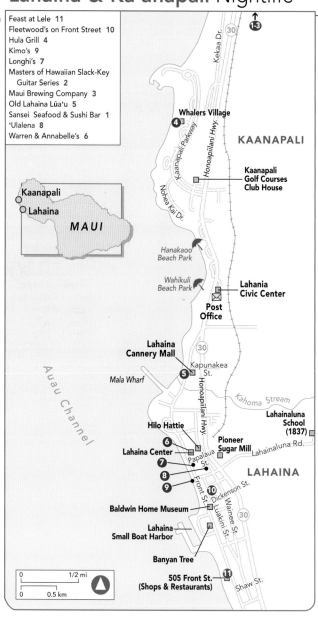

Maui Nightlife A to Z

Bars & Cocktail Lounges
★★ Casanova MAKAWAO
Expect good blues, rock 'n' roll, reggae, jazz, Hawaiian, and the top names in local and visiting entertainment. Call to ask if they are doing Sunday afternoon live jazz. *1188 Makawao Ave. www.casanovamaui. com.* ☎ *808/572-0220. Map p 135.*

★ Charley's Restaurant PĀʻIA
This local pub features an eclectic selection of music most nights, from country and western (Willie Nelson and son Lukas occasionally sit in) to fusion/reggae to rock 'n' roll. Call or visit online to see what's on. *142 Hāna Hwy. www.charleys maui.com.* ☎ *808/579-8085. Map p. 135.*

★★ Four Seasons Lobby Lounge WAILEA
For a quiet evening with gentle jazz or soft Hawaiian music, sink into the plush furniture and order an exotic drink. Nightly live music from 5:30 to 7:30pm and 8:30 to 11:30pm. *Four Seasons Wailea, 3900 Wailea Alanui Dr.* ☎ *808/874-8000. Map p 135.*

★ Hula Grill KAʻANAPALI
At the oceanfront Hula Grill's Barefoot Bar, live music starts daily at 11am and goes until 9:15pm, and happy hour starts at 3pm. *Whalers Village. 2435 Kaʻanapali Pkwy. Hula Grill. www.hulagrillkaanapali.com.* ☎ *808/667-6636. Map p 136.*

★ Kahului Ale House KAHULUI
Locals gather here for live music starting at 10pm. *355 E. Kamehameha Ave.* ☎ *808/877-0001. Map p 135.*

★ Kimo's LAHAINA
For the sweet sounds of Hawaiian music, call Kimo's to see who's on for the night. *845 Front St.* ☎ *808/661-4811. Map p 136.*

★ Longhi's LAHAINA
Live music spills out into the streets from 10pm Thursday and Friday, and Sunday jazz goes from 7 to 10pm. I love people-watching here. It's a real mix, with everyone from Midwestern tourists to the occasional rock star. *888 Front St.* ☎ *808/667-2288. Map p 136.*

★★ Luana Lounge at the Fairmont Kea Lani WAILEA
Catch the sunset from this swank lobby bar, with live entertainment weekends from 7 to 10pm. *Fairmont Kea Lani, 4100 Wailea Alanui Dr. www. fairmont.com/kea-lani-maui/dining/ luana.* ☎ *808/875-4100. Map p 135.*

★ Maui Brewing Company
KĪHEI, KAHANA Sample a variety of local brews at the Kīhei brewery and tasting room or the Kahana brewpub. Favorites include tasty coconut porter, Bikini Blonde lager, and numerous seasonal beers. *605 Līpoa Pwy., Kīhei* ☎ *808/213-3002 and 4405 Honoapiʻilani Hwy., Kahana. www.mauibrewingco.com.* ☎ *808/669-3474. Map p 136.*

★★ Monkeypod Kitchen
WAILEA The fancy signature mai tai with honey-lilikoi foam is a good enough reason to stop here for a beverage or two—and who can

The oceanfront Hula Grill.

Maui Movie Magic

Movie lovers: Try to time your trip with the ★★★ **Maui Film Festival** (www.mauifilmfestival.com; (☎ **808/579-9244**), which always starts the Wednesday before Father's Day in June. The 5-day festival premieres films nightly in the Celestial Cinema, a peerless outdoor theater on the Wailea Golf Course. Sit under the stars and watch great films on the 50-foot-wide (15m) screen with Dolby Digital Surround Sound. Catch celebrities at the festival's multiple parties and special screenings.

Enjoy movies under the stars in the Celestial Cinema.

resist a libation with mezcal and honey called When Doves Cry? *10 Wailea Gateway Pl., Wailea. www. monkeypodkitchen.com/wailea.* ☎ *808/891-2322. Map p 135.*

★★ Mulligan's On the Blue
WAILEA   Toss back a pint of Guinness and catch Uncle Willie K or the Celtic Tigers at this rollicking Irish pub. *100 Kaukahi St., Wailea. www. mulligansontheblue.com.* ☎ *808/ 874-1131. Map p 135.*

South Shore Tiki Lounge KĪHEI This tiny, fun bar features live music nightly from 4-6pm and dancing on the outdoor patio from 10pm to 1:30am. *1913 S. Kīhei Rd., Kīhei. www.southshoretikilounge.com.* ☎ *808/874-6444. Map p 135.*

**Dance, Theater & Shows
'Iao Theater** WAILUKU   It's not Broadway, but Maui does have live community theater, ranging from locally written productions to well-known plays and musicals. *68 N. Market St. www.mauionstage.com.* ☎ *808/244-8680. Map p 135.*

★★★ Maui Arts and Cultural Center KAHULUI   Bonnie Raitt, Pearl Jam, Ziggy Marley, Tony Bennett, the American Indian Dance Theatre, the Maui Symphony Orchestra, and Jonny Lang have all performed here, in addition to the finest in local talent. The center has a visual arts gallery, an outdoor amphitheater, and two theaters. *1 Cameron Way. www.mauiarts.org.* ☎ *808/242-7469. Ticket prices vary. Map p 135.*

★★★ kids 'Ulalena LAHAINA
The whole family will be riveted by this incredible show, which weaves Hawaiian history and mythology together on a state-of-the-art stage.

Maui Arts and Cultural Center.

The cast performs original music, acrobatics, hula and chant in an interactive experience that often leaves the audience breathless. *Maui Theatre, 878 Front St. www.ulalena. com.* ☎ *808/856-7900 or 808/661-9913. Mon, Tues, Thurs, and Fri 6:30pm. Tickets $70–$115 adults, $30–$115 children 6–12. Map p 136.*

★★ Warren & Annabelle's
LAHAINA   This unusual magic/comedy cocktail show stars illusionist Warren Gibson and "Annabelle," a ghost from the 1800s. She plays the grand piano as Warren dazzles with his sleight-of-hand magic. *900 Front St. www.warrenandannabelles.*

Hawaiian history and mythology come to life at the interactive 'Ulalena show.

com. ☎ *808/667-6244. Tickets $60–$100. Map p 136.*

Hawaiian Music
★★★ kids Masters of Hawaiian Slack-Key Guitar Series
NAPILI   For a chance to see a side of Hawai'i that few visitors do, come to this Wednesday night production, where host George Kahumoku, Jr., introduces a new slack-key master (see p 140) every week. George and his guests also "talk story" about old Hawai'i, music, and Hawaiian culture. *In the Nāpili Kai Beach Resort, 5900 Lower Honoapi'ilani Rd, Nāpili. www.slack keyshow.com.* ☎ *808/669-3858. Tickets $38–$95. Map p 136.*

Karaoke
★★ Sansei Seafood Restaurant & Sushi Bar KĪHEI, KAPALUA
This super popular Japanese restaurant hosts fun karaoke nights Thursday through Saturday 10pm to 1am. The bonus? Sushi and appetizers are half off. *1881 S. Kīhei Rd., Kīhei,* ☎ *808/879-0004, and 600 Office Rd., Kapalua. www.sansei hawaii.com.* ☎ *808/669-6286 or 808/667-5353. Map p 136.*

Lū'au
★★ The Feast at Lele LAHAINA
Already been to a lū'au? The Feast at Lele takes it to the next level. Brought to you by the people

Slack-key master and two-time Grammy winner Keoki Kahumoku.

behind Old Lāhaina Lūʻau (see below), the Feast at Lele presents food and dances from Hawaiʻi, Tonga, Tahiti, Cook, New Zealand, and Samoa in an outdoor seaside setting with white-clothed, candlelit tables. *505 Front St. www.feast-atlele.com. ☎ 886/244-5353 or 808/667-5353. Set 5-course menu $115 adults, $85 children 2–12; gratuity not included. AE, MC, V. Dinner daily. Map p 136.*

★★★ kids **Old Lāhaina Lūʻau**
LAHAINA This heartfelt, ocean-front show is the best lūʻau in the state. Festivities begin at sunset and feature Tahitian and Hawaiian entertainment, including ancient hula, modern hula, and an intelligent narrative on the dance's rocky survival into modern times. The food, served from an open-air thatched structure, is as much Pacific Rim as Hawaiian, and mixes in some well-known western favorites. *1251 Front St. www.oldlahaina luau.com. ☎ 800/248-5828 or 808/667-1998. Tickets $99 adults, $69 children 12 and under. Map p 136. ●*

Slackers Welcome!

Unique to Hawaiʻi, slack-key guitar, or *kī hoʻalu* (which translates to "loosen the key") is a style achieved by loosening the guitar strings (or keys) to produce a very different sound when major chords are struck. Check it out at the **Masters of Hawaiian Slack Key Guitar Series** (p 139) or at the free **Kī Hoʻalu Festival** held each June at the Maui Arts & Cultural Center.

Lodging Best Bets

Most Romantic
★★★ **Hotel Wailea** $$$ *555 Kaukahi St., Wailea (p 147)* and ★★★ **Travaasa Hāna** $$$$$ *Hāna Hwy., Hāna (p 150)*

Most Charming B&B
★★ **Old Wailuku Inn at Ulupono** $$ *2199 Kahoʻokele St., Wailuku (p 149)*

Most Luxurious Condo
★★ **Kaʻanapali Aliʻi** $$$$ *50 Nohea Kai Dr., Kaʻanapali (p 148)*

Best Family Condo
★ **Outrigger Maui Eldorado** $$$ *2661 Kekaʻa Dr., Kaʻanapali (p 149)*

Best for Kids
★★★ **Four Seasons Resort Maui at Wailea** $$$$$ *3900 Wailea Alanui Dr., Wailea (p 146)* and ★★★ **Grand Wailea Resort Hotel & Spa** $$$$$ *3850 Wailea Alanui Dr., Wailea (p 147)*

Best for Foodies
★★★ **Andaz Maui at Wailea** $$$$$ *3550 Wailea Alanui Dr., Wailea (p 146)*

Best View
★★★ **Napili Kai Beach Resort** $$$ *5900 Honoapiʻilani Rd., Napili (p 148)*

Most Serene Location
★★ **Hāmoa Bay House & Bungalow** $$ *Hāna Hwy., btwn Haneoʻo loop Road, Hāna (p 147)*

Best Retreat
★★ **Lumeria** $$$$ *1813 Baldwin Ave., Makawao (p 148)*

Best Club-Level Amenities
★★★ **Ritz-Carlton Kapalua** $$$$ *1 Ritz-Carlton Dr., Kapalua (p 149)*

Best Service
★★★ **Four Seasons Resort Maui at Wailea** $$$$$ *3900 Wailea Alanui Dr., Wailea (p 146)*

Best Spa
★★★ **Grand Wailea Resort Hotel & Spa** $$$$$ *3850 Wailea Alanui Dr., Wailea (p 147)*

Most Hawaiian Resort
★★ **Kaʻanapali Beach Hotel** $$ *2525 Kaanapali Pkwy., Kaanapali (p 148)*

Best Boutique Inn
★★ **The Inn at Mama's Fish House** $$ *799 Poho Place, Kuau (p 147)*

Most Ecofriendly
★★★ **The Fairmont Kea Lani Maui** $$$$$ *4100 Wailea Alanui Dr., Wailea (p 146)*

Best for Groups
★★ **Kapalua Villas** $$–$$$$ *500 Office Rd., Kapalua (p 148)*

Best Value on a Budget
★ **Nona Lani Cottages** $ *455 S. Kīhei Rd., Kīhei (p 149)* and ★★ **Pineapple Inn Maui** $ *3170 Akala Dr., Kīhei (p 149)*

Previous page: The stylish pool at the Four Seasons Resort Maui at Wailea.

Maui & Kapalua Lodging

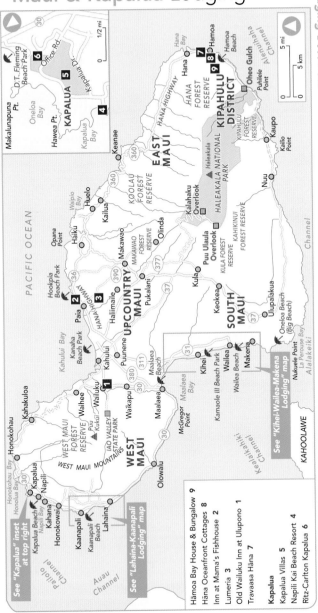

Hāmoa Bay House & Bungalow 9

Hāna Oceanfront Cottages 8

Inn at Mama's Fishhouse 2

Lumeria 3

Old Wailuku Inn at Ulupono 1

Travaasa Hāna 7

Kapalua

Kapalua Villas 5

Napili Kai Beach Resort 4

Ritz-Carlton Kapalua 6

See "Kapalua" inset at top right

See "Lahaina-Kaanapali Lodging" map

See "Kihei-Wailea-Makena Lodging" map

Lahaina & Ka'anapali Lodging

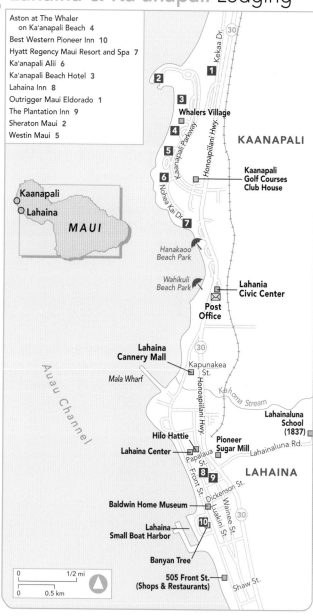

Aston at The Whaler
on Ka'anapali Beach 4
Best Western Pioneer Inn 10
Hyatt Regency Maui Resort and Spa 7
Ka'anapali Alii 6
Ka'anapali Beach Hotel 3
Lahaina Inn 8
Outrigger Maui Eldorado 1
The Plantation Inn 9
Sheraton Maui 2
Westin Maui 5

Kekaa Dr.

1

2

3

Whalers Village

4

5

6

Kaanapali Parkway

Honoapiilani Hwy.

KAANAPALI

Kaanapali
Golf Courses
Club House

Nohea Kai Dr.

7

Hanakaoo
Beach Park

Wahikuli
Beach Park

Lahaina
Civic Center

Post
Office

Kaanapali

Lahaina

MAUI

Auau Channel

Lahaina
Cannery Mall

Mala Wharf

Kapunakea
St.

Honoapiilani Hwy.

Kahoma Stream

Lahainaluna
School
(1837)

Hilo Hattie

Lahaina Center

Papalaua
St.

Pioneer
Sugar Mill

Lahainaluna Rd.

LAHAINA

8 9

Front St.

Dickenson St.

Baldwin Home Museum

Wainee St.

Lahaina
Small Boat Harbor

10

Liakini St.

Banyan Tree

505 Front St.
(Shops & Restaurants)

Shaw St.

0   1/2 mi
0   0.5 km

Kīhei & Wailea Lodging

Andaz Maui at Wailea **3**
The Fairmont Kea Lani Maui **7**
Four Seasons Resort Maui at Wailea **6**
Grand Wailea Resort Hotel & Spa **5**
Hotel Wailea **8**
Nona Lani Cottages **1**
Pineapple Inn Maui **2**
Wailea Marriott Resort & Spa **4**

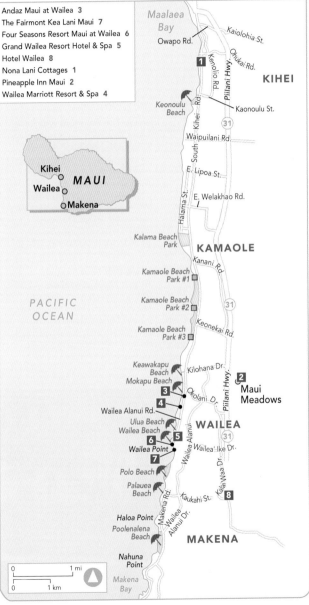

Maui Hotels A to Z

★★★ Andaz Maui at Wailea

WAILEA Gourmands will love this sexy resort's two restaurants: Morimoto Maui (p 129) and Ka'ana Kitchen (p 128). The apothecary-style spa is also wonderful. *3550 Wailea Alanui Dr. www.maui.andaz. hyatt.com.* ☎ *808/573-1234. 198 units. Doubles $409–$604; suites from $553; call for villa price. AE, DC, DISC, MC, V. Map p 145.*

★ Aston at The Whaler on Ka'anapali Beach KA'ANAPALI

In the heart of Ka'anapali, right on the world-famous beach, lies this condo oasis of elegance, privacy, and luxury. *2481 Ka'anapali Pkwy. (next to Whalers Village). www. whalerkaanapali.com.* ☎ *888/671-5310 or 808/661-4861. 360 units. Studio $306–$365 studio; 1 bedroom (up to 4 guests) $325–$589; 2 bedroom (up to 6) $535–$885. AE, DC, DISC, MC, V. Map p 144.*

🔲 Best Western Pioneer Inn

LAHAINA This turn-of-the-19th-century, two-story, plantation-style hotel overlooking Lahaina Harbor has been remodeled with vintage bathrooms. *658 Wharf St. (in front of Lahaina Pier). www.pioneerinnmaui. com.* ☎ *800/457-5457 or 808/661-3636. 34 units. Doubles $168–$217. Suites from $185. Extra person $20 (ages 12 and over). AE, DC, DISC, MC, V. Map p 144.*

★★★ The Fairmont Kea Lani Maui

WAILEA You get your money's worth at this luxurious resort: an entire suite with kitchenette, entertainment center, spacious bedroom, and large lānai facing semi-private Polo beach. *4100 Wailea Alanui Dr. www.fairmont.com/ kealani.* ☎ *800/257-7544 or 808/875-4100. 450 units. Doubles $459–$1,100. Villas from $1,175. AE, DC, DISC, MC, V. Map p 145.*

★★★ 🔲 Four Seasons Resort Maui at Wailea

WAILEA Service at this stylish resort is unparalleled, and it's the most kid-friendly hotel on Maui—cookies and milk on arrival, complimentary baby gear, and a stellar kids camp. Adults get a swank

Porch deck at the Four Seasons Resort.

The pool at the Grand Wailea Resort.

infinity pool with swim-up bar and underwater music. *3900 Wailea Alanui Dr. www.fourseasons.com/maui.* ☎ *800/311-0630 or 808/874-8000. 380 units. Doubles $539–$1,059; club floor doubles $1,349–$4,500; suites from $1,169. AE, DC, MC, V. Map p 145.*

★★★ kids Grand Wailea Resort Hotel & Spa WAILEA

This dazzling resort boasts Hawai'i's largest and most luxurious spa, and its most elaborate swimming pools with slides, waterfalls, rapids, a Tarzan swing, swim-up bar, even a hot tub atop a manmade volcano. *3850 Wailea Alanui Dr. www.grandwailea.com.* ☎ *800/888-6100 or 808/875-1234. 780 units. Doubles $523–$1,130; Club floor from $1,036. Daily $30 resort fee AE, DC, DISC, MC, V. Map p 145.*

★★ Hāmoa Bay House & Bungalow HĀNA

Romance blooms in these gorgeous units, both with hot tubs, big lānai, and Balinese furnishings. Plus, you're close to Hāmoa Beach. *Hāna Hwy.* ☎ *808/248-7884. fax 808/248-7853. 2 units. Doubles $225–$285. MC, V. Map p 143.*

★★ Hāna Oceanfront Cottages HĀNA

Serenity reigns at this plantation-style cottage and villa overlooking Hāmoa Bay. Both have gourmet kitchens and huge lānais for admiring the panoramic view. *522 Haneo'o Rd., Hāna. www.hanabythesea.com.* ☎ *808/248-7558.*

2 units. Doubles $335–$375. $60 cleaning fee. 3-night minimum MC, V, D. Map p 143.

★★★ Hotel Wailea WAILEA

Secluded and serene, with a falcon's view of the Wailea coastline, this stylish boutique hotel is a sexy honeymooners' paradise. *555 Kaukahi St. www.hotelwailea.com.* ☎ *866/970-4167 or 808/874-0500. 72 units. Suites $499–$799; Daily $30 resort fee AE, DC, DISC, MC, V. Map p 145.*

★★ kids Hyatt Regency Maui Resort and Spa KA'ANAPALI

This palatial resort has a ½-acre (.2ha) outdoor pool with a lava tube slide, a cocktail bar under the falls, 9 waterfalls, an Asian and Pacific art collection, and (try to top this) South African penguins in the lobby. *200 Nohea Kai Dr. www.maui.hyatt.com.* ☎ *800/233-1234 or 808/661-1234. 806 units. Doubles $279–$509. AE, DC, DISC, MC, V. Map p 144.*

★★ The Inn at Mama's Fish House PĀ'IA

Nestled in a coconut grove on a secluded beach in Kū'au, these expertly decorated duplexes next to Mama's Fish House (p 129) exude the same South Pacific charm. *799 Poho Place (off the Hāna Hwy. in Kū'au). www.mamasfishhouse.com.* ☎ *800/860-HULA (4852) or 808/579-9764. 8 units. Double $250; 1-bedroom $300; suites $425; 2-bedroom cottages $350–$850. AE, DISC, MC, V. Map p 143.*

Napili Kai Beach Resort.

★★ kids Ka'anapali Ali'i

KA'ANAPALI These oceanfront condo units sit on 8 landscaped acres (3.2ha) right on Ka'anapali Beach, combining the amenities of a luxury hotel (yoga classes on the lawn, anyone?) with the convenience of a condominium. *50 Nohea Kai Dr. www.kaanapalialii.com. ☎ 866/664-6410 or 808/667-1400. 264 units. 1 bedroom $550–$695; 2 bedroom $800–$1100. AE, DC, DISC, MC, V. Map p 144.*

★★ kids Ka'anapali Beach Hotel

KA'ANAPALI Old Hawai'i customs reign here, in everything from the nightly Hawaiian hula and music to the extensive cultural program (learn to weave *lauhala*, string lei, and even speak a little *'ōlelo Hawai'I*, the Islands' native language). *2525 Kaanapali Pkwy. www. kbhmaui.com. ☎ 800/262-8450 or 808/661-0011. 430 units. Doubles $195–$332; suites from $311. AE, DC, DISC, MC, V. Map p 144.*

★★ Kapalua Villas

KAPALUA The stately townhouses dotting the

Learning hula at the Kaanapali Beach Hotel.

oceanfront cliffs and fairways of this idyllic coast are a (relative) bargain, especially for couples traveling together. *500 Office Rd. www. outrigger.com. ☎ 800/545-0018 or 808/669-8088. 1 bedroom $174–$329; 2 bedroom $279–$415; 3-bedroom $439–$599. Cleaning fee $175-$245. AE, DC, DISC, MC, V. Map p 143.*

★ Lahaina Inn

LAHAINA These Victorian antique–stuffed rooms are a rare bargain on Maui, with an excellent restaurant and bar downstairs (Lahaina Grill, p. 128). However, rooms are on the small side. *127 Lahainaluna Rd. (off Front St.). www.lahainainn.com. ☎ 800/222-5642 or 808/661-0577. 12 units. Doubles $145–$221. AE, MC, V. Map p 144.*

★★ Lumeria

MAKAWAO If crystals, sacred artwork, daily yoga classes, and organic breakfasts are your jam, this is your spot, a lavishly converted women's college just above Maui's scenic north shore. *1813 Baldwin Ave. www.lumeriamaui. com. ☎ 808/579-8877. 25 units. Doubles $329–$419; suite from $899. Daily $25 resort fee. AE, MC, V. Map p 143.*

★★★ kids Napili Kai Beach Resort

NAPILI A secluded gold-sand beach, a weekly schedule full of entertainment and activities, units with full kitchens, and jaw-dropping views of Moloka'i and Lāna'i make this vintage resort very popular. *5900 Honoapi'ilani Rd. (far north end of Nāpili, next to Kapalua Resort). www.napilikai.com.* ☎ *800/367-5030 or 808/669-6271. 162 units. Doubles from $351; studio double (sleeps 3–4) from $482; 1-bedroom suite from $720; 2-bedroom suite from $1,156; 3-bedroom suite from $1,380. AE, DISC, MC, V. Map p 143.*

★ **Nona Lani Cottages** KĪHEI These vintage cottages, tucked among palm, fruit, and plumeria trees across the street from Sugar Beach, are a pretty sweet deal. Wi-Fi is spotty, though. *455 S. Kīhei Rd. (just south of Hwy. 31). www.nonalanicottages.com.* ☎ *800/733-2688 or 808/879-2497. 11 units. Double $179–$220. 2-night minimum or $55 cleaning fee. DISC, MC, V. Map p 145.*

★★ **Old Wailuku Inn at Ulupono** WAILUKU This lovingly restored 1924 former plantation manager's home offers a genuine old Hawai'i experience, plus a gourmet breakfast. *2199 Kaho'okele St. (at High St.). www.mauiinn.com.* ☎ *800/305-4899 or 808/244-589710 units. Doubles $175–$215. MC, V. Map p 143.*

★ **kids Outrigger Maui Eldorado** KA'ANAPALI These are great condos for families: spacious units, grassy play areas outside, safe swimming, and a beachfront with cabanas and barbecue area. *2661 Keka'a Dr. www.outrigger.com.* ☎ *888/339-8585 or 808/661-0021. 204 units. Studio $135–$239; 1 bedroom $169–$345; 2 bedroom $239–$509. Daily $15 resort fee and $115-$175 cleaning fee. AE, DC, DISC, MC, V. Map p 144.*

★★ **Pineapple Inn Maui** KĪHEI This charming inn offers impeccably decorated, soundproof rooms, a giant saltwater pool and Jacuzzi overlooking the ocean, and walletpleasing prices. *3170 Akala Dr. www.pineappleinnmaui.com.* ☎ *877/212-MAUI (6284) or 808/298-4403. 5 units. Doubles $159–$189; cottage $215-$255. 3-night minimum. No credit cards. Map p 145.*

★★ **The Plantation Inn** LAHAINA This romantic, Victorian-style inn features period furniture and four-poster canopy beds. It's next door to one of Lahaina's best French restaurants, Gerard's (p 126), where guests get a discount. *174 Lahainaluna Rd. (1 block from Hwy. 30). www.theplantationinn.com.* ☎ *800/433-6815 or 808/667-9225. 19 units. Doubles $160–$318. AE, DC, DISC, MC, V. Map p 144.*

★★★ **kids Ritz-Carlton Kapalua** KAPALUA If you can afford it, stay on the Club Floor,

The pool at the Ritz-Carlton.

which offers the best amenities in the state, including morning coffee, a lunch buffet, cookies in the afternoon, and *pūpū* and drinks at sunset. *1 Ritz-Carlton Dr. www. ritzcarlton.com.* ☎ *800/262-8440 or 808/669-6200. 463 units. Doubles from $520; Club Floor from $920. Daily $35 resort fee. AE, DC, DISC, MC, V. Map p 143.*

★★★ kids Sheraton Maui

KA'ANAPALI   The family suites are great for those traveling with kids: three beds, a sitting room with full-size couch, and two TVs (both equipped with Nintendo); plus fun activities onsite and nearby. Honeymooners enjoy the spa's couples treatments. *2605 Ka'anapali Pkwy. www.sheraton-maui.com.* ☎ *866/ 716-8109 or 808/661-0031. 508 units. Doubles from $503; suites from $769. Daily $25 resort fee. Parking $25. AE, DC, DISC, MC, V. Map p 144.*

★★★ kids Travaasa Hāna

HĀNA   This heavenly 66-acre resort wraps around Kau'iki Hill overlooking the sea. The bungalows are dreamy refuges stocked with homemade banana bread. No TVs here; instead listen to the crashing surf. *5031 Hāna Hwy. www. travaasa.com/hana.* ☎ *800/321-HĀNA (4262) or 808/248-8211. 66 units. Doubles $425–$750. AE, DC, DISC, MC, V. Map p 143.*

★★ Wailea Beach Marriott Resort & Spa

WAILEA   This meandering resort's infinity pool is an ideal spot to spend your day(s). Or hit neighboring Ulua Beach for A+ snorkeling. *3700 Wailea Alanui Dr. www.marriotthawaii.com.* ☎ *800/ 367-2960 or 808/879-1922. 545 units. Doubles from $430–$585; suites from $579. Daily $30 resort fee. Parking $25. AE, DC, DISC, MC, V. Map p 145.*

★★ kids Westin Maui

KA'ANAPALI   Kids love the aquatic playground here, with slides, waterfalls, live flamingos, and black swans. Adults love the trademark Heavenly beds and the decked-out spa and fitness center. *2365 Ka'anapali Pkwy. www.westinmaui. com.* ☎ *866/716-8112 or 808/667-2525. 759 units. Doubles $550–$830. Daily $30 resort fee. AE, DC, DISC, MC, V. Map p 144.* ●

A room at Travaasa Hāna.

The Best of Lāna'i **in One Day**

1. Mānele Bay Harbor
2. Lāna'i Culture & Heritage Center
3. Keahikawelo (Garden of the Gods)
4. Shipwreck Beach
5. Lāna'i City
6. Hulopo'e Beach

The smallest of the main Hawaiian Islands, Lāna'i is quiet and quaint with stunning beaches, ancient petroglyphs, two posh resorts, and 3,000 of the friendliest people you will ever meet. It's possible to get an overview of the island in a single day if you catch the first ferry departing from Lahaina at 6:45am. You'll want to either a) book a tour with Rabaca's Limousine Service (see p 155) or b) rent a Jeep to access the island's off-road sites. The tour is the better bet, with friendly and informative drivers who know how to navigate the often washed-out roads to take you wherever you like.
START: **Mānele Bay Harbor. Trip length: 68 miles (109km).**

❶ Mānele Bay Harbor. To make the most of your day on Lāna'i, take the 6:45am ferry from Lahaina Harbor. Arrive early enough in Lahaina to find all-day parking (check out side streets such as Waine'e). The ferry dock is at the north end of the harbor, next to the lighthouse. Once on board, look for dolphins, flying fish, and whales (in

winter) as you travel across the channel. Rabaca's Limousine Service (p 155) will pick you up at the **Mānele** harbor to start your tour or deliver you to Dollar Rent A Car (p 155) in Lāna'i City, a 20-minute trip.

❷ ★★ Lāna'i Culture & Heritage Center. One of your first stops on

Previous page: Sunrise over Mānele Bay on the island of Lāna'i.

Garden of the Gods.

Lāna'i should be this tiny, well-curated museum in the heart of Lāna'i City, where you can orient yourself to the island's cultural and natural history. See relics from the past, get directions to the island's petroglyph fields, and ask docents to recount local legends passed down in their families. ⏱ *30 min. 730 Lāna'i Ave. www.lanaichc.org.* ☎ *808/565-7177. Open 8:30am–3:30pm.*

From Lāna'i City, it's 14 miles (23km) to Keahiakawelo. Turn right onto Lāna'i Avenue, then left (north) to Hwy. 430 (Keōmuku Hwy.). Turn left on Polihua Road, just past the stables. Look for the rock sign that says GARDEN OF THE GODS. Allow about 25 minutes.

❸ ★★★ kids **Keahiakawelo (Garden of the Gods).** Boulders strewn by volcanic forces have been sculpted by the elements into varying shapes and colors—brilliant reds, oranges, ochers, and yellows—in this rugged, beautiful landscape. Modern visitors nicknamed this otherworldly place "the Garden of the Gods," but its ancient Hawaiian name, Ke-ahi-a-kawelo, means "the fire of Kawelo."

According to legend, it's the site of a sorcerers' battle.

Return to Hwy. 430 (Keōmuku Hwy.) and turn left. Continue down towards the ocean. At the junction, turn left and drive to the end of the road. Allow 1 hour to drive these 20 miles (32km) on winding, unimproved roads.

❹ ★★ kids **Shipwreck Beach.** This 8-mile-long (13km) windswept

Shipwreck Beach and the rusting offshore hulk for which it is named.

strand on Lāna'i's northeastern shore—named for the rusty ship "Liberty" stuck on the coral reef—is a sailor's nightmare and a beachcomber's dream. The swimming isn't great here, nor is the snorkeling (too murky), but this is the best place in Hawai'i to beachcomb. Strong currents yield all sorts of flotsam, from glass fishing floats and paper nautilus shells to lots of junk. At the end of the road, a trail leads about 200 yards inland to the **Kukui Point petroglyphs;** follow the stacked rock ahu (altars) to the large boulders. Respect this historic site by not adding anything to it or taking anything away. Most important, do not touch the petroglyphs.

It takes about 45 minutes to retrace your route back up Hwy. 430 into Lāna'i City.

There's an App For That

The Lāna'i Culture & Heritage Center helped create the Lāna'i Guide, a GPS-enabled app that directs you to historic sites, replete with old photos, aerial videos, and chants. It's free on iTunes.

⑤ ★★ kids Lāna'i City. This quaint old-fashioned town centered on Dole Square sits at 1,645 feet (501m) above sea level, perched amidst the Cook Island pines. Built in 1924, the former pineapple plantation village is a tidy grid of tin-roofed cottages in bright pastels, with tropical gardens of banana, *lilikoi,* and papaya. The charming village square has two general stores selling basic necessities, a smattering of restaurants, an art gallery, an art center, and a movie

Colorful signpost in quaint Lāna'i City.

theater. Give yourself an hour or two to check out the shops, then catch a shuttle down to Hulopo'e Beach.

Follow Eighth Avenue to Fraser Avenue and turn left. Go right at Hwy. 440 (Kaumalapau Hwy.). Turn left at Mānele Road, staying on Hwy. 440 to the end at Hulopo'e Beach Park. Allow 30 minutes for the 11-mile (18km) trip.

⑥ ★★★ kids Hulopo'e Beach. This wide beach is one of my favorites in the entire state. Not only is it a terrific snorkeling spot (especially along the rocks to your left as you face the ocean), but it is a marine preserve, where fishing and

Getting To & Around Lāna'i

To fly to Lāna'i, you'll have to make a connection on O'ahu or Maui, where you catch a puddle-jumper for the 25-minute flight. **Hawaiian Airlines** (www.hawaiianairlines.com; ☎ 800/367-5320) flies five times daily to Lāna'i; **Mokulele Airlines** (www.mokuleleairlines.com; ☎ 866/260-7070) offers charter flights to the island on 9-passenger Cessnas.

The **Expeditions Lahaina/Lāna'i Passenger Ferry** (http://go-lanai.com; ☎ 800/695-2624) runs five times a day, 365 days a year, between Lahaina, Maui, and the Mānele Small Boat Harbor on Lāna'i. The 9-mile channel crossing takes 45 minutes to an hour, depending on sea conditions. One-way tickets cost $30 adults and $20 children. Reservations are strongly recommended.

The island has very little infrastructure, so plan your transportation in advance. **Rabaca's Limousine Service** (☎ 808/565-6670) will retrieve you from the airport or harbor for $10 per person and also offers 3 ½-hour tours ($75 per person). Guests at the **Four Seasons Lāna'i** (p 137) can hire a luxury shuttle ($22 per person from the harbor, $49 from the airport) or a private SUV ($85 per vehicle, limit 4 passengers). If you plan to explore the island's uninhabited areas (which I highly recommend), you'll need a four-wheel-drive (4WD) vehicle for at least a day. Book a tour and let Rabaca's do the driving, or contact **Dollar Rent A Car,** 1036 Lāna'i Ave. (http://dollarlanai.com; ☎ 800/533-7808) or **Dreams Come True** (www.dreamscometruelanai.com; ☎ 808/565-6961). Reserve far in advance; cars are in short supply.

Hulopo'e Beach.

collecting marine critters is forbidden. Boats cannot anchor in the bay, so you have the entire ocean to yourself. For a bit of glamour, walk up to the **Four Seasons** (p 137) for a cocktail.

Take the 5-minute walk from Hulopo'e Beach Park to Mānele Bay to catch the last ferry back to Lahaina at 6:45pm.

The Best of Lāna'i in Three Days

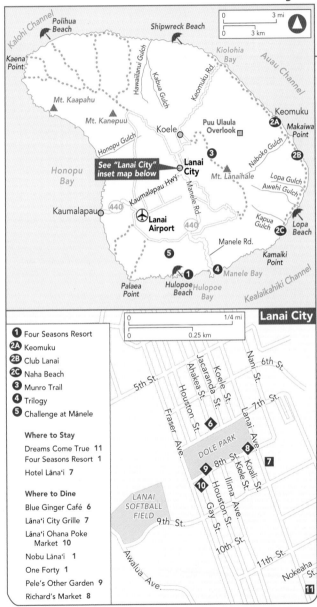

1 Four Seasons Resort
2A Keomuku
2B Club Lanai
2C Naha Beach
3 Munro Trail
4 Trilogy
5 Challenge at Mānele

Where to Stay

Dreams Come True **11**
Four Seasons Resort **1**
Hotel Lāna'i **7**

Where to Dine

Blue Ginger Café **6**
Lāna'i City Grille **7**
Lāna'i Ohana Poke
   Market **10**
Nobu Lāna'i **1**
One Forty **1**
Pele's Other Garden **9**
Richard's Market **8**

Three days is ideal for Lāna'i, giving you enough time to explore the island, relax on the beach, and sample one of many outdoorsy activities, such as scuba diving, golfing, clay shooting, hiking, or horseback riding. Spend your first day scouting out the sights outlined in the 1-day tour on p 152. On your following days, depending on the weather, choose any of the five options described below. START: **Lāna'i City or at your Lāna'i lodgings.**

The beach at the Four Seasons Resort Lāna'i offers good snorkeling in Hulopo'e Bay.

❶ ★★★ kids Four Seasons Resort and **Hulopo'e Beach.** Indulge in luxury at the Four Seasons and Hulopo'e Beach. Even if you're not a guest at the resort, you can have a resplendent brunch at **One Forty** (p 160); gorge on made-to-order omelets, smoothies, and mala-sadas. Gaze out at the bay where dolphins and whales often come to rest and play. Migrate down to the beach. Watch the kids play in the surf, snorkel at the edges of the bay, and take a relaxing stroll up to **Pu'u Pehe** (Sweetheart Rock). If you're feeling energetic in the afternoon, book a horseback ride or spin around the clay-shooting course at the Four Seasons' **Island Adventure Center** (see below). For dinner, dress up and wander over to **Nobu Lāna'i** (p 160) for the exquisite Japanese cuisine of Chef Nobu Matsuhisa, and a view of the sun sinking into the ocean.

Activity Central

The **Island Adventure Center** (1 Mānele Bay Rd., Lāna'i City; www.fourseasons.com/lanai; ☎ 808/565-2072) at the Four Seasons Resort Lāna'i offers fun activities for guests and non-guests alike. Book a horse-back ride through the forest, a spin around the 14-station clay-shooting course, an archery lesson, or an ATV ride.

From Lāna'i City, follow Keōmoku Road (Hwy. 430) 8 miles to the coast. Here the road turns to dirt, mud, or sand; proceed with caution. Head right past beaches and old villages to the road's end. Return the way you came.

❷ The East Side of the Island. If it hasn't rained recently, rent a 4×4 vehicle and explore Lāna'i's untamed east side. Bring snacks and extra water; there are no facilities out here and cell service is scarce.

Explore the east side's string of empty beaches and abandoned villages, including **❷A Keōmoku ★★**, which is about 5¾ miles down the dirt road running parallel to the shore. This former ranching and fishing community of 2,000 was home to the first non-Hawaiian settlement on Lāna'i. A ghost town since the mid-1950s, it dried up after droughts killed off the Maunalei Sugar Company. Check out **Ka Lanakila ★**, the village's sweetly restored church that dates back to 1903, and investigate the driftwood beach forts.

Continue another 2 miles south to the deserted remains of **2B** **Club Lāna'i** ★★. A lonely pier stretches into the Pacific from a golden-sand beach populated by coconut palms, a few gazebos, and an empty bar floating in a lagoon. You can pretend you're on the set of *Gilligan's Island* here. The road ends at **2C** **Naha Beach** ★ with its ancient fishponds. Return the way you came and take any trash with you.

From Lāna'i City, take Keōmoku Rd. (Hwy. 430) about 2.3 miles (3.7km) to the Lāna'i Cemetery, where you'll find the Munro Trail trailhead.

3 ★★ **Munro Trail**. Fit and ambitious hikers can spend the day (plan on at least 7 hours) climbing to the top of Lānaihale on the well-marked Munro Trail. This tough, 11-mile (18km) round-trip, uphill climb through groves of Norfolk pines is a lung buster, but if you reach the top, you'll be rewarded with a breathtaking view of Kaho'olawe, Maui, Hawai'i Island, and Molokini's tiny crescent. The trail follows Lāna'i's ancient caldera rim, ending up at the island's highest point, Lānaihale. Go in the morning for the best visibility. After 4 miles (6.4km), you'll get a view of Lāna'i City. If you're tired, you can retrace your steps from here, otherwise, continue the last 1¼ miles (2km) to the top. Die-hards can head down Lāna'i's steep south-crater rim to join the highway to Mānele Bay. Soak in a hot tub on your return.

From Lāna'i City take the Kaumalapau Hwy. 440 to the end of the road at Mānele Harbor. Allow 30–35 min. for the 11-mile/18km trip.

4 ★★★ **Sail-snorkel Excursion.** To go out on (or into) the water, contact **Trilogy Lāna'i Ocean Sports** (www.visitlanai.com; ☎ 888/MAUI-800 [628-4800]) about their sailing-snorkeling, whale-watching, or scuba trips from Mānele Boat Harbor. Diving is particularly magical at two sites: Cathedrals I and II.

From Lāna'i City take Kaumalapau Hwy. 440 to the end of the road at Mānele Harbor. Allow 30–35 min. for the 11-mile/18km trip.

5 ★★★ **Golf at Challenge at Mānele.** Golfers can test their mettle at this target-style, desert-links course designed by Jack Nicklaus, one of the toughest and most beautiful golf courses in the state. Located next to the Four Seasons–Lāna'i at Mānele in Hulopoe Bay (p 159), the Challenge course charges greens fees of $425 or $350 for resort guests. To reserve a tee time, visit www.golfonlanai.com/manele or call ☎ 808/565-2222.

Hike to Lāna'i's highest point on the Munro Trail.

Where to **Stay & Eat**

The Blue Ginger Café.

Hotels

★★ Dreams Come True Lāna'i

LĀNA'I CITY   This nicely renovated 1925 plantation house is roomy and quaint, with four bedrooms, four bathrooms, and a backyard orchard. Among the many perks: marble bathrooms, fresh *lilikoi* juice served with the delicious breakfast each morning, and private four-wheel-drive rentals—a real bonus on this car-deficient island! *1168 Lāna'i Ave., Lāna'i City. www.dreams cometruelanai.com.* ☎ *808/565-6961. 4 rooms. Doubles $141–$160; entire house from $564, plus $100 cleaning fee. AE, DC, MC, V. Map p 156.*

★★★ Four Seasons Resort

Lāna'i MĀNELE   A conch shell's trumpeting call announces your arrival at this oceanfront retreat, where everyone magically knows your name—even the computer screen in your bathroom mirror. Every inch of this opulent oasis reflects the latest in tech-savvy luxury, from the wristband room keys to the Toto toilets. Service is impeccable: The concierge texts you when dolphins or whales appear in the bay. Beach attendants set up umbrellas in the sand for you, spritz you with Evian, and deliver smoothie samples. *1 Mānele Bay Rd. www.fourseasons.com/lanai.* ☎ *808/565-2000. 236 units. Doubles from $1,075, suites from $2,200. AE, DC, MC, V. Map p 156.*

★★ kids Hotel Lāna'i LĀNA'I

CITY   This hotel is perfect for families and other vacationers looking for a good deal. Built in the 1920s, it's a clapboard plantation-era relic that has retained its quaint character. *828 Lān'ai Ave., Lanai City. www. hotellanai.com.* ☎ *800/795-7211. 11 units. Doubles $174–$304 include continental breakfast; separate cottage $254–$279. AE, MC, V. Map p 156.*

Restaurants

Blue Ginger Café LĀNA'I CITY *COFFEE SHOP*   This cafe is a casual, inexpensive alternative to Lāna'i's fancy hotel restaurants. Try the burgers on homemade buns. *409 7th St. (at Ilima St.), Lāna'i City. www.bluegingercafelanai.com.* ☎ *808/565-6363. Breakfast and lunch items under $17; dinner entrees under $18. Cash only. Breakfast, lunch & dinner Thurs–Mon; breakfast & lunch Tues–Wed. Map p 156.*

★ kids **Lāna'i City Grill** LANAI CITY AMERICAN Local venison is the star at this cozy restaurant in the heart of town. Bring a jacket if you want to sit outside by the fire pits and soak up the friendly Lāna'i ambiance and fantastic live music. In the Hotel Lāna'i, 828 Lāna'i Ave., L āna'i City. www.hotellanai.com. ☎ 808/565-7211. Entrees $18–$38. MC, V. Dinner Wed–Sun. Map p 156.

Lāna'i Ohana Poke Market LĀNA'I CITY FISH DELI Poke is a delicacy in Hawai'i consisting of raw fish cut into small pieces and sea-soned with seaweed, onions, and spices. Visit this tiny to-go window for the freshest poke on the island. 834 Gay St. (between 8th and 9th aves), Lāna'i City. ☎ 808/559-6265. Bowl of poke $7.50, with rice and macaroni salad $9. No credit cards. Mon–Fri lunch. Map p. 156.

★★★ **Nobu Lāna'i** MĀNELE JAPANESE At this classy dining room in the Four Seasons Resort, every dish is as delicious as it is art-ful: the smoked Wagyu gyoza with jalapeño miso, the immaculate plates of nigiri sushi, and the ahi avocado salad with greens grown at Alberta's farm up the road. Vegetarian? Nobu has a sophisti-cated menu just for you, featuring fusion tacos and tofu tobanyaki anticucho—a melting pot of Japa-nese and Peruvian flavors. 1 Mānele Bay Rd. www.fourseasons.com/lanai. ☎ 808/565-2832. Entrees $18–$58. Tasting menu $120 per person. AE, DC, MC, V. Dinner Tues–Sat. Map p 156.

★ **One Forty** MĀNELE STEAK & SEAFOOD Located just off the pool in the Four Seasons Lāna'i at Mānele Bay, this casual, open-air, Hawaii-style bistro serves breakfast and dinner. The dinner menu focuses on steaks and Hawaiian seafood, but I also love the orange and ginger roasted chicken. If you're up for it, Chef Matthew Brennan offers a 5-course tasting, with or without wine pairings. Book a table for dinner and watch the sun set and the stars come out. 1 Mānele Bay Rd. www.fourseasons. com/lanai. ☎ 808/565-2290. Break-fast entrée $12–$24; buffet $52; din-ner $32–$95. AE, DC, MC, V. Breakfast and dinner daily. Map p 156.

★ **Pele's Other Garden** LĀNA'I CITY DELI/BISTRO The check-ered floor and vanity license plates decorating the walls set an upbeat tone at this casual bistro. For lunch, dig into an avocado and feta wrap or an Italian hoagie. Cheese lovers will swoon over the thin-crusted four-cheese pizza. 811 Houston St., Lāna'i City. ☎ 808/565-9628. Entrees $8–$13 lunch, $17–$20 din-ner; pizza slice from $9. AE, DISC, MC, V. Lunch Mon–Sat; lunch & din-ner. Map p 156.

★★ **Richards Market** LĀNA'I CITY GROCERY This 1946 grocery got a gourmet makeover when Larry Ellison came to town. Now find fancy wine and chocolates alongside fresh poke (raw seasoned fish), local produce, and on Tues-days, delicious barbecue plates. 434 Eighth St., Lāna'i City. ☎ 808/ 565-3780. AE, DISC, MC, V. Open 6am–10pm. Map p 156. ●

The **Savvy Traveler**

Before You Go

Government Tourist Offices

On Maui: Maui Visitors Bureau (1727 Wili Pa Loop, Wailuku, HI 96793; www.gohawaii.com/maui and @mauivisit on Twitter; ☎ 800/525-MAUI [6284]). **On Lānaʻi: Lanai Visitors Bureau** (1727 Wili Pa Loop, Wailuku, Maui 96793; www.gohawaii.com/lanai and @visitlanai on Twitter; ☎ 800/947-4774).

The Best Times to Go

Most visitors come to Hawaiʻi when the weather is lousy elsewhere. Thus, the **high season**—when prices are up and resorts are often booked to capacity—is generally from mid-December to March or mid-April. In particular, the last 2 weeks of December and the first week of January are prime time for travel to Hawaiʻi. Spring break is also jam-packed with families taking advantage of the school holiday.

If you're planning a trip during peak season, make hotel and rental car reservations as early as possible, expect crowds, and prepare to pay top dollar. The winter months tend to be a little rainier and cooler. But there's a perk to travelling during this time: Hawaiian humpback whales are here, too.

The **off season,** when the best rates are available and the islands are less crowded, is late spring (mid-April to early June) and fall (September to mid-December).

If you plan to travel in **summer** (June–August), don't expect to see the fantastic bargains of spring and fall—this is prime time for family travel. But you'll still find much better deals on packages, airfare, and accommodations than in the winter months.

Festivals & Special Events

WINTER. Banyan Tree Lighting Celebration is when Lahaina's historic Banyan Tree is lit up with thousands of Christmas lights in early December (www.visitlahaina.com; ☎ 808/667-9175). The end of December and early January brings the Academy of Motion Pictures' major screenings of top films with the **First Light,** at the Maui Arts and Cultural Center (www.mauifilmfestival.com; ☎ 808/579-9244). To celebrate **Chinese New Year** (January–February), the historic Wo Hing Temple in Lahaina town holds a traditional lion dance plus fireworks, food booths, and a host of activities (www.visitlahaina.com; ☎ 808/661-5553). **Maui Whale Festival,** in February, is a month-long celebration on Maui with a variety of activities including a parade, craft fairs, games, and food (www.worldwhaleday.org; ☎ 808/249-8811).

SPRING. In mid-March, the entire town of Lahaina celebrates the **Whale and Ocean Arts Festival** in Banyan Tree Park, with Hawaiian musicians and hula troupes, marine-related activities, games, and a "creature feature" touch-pool exhibit for children (www.visitlahaina.com; ☎ 808/667-9175). At the end of March or beginning of April, Hāna holds the **East Maui Taro Festival,** serving taro in many different forms, from fresh poi to chips. Stroll around the ballpark and check out the Hawaiian exhibits, hula demonstrations, and food booths (www.tarofestival.org; ☎ 808/264-1553). Easter weekend brings the **Annual Ritz-Carlton Kapalua Celebration of the Arts**

Previous page: Driving the Hāna Highway.

LAHAINA-KA'ANAPALI'S AVERAGE TEMPERATURE & RAINFALL

	JAN	FEB	MAR	APR	MAY	JUNE
Daily High (°F/°C)	82/28	80/27	83/28	84/29	85/29	87/31
Daily Low (°F/°C)	64/18	6317	64/18	65/18	67/19	68/20
Water Temp	75/24	74/23	74/23	75/24	76/24	77/25
Rain in Inches	3.5	2.4	1.8	1.1	1.1	0.1

	JULY	AUG	SEPT	OCT	NOV	DEC
Daily High (°F/°C)	88/31	88/31	89/32	88/31	86/30	83/28
Daily Low (°F/°C)	69/21	69/21	70/21	69/21	67/19	65/18
Water Temp	78/26	79/26	80/27	79/26	77/25	76/24
Rain in Inches	0.2	0.2	0.3	1.1	2.2	3.2

KĪHEI-WAILEA'S AVERAGE TEMPERATURE & RAINFALL

	JAN	FEB	MAR	APR	MAY	JUNE
Daily High (°F/°C)	81/27	81/27	83/28	84/29	85/29	87/31
Daily Low (°F/°C)	63/17	63/17	64/18	64/18	65/18	67/19
Water Temp	75/24	74/23	74/23	75/24	76/24	77/25
Rain in inches	4.1	2.9	2.7	1.8	0.8	0.3

	JULY	AUG	SEPT	OCT	NOV	DEC
Daily High (°F/°C)	8831	89/32	88/31	87/31	85/29	82/28
Daily Low (°F/°C)	69/21	69/21	69/21	68/20	67/19	65/18
Water Temp	78/26	79/26	80/27	79/26	77/25	76/24
Rain in inches/cm	0.4	0.5	0.4	1.3	2.6	3.3

to the West Maui resort. Contemporary and traditional Hawaiian artists give free hands-on lessons during this 3-day festival, which also features song contests and rousing debates on what it means to be Hawaiian. (www.celebrationofthe arts.org; ☎ 808/669-6200). On the first Saturday in April, the **Maui County Ag Fest** celebrates farmers and their bounty. Kids enjoy barnyard games while parents sample top chefs' collaborations with local farmers. (www.mauicountyfarm bureau.org/maui-county-agricultural-festival-2; **808/243-2290).**

May 1 is **Lei Day** in Hawai'i. Across the state, schoolchildren and public officials will be decked out in flowers. Join the fun at the **Lei Day Heritage Festival** at the Bailey House Museum, 10am–4pm (www.maui museum.org; ☎ 808/244-3326).

SUMMER. A state holiday on June 11, **King Kamehameha Day,** jumpstarts the summer with a massive floral parade and *ho'olaule'a* (party) (www.visitlahaina.com; ☎ 808/667-9175). Just before Father's Day weekend in June, the **Maui Film Festival** at the Wailea Resort features 5 days and nights of celebrity-splashed premieres and special films, along with fancy soireés, feasts, and stargazing. (www.mauifilmfestival. com; ☎ 808/579-9244). On the last Saturday in July, on Lāna'i, the **Pineapple Festival** celebrates Lāna'i's history of pineapple plantation and ranching and includes eating and cooking contests, entertainment, arts and crafts, food, and fireworks (www.gohawaii.com/lanai; ☎ 808/565-7600). The **Fourth of July** is celebrated on Maui with various activities (www.gohawaii.com/maui;

☎ 800/525-MAUI [6284]). Every weekend in June and July, a different Buddhist church on Maui hosts an **Obon Dance and Ceremony** to honor the souls of departed ancestors. The Lahaina Jodo Mission's ceremony is the prettiest, with glowing lanterns released into the sea after sunset. (☎ 808/661-4304). In early July, famous wine and food experts and oenophiles gather at the **Kapalua Wine and Food Festival** (www.kapaluaresort.com; ☎ 800/KAPALUA [527-2582]), for tastings, panel discussions, and samplings of new releases.

FALL. The statewide **Aloha Festivals** (www.festivalsofaloha.com; ☎ 800/268-9285), a series of celebrations, parades, and other events honoring the Hawaiian culture, takes place in September and October. Early September brings **A Taste of Lahaina,** where Maui's premier chefs serve up 40 signature entrees. The event includes cooking demonstrations, wine tastings, and live entertainment (www.visit lahaina.com; ☎ 888/310-1117).

The Weather

Because Maui lies at the edge of the tropical zone, it technically has only two seasons, both of them warm. The dry season corresponds to summer, and the rainy season generally runs from November to March. The rainy season can cause gray weather and spoil your tanning opportunities. Fortunately, it seldom rains for more than 3 days straight, and rainy days often just consist of a mix of clouds and sun, with very brief showers.

The **year-round temperature** typically varies no more than 15 degrees, but it depends on where you are. Maui's **leeward** sides (the west and south) are usually hot and dry, whereas the **windward** sides (east and north) are generally cooler and moist. If you want arid,

desertlike weather, go leeward. If you want lush, often wet, junglelike weather, go windward. Your best bets for total year-round sun are the Kīhei-Wailea and Lahaina-Kapalua coasts.

Maui is also full of **microclimates,** thanks to its interior valleys, coastal plains, and mountain peaks. If you travel into the mountains, it can change from summer to winter in a matter of hours, because it's cooler the higher up you go.

Useful Websites

- **www.gohawaii.com:** The Hawai'i Tourism Authority's all-around guide to islands, with pages devoted to Maui and Lāna'i.

- **www.hawaiiradiotv.com:** Hawaii's radio and television guide.

- **www.calendarmaui.com:** A comprehensive look at events on Maui, with some advertisements for accommodations.

- **www.mauinow.com:** Maui's online news source.

- **www.omaui.com:** Daily surf report for Maui.

- **www.weather.com:** Up-to-the-minute worldwide weather reports.

Restaurant & Activity Reservations

If you've got your heart set on a particular restaurant or activity (like dinner at the Old Lahaina Lū'au or the Trilogy trip to Lāna'i), book well in advance. For popular restaurants, try asking for early or late hours—often tables are available before 6:30pm and after 8pm.

Cellphones

In general it's a good bet that your cellphone will work in Maui, although coverage may not be as good as in your hometown. Cell coverage on Lāna'i may be spotty (few towers). If you're not from the U.S., you'll be appalled at the poor reach of the GSM (Global System for Mobiles) wireless network, which is used by much of the rest of the world. Assume nothing—call your wireless provider and get the full scoop. In a worst-case scenario, you can always rent a phone from **InTouch USA** (www.intouchglobal. com; ☎ **800/872-7626**), but be aware that you'll pay $1 a minute or more for airtime.

Getting **There**

By Plane
If possible, fly directly to Maui. Doing so can save you a 2-hour lay-over in Honolulu and another plane ride.

If you think of the island of Maui as the shape of a person's head and shoulders, you'll probably arrive near its neck, at **Kahului Airport** (OGG). Many airlines offer direct flights to Maui from the mainland U.S., including **Hawaiian Airlines** (www.hawaiianair.com; ☎ **800/367-5320**), **Alaska Airlines** (www.alaskaair.com; ☎ 800/252/7522), **United Airlines** (www.united.com; ☎ 800/241-6522), **Delta Air Lines** (www.delta. com; ☎ 800/221-1212), **American Airlines** (www.aa.com; ☎ **800/882-8880**), and **Virgin America** (www.virginamerica.com; ☎ 877/359-8474). The only international flights to Maui originate in Canada, via **Air Canada** (www.aircanada.com; ☎ 888/247-2262) and **West Jet** (www.westjet.com; ☎ 888/937-8538), which both fly from Vancouver.

Other major carriers stop in Honolulu, where you'll catch an interisland flight to Maui on **Hawaiian Airlines** or **Island Air** (www. islandair.com; ☎ 800/652-6541).

If you're staying in Lahaina or Ka'anapali, you might consider flying in or out of **Kapalua–West Maui Airport** (JHM). From this tiny airfield, it's only a 10- to 15-minute drive to most hotels in West Maui, as opposed to an hour or more from Kahului. Same story with **Hāna Airport** (HNM): Flying directly here will save you a 3-hour drive.

A small commuter service, **Mokulele Airlines** (www.mokulele airlines.com; ☎ 866/260-7070) flies between Honolulu, Kahului, Kapalua, Hāna, Kona, Waimea (Hawaii Island), and Ho'olehua (Moloka'i), and by charter to Lāna'i City. Check-in is a breeze: no security lines (unless leaving from Honolulu). You'll be weighed, ushered onto the tarmac, and welcomed aboard a nine-seat Cessna. The plane flies low, and the views between the islands are outstanding.

Getting **Around**

By Car
The best way to get around Maui is to rent a car and you'll find the best rates online. Rental cars run from $40 to $75 a day (including all state taxes and fees). Cars are usually plentiful, except on holiday week-ends, which in Hawai'i also means

King Kamehameha Day (June 11), Prince Kūhiō Day (March 26), and Admission Day (3rd Friday in August). Rental cars on Lāna'i are expensive and in short supply, so book well ahead.

All the major car-rental agencies have offices on Maui: **Alamo** (www.goalamo.com; ☎ 877/222-9075), **Avis** (www.avis.com; ☎ 800/331-1212), **Budget** (www.budget.com; ☎ 800/214-6094), **Dollar** (www.dollarcar.com; ☎ 800/800-4000), **Hertz** (www.hertz.com; ☎ 800/654-3131), and **National** (www.nationalcar.com; ☎ 800/227-7368).

There are also a few frugal car-rental agencies offering older cars at discount prices. **Aloha Rent a Car** (www.aloharentacar.com; ☎ 877/5452-5642 or 808/877-4477) has used, older vehicles and requires a 4-day minimum rental. Rates start at $31 a day, with free airport pickup and drop-off included. **Maui Cruisers,** in Wailuku (www.mauicruisers.net; ☎ 877/749-7889 or 808/249-2319), also offers free airport pickup and return; rentals start at $28 a day (4-day minimum) or $122 a week (including tax and insurance).

To rent a car in Hawai'i, you must be at least 25 years old and have a valid driver's license and a credit card.

One more thing on car rentals: Hawai'i is a no-fault state, which means that if you don't have collision-damage insurance, you are required to pay for all damages before you leave the state, whether or not the accident was your fault. Your personal car insurance back home may provide rental-car coverage; read your policy or call your insurer before you leave home. Bring your insurance card if you decline the optional insurance, which usually costs from $12 to $20 a day. Obtain the name of your company's local claim

representative before you go. Some credit card companies also provide collision-damage insurance for their customers; check with yours before you rent.

By Bus
The **Maui Bus** (www.mauicounty.gov/bus; ☎ **808/871-4838**) provides limited public transit across the island. Expect hour-long waits between rides. Air-conditioned buses serve 13 routes, including several that stop at the airport. Simply cross the street at baggage claim and wait under the awning. Unfortunately, bus stops are few and far between, so you may end up lugging your suitcase a long way to your destination. All routes operate daily, including holidays. Suitcases (one per passenger) and bikes are allowed; surfboards are not. The fare is $2.

By Airport Shuttle
You can choose to get a shuttle van from the airport to your destination from **Roberts Hawai'i Airport Express Shuttle** (www.airportshuttlehawaii.com/shuttles/maui; ☎ 800/831-5541 or 808/954-8630), which offers curb-to-curb service in a shared van or small bus. Booking is a breeze on their new website. Plan to pay $26 (one-way) to Wailea and $36 to Ka'anapali. Prices drop if you book round-trip. Another option is **SpeediShuttle Maui** (www.speedishuttle.com; ☎ 877/242-5777); prices (one-way, from the airport, for a shared van) range from $42 to Wailea or $58 to Ka'anapali. You need to book in 24 hours in advance. Bonus: You can request a fresh flower-lei greeting for an added fee.

By Taxi
Taxi service on Maui is quite expensive—expect to spend around $80 for a ride from Kahului to

Ka'anapali and $60 from the airport to Wailea. For islandwide 24-hour service, call **Alii Cab Co.** (☎ 808/661-3688 or 808/667-2605). You can also try **Kīhei Taxi** (☎ 808/879-3000), **Wailea Taxi** (☎ 808/874-5000), or **Maui Central Cab** (☎ 808/244-7278).

Fast **Facts**

ATMS You'll find **ATMs** at most banks, in supermarkets, and in most resorts and shopping centers.

BABYSITTING The first place to check is with your hotel. Many hotels have babysitting services or will provide you with lists of reliable sitters. The **Nanny Connection** (www.thenannyconnection.com; ☎ 808/875-4777) on Maui is a reputable business that sends Mary Poppins–esque nannies to resorts and beaches to watch children ($17 per hour and up, with a 3-hour minimum and booking fee). Tutoring services are also available. You can also call **People Attentive to Children** (PATCH; www.patchhawaii. org; ☎ 808/242-9232 [Maui] or 800/498-4145 [Lāna'i]), which will refer you to individuals who have taken their childcare training courses.

BANKING HOURS Banks are open Monday through Thursday from 8:30am to 5pm and Friday from 8:30am to 6pm. Many banks are open until noon on Saturday.

BUSINESS HOURS Most offices are open from 8am to 5pm. Shopping centers are open Monday through Friday from 10am to 9pm, Saturday from 10am to 5:30pm, and Sunday from 10am to 5 or 6pm.

CONDOMINIUM & VACATION HOME RENTALS **Condominium Rentals Hawai'i** (www.crhmaui.com; ☎ 800/367-5242) offers affordable, quality properties primarily in Kīhei, with a few in Wailea and Lahaina. **Bello Realty** (www.bellomauivacations.com; ☎ 800/541-3060) also offers a variety of condos. For vacation rentals, contact **Hawaiian Beach Rentals** (www.hawaiianbeachrentals.com; ☎ 844/261-0464).

CUSTOMS Visitors from other countries arriving by air, no matter what the port of entry, should cultivate patience and resignation before setting foot on U.S. soil. Getting through customs and immigration control can take as long as 2 hours on some days.

DENTISTS If you have dental problems, a nationwide referral service known as **1-800-DENTIST** (☎ 800/336-8478) will provide the name of a nearby dentist or clinic. Emergency dental care is available at **Hawaii Family Dental** (1847 S. Kīhei Rd., Kīhei; ☎ 808/856-4625 and 95 Lono Av., Ste. 210, Kahului ☎ 808/856-4626), or in Lahaina at the **Aloha Lahaina Dentists** (134 Luakini St., in the Maui Medical Group Bldg.; ☎ 808/661-4005).

DOCTORS **Urgent Care West Maui,** located in the Fairway Shops, 2580 Keka'a Dr., Suite 111, Ka'anapali (www.westmauidoctors.com; ☎ 808/667-9721), is open 365 days a year; no appointment necessary. In Kīhei, call **Urgent Care Maui** (http://medicalclinicinmaui.com; ☎ 808/879-7781), open daily 8am to 6pm at 1325 S. Kīhei Rd., Suite 103 (at Lipoa St., across from Times Market).

ELECTRICITY The United States uses 110 to 120 volts AC (60 cycles), compared to 220 to 240 volts AC (50 cycles) in most of Europe, Australia, and New Zealand. Downward converters that change 220–240 volts to 110–120 volts are difficult to find in the United States, so bring one with you.

EMBASSIES & CONSULATES All embassies are located in Washington, D.C. The embassy of **Australia** is at 1601 Massachusetts Ave. NW, Washington, DC 20036 (www.usa. embassy.gov.au; ☎ 202/797-3000). The embassy of **Canada** is at 501 Pennsylvania Ave. NW, Washington, DC 20001 (www.canadian embassy.org; ☎ 202/682-1740). The embassy of **Ireland** is at 2234 Massachusetts Ave. NW, Washington, DC 20008 (www.embassyof ireland.org; ☎ 202/462-3939). The embassy of the **United Kingdom** is at 3100 Massachusetts Ave. NW, Washington, DC 20008 (www.gov. uk/government/world/usa; ☎ 202/588-6500). For other countries, call directory information in Washington, D.C. (☎ 202/555-1212), for the number of your national embassy.

EMERGENCIES Dial ☎ 911 for the police, an ambulance, and the fire department. District stations are located in Lahaina (☎ 808/661-4441) and in Hāna (☎ 808/248-8311). For the **Poison Control Center,** call ☎ 800/222-1222.

EVENT LISTINGS The best source for listings is the Friday edition of the local daily newspaper, **Maui News** (www.mauinews.com). There are also several tourist publications with listings, including **This Week on Maui** (www.thisweek.com) and **Maui Visitor Magazine** (www.aloha visitorguides.com). You can also check small, local community newspapers, such as **Maui Time Weekly** (www.mauitime.com), **Maui Weekly** (www.mauiweekly.com), and **Lahaina News** (www.lahainanews.com).

FAMILY TRAVEL Look for the kids icon throughout this book for tips on the best activities, hotels, and restaurants for families with kids. For up-to-date family-friendly events, check out **Maui Mama** (www.maui mama.com), also available in print at many island locations. **Baby's Away** (www.babysaway.com; ☎ 800/942-9030 or 808/631-8618) rents cribs, strollers, highchairs, playpens, and infant seats. The staff will deliver whatever you need to wherever you're staying and pick it up when you're done.

GAY & LESBIAN TRAVELERS **Pride Guide Hawai'i** (www.gogayhawaii. com) features gay and lesbian news, blogs, business recommendations, and other information for the entire state. Also check out the website for **Out in Hawai'i** (www.outinhawaii. com), which calls itself "Queer Resources and Information for the State of Hawai'i," with vacation ideas, a calendar of events, information on Hawai'i, and even a chat room.

HOLIDAYS Federal, state, and county government offices are closed on all federal holidays: January 1 (New Year's Day), third Monday in January (Martin Luther King Day), third Monday in February (Presidents' Day, Washington's Birthday), last Monday in May (Memorial Day), July 4th (Independence Day), first Monday in September (Labor Day), second Monday in October (Columbus Day), November 11 (Veterans Day), fourth Thursday in November (Thanksgiving Day), and December 25 (Christmas). State and county offices also are closed on local holidays, including Prince Kūhiō Day (March 26), King Kamehameha Day (June 11), and Admission Day (third Friday in August). Other special days are celebrated by many people in Hawai'I, but do not involve the closing of federal, state, or county offices: They include Chinese New Year (in January or February), Girls' Day (March 3),

Buddha's Birthday (April 8), Father Damien's Day (April 15), Boys' Day (May 5), Samoan Flag Day (in August), Aloha Festivals (September or October), and Pearl Harbor Day (December 7).

INSURANCE   Trip-cancellation insurance helps you get your money back if you have to back out of a trip, if you have to go home early, or if your travel supplier goes bankrupt. For information, contact one of the following insurers: **Allianz Global Assistance** (www.allianz travelinsurance.com; ☎ 800/284-8300), **Travel Guard International** (www.travelguard.com; ☎ 800/826-4919), **Travel Insured International** (www.travelinsured.com; ☎ 800/243-3174), and **Travelex Insurance Services** (www.travelexinsurance. com; ☎ 800/228-9792).

Although it's not required of travelers, health insurance is highly recommended. Unlike many European countries, the United States does not usually offer free or low-cost medical care to its citizens or visitors. Doctors and hospitals are expensive, and in most cases require advance payment or proof of coverage before they treat patients. Lack of health insurance may prevent you from being admitted to a hospital in non-emergencies, but don't worry about being left on a street corner to die: The American way is to fix you now and bill the living daylights out of you later.

INTERNET ACCESS   Most hotels and even small B&Bs have Wi-Fi, sometimes for a fee. **Whole Foods** (www.wholefoodsmarket.com/ stores/maui) at the Maui Mall in Kahului has free Wi-Fi, as does **Starbucks** (www.starbucks.com/ store-locator) with stores in Kahului, Pukalani, Lahaina, and Kīhei. If you need a computer, visit a **public library** (to find the closest location,

check www.publiclibraries.com/ hawaii.htm). A library card gets you free access; purchase a 3-month visitor card for $10.

MAIL & POSTAGE   At press time, domestic postage rates were 34¢ for a postcard and 47¢ for a letter. For international mail, a first-class postcard or letter up to 1 ounce costs $1.15. For more information go to **www.usps.com**. To find the nearest post office, call ☎ **800/ ASK-USPS** [275-8777] or log on to www.usps.gov. In Lahaina the main post office is at the Lahaina Civic Center (1760 Honoapiʻilani Hwy.), in Kahului there's a branch at 138 S. Puʻunēnē Ave., and in Kīhei there's one at 1254 S. Kīhei Rd. Mail can be sent to you, in your name, c/o General Delivery, at the post office. Most post offices will hold your mail for up to 1 month.

PASSPORTS   Anyone traveling to Hawaiʻi from outside of the U.S. is required to show a passport. Bring a photocopy of your passport with you and store it separately; if your passport is lost or stolen, the copy will help you get a new one reissued at your consulate. If you are an American citizen flying to Hawaiʻi from the U.S. mainland, a driver's license or state ID will suffice. *Note:* Effective January 22, 2018, all travelers must show identification that complies with the REAL-ID Act: either a passport or an ID/driver's license from a REAL-ID compliant state. Check with the Department of Homeland Security to see if your ID is compliant (www. dhs.gov/real-id-enforcement-brief; ☎ **202/282-8000**). As of publication, drivers' licenses from 5 states—Maine, Minnesota, Missouri, Montana, and Washington State—were not yet deemed compliant.

PHARMACIES   **Longs Drugs** (www. cvs.com) has five pharmacies, two of which are open 24 hours: in Kīhei (41 E. Līpoa St. ☎ 808/879-8499), and in Kahului at the Maui Mall Shopping Center (70 E. Kaahumanu Ave.; ☎ 808/877-0068). See website for other locations.

SAFETY Although Hawai'i is generally a safe tourist destination, visitors have been crime victims, so stay alert. The most common crime against tourists is rental-car break-ins. Never leave any valuables in your car, not even in your trunk. Be especially careful in high-risk areas, such as beaches and resorts. Never carry large amounts of cash with you. Stay in well-lighted areas after dark. Don't hike on deserted trails or swim in the ocean alone.

SENIOR TRAVELERS Discounts for seniors are available at almost all of Maui's major attractions, and occasionally at hotels and restaurants. The Outrigger hotel chain, for instance, offers travelers ages 50 and older a 20% discount on regular published rates—and an additional 5% off for members of AARP. Always inquire when making hotel reservations or buying air tickets and carry proof of your age with you—it can really pay off. Most major domestic airlines offer senior discounts. Members of **AARP** (www.aarp.org; ☎ 800/424-3410 or 202/434-2277) are usually eligible for extra discounts. AARP also puts together organized tour packages at moderate rates. Some great, low-cost trips to Hawai'i are offered to people 55 and older through **Road Scholar** (formerly Elderhostel; 11 Avenue de Lafayette., Boston, MA 02111; www.roadscholar.org; ☎ 800/454-5768), a nonprofit group that arranges travel and study programs around the world.

 If you're planning to visit Haleakalā National Park, you can save sightseeing dollars if you're 62 or older by picking up a **Golden Age Passport** from any national park, recreation area, or monument. This lifetime pass has a one-time fee of $10 and provides free admission to all of the parks in the system, plus a 50% savings on camping and recreation fees.

SPECTATOR SPORTS Maui hosts a slew of professional and amateur sports events that are exciting to watch. Golf fans can witness the annual **SBS Tournament of Champions** in Kapalua (www.golfat kapalua.com; ☎ 808/669-8044); kite-surfing aficionados can catch the **Red Bull King of the Air** competition at Ho'okipa (www.redbull kingoftheair.com); and basketball fans get front row bleacher seats at the annual **Maui Invitational** college basketball tournament (www. mauiinvitational.com). There are even rousing **polo** matches to rally behind in Makawao (www. maui poloclub.com; ☎ 808/877-7744).

TAXES The United States has no value-added tax (VAT) or other indirect tax at the national level. Local taxes, however, may be levied on purchases, including hotel and restaurant checks and airline tickets. These taxes will not appear on price tags. Hawai'i state has a general excise tax of 4.166%, which applies to all items purchased (including hotel rooms). On top of that, the state's transient Accommodation Tax (TAT) is 9.25%. These taxes, combined with various resort fees, can add up to 17% to 18% of your room rate. Budget accordingly.

TELEPHONE For directory assistance, dial ☎ 411; for long-distance information, dial 1, then the appropriate area code, and then 555-1212. The area code for all of Hawai'i (not just Maui) is 808. Calls to other islands are considered long distance. For calls to other islands you have to dial 1 + 808 + the 7-digit phone number.

TIPPING Tips are a major part of certain workers' income, and gratuities are the standard way of showing appreciation for services provided. (Tipping is certainly not compulsory if the service is poor!) In hotels, tip bellhops at least $2 per bag ($3–$5 if you have a lot of luggage) and tip the housekeepers $2 per person per day (more if you've left a disaster area for him or her to clean up). Tip the doorman or concierge only if he or she has provided you with some specific service (for example, calling a cab for you or obtaining difficult-to-get theater tickets). Tip the valet-parking attendant $2 to $5 every time you get your car.

In general, tip service staff such waiters, bartenders, and hairdressers 18% to 20% of the bill. Tip cab drivers 15% of the fare.

TOILETS You won't find public toilets on the streets in Hawai'i, but you can find them in hotel lobbies, restaurants, museums, department stores, service stations, and at most beaches (where you'll find showers, too). Large hotels and fast-food restaurants are often the best bet for clean facilities. Restaurants and bars in heavily visited areas may reserve their restrooms for patrons.

TRAVELERS WITH DISABILITIES Travelers with disabilities will feel welcome in Maui. Hotels are usually equipped with wheelchair-accessible rooms and swimming pools, and tour companies provide many special services. Beach wheelchairs are available at Kama'ole I in Kīhei (ask lifeguard). For tips on accessible travel in Hawai'i, go to the **Hawai'i Tourism Authority** website (www.travelsmarthawaii.com/en/practical-travel-info/before-traveling/travelers-with-special-needs). The only travel agency in Hawai'i specializing in needs for travelers with disabilities is **Access Aloha Travel** (www.accessalohatravel.com; ☎ 800/480-1143), which can book anything, including rental vans, accommodations, tours, cruises, airfare, and just about anything else you can think of. Travelers with disabilities who wish to do their own driving can rent hand-controlled cars from **Avis** (www.avis.com; ☎ 800/331-1212) and **Hertz** (www.hertz.com; ☎ 800/654-3131). The number of hand-controlled cars in Hawai'i is limited, so be sure to book well in advance. Maui recognizes other states' windshield placards indicating that the driver of the car is disabled, so be sure to bring yours with you. Vision-impaired travelers who use a Seeing Eye dog need to present documentation that the dog is a trained Seeing Eye dog and has had rabies shots. For more information, contact the **Animal Quarantine Facility** (http://hdoa.hawaii.gov/ai/aqs/animal-quarantine-information-page; ☎ 808/483-7151).

A Brief **History**

BETWEEN A.D. **300 AND 1200** Using the stars and currents as their guides, Polynesian wayfinders sail double-hulled canoes across the sea to Hawai'i. They bring with them everything needed for survival, including tools, medicine, animals, and around 30 different plant species.

AROUND 1300 Transoceanic voyages halt; Hawai'i begins to develop its own culture in earnest. Sailors become farmers and fishermen, and build temples, fishponds, and aqueducts to irrigate *kalo lo'i* (taro paddies). Each island is a separate kingdom, divided into smaller districts called *ahupua'a*. Each wedge-shaped *ahupua'a* runs from the mountain to the sea, granting its residents access to a wide range of natural resources. The *ali'i* (chiefs) create a caste system with numerous *kapu* (restrictions). The arts flourish; Hawaiians develop sophisticated dances, chants, weaving techniques, and *kapa* (barkcloth) patterns.

AROUND 1400 Work begins on a massive *heiau* (temple) later known as Pi'ilanihale in Hāna. When complete, it will span 3 acres with 50-foot-tall walls.

AROUND 1577 Pi'ilani, a high chief from Hāna, is born. He unites Maui under single rule, builds fishponds and irrigation fields, and begins paving a road of smooth stones 4 to 6 feet (1.2–1.8km) wide around the entire island. His sons and grandson complete the project.

MID-1700S A pregnant woman in Kona craves the eyeball of a man-eating shark, signifying that her unborn son is destined to be a powerful chief. She gives birth to Kamehameha I in Kohala on Hawai'i Island. Fulfilling many prophecies, the boy grows into a great warrior.

1768 Ka'ahumanu is born, reportedly in a cave at Pu'u Kauiki in Hāna. She later becomes the favorite wife of Kamehameha I and an influential figure in the Hawaiian monarchy.

1778 Captain James Cook sails into Waimea Bay on Kaua'i, where he is welcomed as the god Lono. His sailors trade nails for fresh water, pigs, and the affections of Hawaiian women.

The foreigners bring syphilis, measles, and other diseases to which the Hawaiians have no natural immunity, thereby unwittingly wreaking havoc on the native population. The Captain and four of his crew are killed the following year during a scuffle over a stolen boat in Kealakekua Bay on Hawai'i Island.

1782 Kamehameha I begins his campaign to conquer the Hawaiian Islands.

1790 During the Battle of Kepaniwai (the damming of the waters) Kamehameha thrashes the Maui forces in 'Iao Valley with western guns and cannons. Maui chiefess Kalola and her granddaughter Keōpūolani (Hawai'i's highest ranking princess) escape through the mountains to Olowalu and continue by canoe to Moloka'i.

1795 Kamehameha I finally conquers Maui. He marries Keōpūolani to establish his dominance, and makes Lahaina the capital of his new kingdom.

1801 Kamehameha I stops on Maui with his fleet of war canoes on his way to do battle on O'ahu and Kaua'i. He stays in Lahaina for a year, constructing the Brick Palace, Hawai'i's first Western-style structure.

1810 Kamehameha I unites the Hawaiian Islands under single rule.

1819 Kamehameha I dies; his son Liholiho is proclaimed Kamehameha II. Under the influence of Queen Ka'ahumanu, Kamehameha II orders the destruction of *heiau* and an end to the *kapu* system, thus overthrowing the traditional Hawaiian religion. Ka'ahumanu and Keōpūolani convert to Christianity, influencing thousands of Hawaiians follow suit. The first whaling ship, *Bellina*, drops anchor in Lahaina.

1820 Missionaries arrive in Lahaina from New England, bent on converting islanders and combating the drunken licentiousness of visiting sailors. To spread the gospel, missionaries create a Hawaiian alphabet and introduce written language. They establish the first high school and newspaper west of the Rockies.

1845 King Kamehameha III moves the capital of Hawai'i from Lahaina to Honolulu, where the natural harbor can accommodate more commerce.

1849 George Wilfong, a sea captain, builds a mill in Hāna and plants some 60 acres of sugar cane, creating Hawai'i's first sugar plantation.

1876 Sugar planters engineer an elaborate ditch system that takes water from rainy Hā'iku and delivers it to the dry plains of Central Maui, cementing the future of sugar in Hawai'i.

JANUARY 17, 1893 A group of American sugar planters and missionary descendants, with the support of U.S. Marines, imprison Queen Lili'uokalani in her own palace in Honolulu and illegally overthrow the Hawaiian government.

JUNE 16, 1897 U.S. President McKinley acts to formally annex the Hawaiian Islands. Queen Liliu'okalani travels to Washington in protest and 21,269 Native Hawaiians (more than half the entire population) sign a petition against annexation. The following year, Congress passes McKinley's resolution.

APRIL 30, 1900 Congress passes the Organic Act, establishing the Territory of Hawai'i with Sanford Dole as its first governor.

NOVEMBER 22, 1935 Pan American Airways offers the first commercial flight from the U.S. mainland to Hawai'i—16 hours from Los Angeles to Honolulu.

DECEMBER 7, 1941 Japanese Zeros bomb American warships based at Pearl Harbor, plunging the U.S. into World War II.

AUGUST 21, 1959 Hawai'i becomes the 50th state of the United States.

1960 Amfac, owner of Pioneer Sugar Company, builds Maui's first destination resort in Ka'anapali.

1967 The state of Hawai'i hosts 1 million tourists.

1975 Maui reaches the 1 million annual tourists mark. Ten years later the number is 2 million.

1990S Hawai'i's economy suffers following a series of events: First, the Gulf War severely curtails air travel to the island; then, Hurricane Iniki slams into Kaua'i, crippling its infrastructure; and finally, sugar-cane companies across the state began shutting down, laying off thousands of workers. Maui weathers this turbulent economic storm.

NOVEMBER 4, 2008 Barack Obama, a Punahou School graduate, becomes the first Hawai'i-born President of the United States.

2009 Hawai'i, the 50th state, celebrates 50 years of statehood.

DECEMBER 2016 Hawai'i's oldest and largest sugar plantation, Hawaiian Commercial & Sugar Company ceases operations, ending 168 years of sugar harvests in the Islands.

The Hawaiian **Language**

Almost everyone in the Islands speaks English. But many folks now speak 'ōlelo Hawai'i, the native language, as well. All visitors will hear the words *aloha* (hello/goodbye/love) and *mahalo* (thank you). If you've just arrived, you're a *malihini*. Someone who's been here a long time is a *kama'aina,* child of the land. When you finish a job or your meal, you are *pau* (finished). On Friday it's *pau hana,* work finished. You eat *pūpū* (appetizers) when you go *pau hana.*

The Hawaiian alphabet, created by the New England missionaries, has only 12 letters: the 5 regular vowels (*a, e, i, o,* and *u*) and 7 consonants (*h, k, l, m, n, p,* and *w*). The vowels are pronounced in the Roman fashion, that is, *ah, ay, ee, oh,* and *oo* (as in "too")—not *ay, ee, eye, oh,* and *you,* as in English. For example, *huhu* is pronounced *who-who*. Most vowels are sounded separately, though some are pronounced together, as in Kalakaua (*Kah-lah-cow-ah*).

Two Hawaiian punctuation marks will help you with pronunciation: The *'okina* is a backwards apostrophe that separates vowels. It's pronounced as a pause or glottal stop. *Ho'okipa*, which means hospitality, is pronounced ho-oh-keepa. The *kahako* is a line above a vowel that indicates stress. For example, Kanahā, a beach near the airport, is pronounced Kah-nah-HA, with emphasis on the final syllable.

Useful Words & Phrases

Here are some basic Hawaiian words that you'll often hear in Hawai'i and see throughout this book. For a more complete list, consult Mary Kawena Pukui's authoritative *Hawaiian Dictionary.*

ali'i: Hawaiian royalty
aloha: greeting or farewell
hālau: school
hale: house or building
heiau: Hawaiian temple or place of worship
kahuna: priest or expert
kama'aina: long-time Hawaii resident
kapa: bark cloth
kapu: taboo, forbidden
keiki: child
lānai: porch or veranda
lomilomi: massage
mahalo: thank you
maika'i: good
makai: a direction, toward the sea
mana: spirit power
mauka: a direction, toward the mountains
mu'umu'u: loose-fitting gown or dress
'ono: delicious
pali: cliff
paniolo: Hawaiian cowboy(s)
wiki: quick

Pidgin: Try Talk Story

If you venture beyond the tourist areas, you might hear another local tongue: Hawaiian Pidgin, a blend of 'ōlelo Hawai'i and the languages of the early sugar plantation workers: Chinese, Japanese, Portuguese, etc. "Broke da mouth" (tastes really good) is a favorite phrase you might hear. If you're lucky you could be invited to hear an elder "talk story" (chat and tell stories).

Eating in Maui

When it comes to dining in Maui, all I can say is: Come hungry and bring a fat wallet. Dining has never been better on the Valley Isle, which is presently producing numerous enterprising and imaginative chefs. The farm-to-table concept has finally taken root on this bountiful island, where in past years up to 90% of the food had been imported. Today chefs and farmers collaborate on menus, filling plates with tender micro-greens and heirloom tomatoes picked that morning. Fishers reel in glistening 'ōpakapaka (pink snapper), and ranchers offer up flavorful cuts of Maui-grown beef.

A new crop of inspired chefs is taking these ripe ingredients to new heights. At **Ka'ana Kitchen** (see p. 128), chef Isaac Bancaco nearly outshines his celebrity neighbor, "Iron Chef" Masaharu Morimoto (who brought his high-octane Japanese fusion cuisine to **Morimoto Maui** in Wailea, p. 129). Both are outstanding; make time for each. On the other side of the island, at Kapalua's **Plantation House** (p. 130), Jojo Vasquez adds exciting molecular gastronomy accents to his gourmet dishes. Stellar dining experiences all, with prices to match.

Haute cuisine is alive and well here, but good-value plate lunch places and food trucks stand ready to satisfy you as well. The **plate lunch**, like Hawaiian Pidgin, is a gift of the plantation era. You'll find plate lunches served in to-go eateries across the islands. They usually consist of some protein—fried mahimahi, say, or teriyaki beef, shoyu chicken, or chicken or pork cutlets served katsu style: breaded, fried, and slathered in tangy sauce—accompanied by "two scoops rice," macaroni salad, and a few leaves of green, typically julienned cabbage.

Chili water and soy sauce are the condiments of choice. Like **saimin**—the local version of noodles in broth topped with scrambled eggs, green onions, and sometimes pork—the plate lunch is Hawai'i's version of comfort food.

Because this is Hawai'i, at least a few fingerfuls of **poi**—steamed, pounded taro (the traditional Hawaiian staple crop)—are a must. Mix it with salty *kālua* pork (pork cooked in a Polynesian underground oven known as an *imu*) or *lomi* salmon (salted salmon with tomatoes and green onions). Other tasty Hawaiian foods include **poke** (pronounced *po-kay*), a popular appetizer made of cubed raw fish seasoned with onions, seaweed, and roasted *kukui* nuts; **laulau,** pork, chicken, or fish steamed in *ti* leaves; **squid lū'au,** cooked in coconut milk and taro tops; **haupia,** creamy coconut pudding; and **kūlolo,** a steamed pudding of coconut, brown sugar, and taro.

A Hawaiian Seafood Primer

To help familiarize you with the menu language of Hawaii, here's a basic glossary of island fish:
'ahi: yellowfin or big-eye tuna
aku: skipjack tuna
hapu'upu'u: grouper, a sea bass
hebi: spearfish
kūmū: goatfish
mahimahi: dolphin fish (the game fish, not the mammal)
monchong: bigscale or sickle pomfret
onaga: ruby snapper
ono: wahoo
opah: moonfish
'ōpakapaka: pink snapper
pāpio: jack trevally
shutome: broadbill swordfish
tombo: albacore tuna
uhu: parrotfish
uku: gray snapper
ulua: large jack trevally

Airline and Car Rental Websites

Airlines on Maui

AIR CANADA
www.aircanada.com

ALASKA AIRLINES
www.alaskaair.com

AMERICAN AIRLINES
www.aa.com

CONTINENTAL AIRLINES
www.continental.com

DELTA AIR LINES
www.delta.com

HAWAIIAN AIRLINES
www.hawaiianair.com

ISLAND AIR
www.islandair.com

MOKULELE AIRLINES
www.mokuleleairlines.com

UNITED AIRLINES
www.ual.com

WEST JET
www.westjet.com

Car Rental Agencies on Maui

ALAMO
www.goalamo.com

AVIS
www.avis.com

BUDGET
www.budget.com

DOLLAR
www.dollarcar.com

HERTZ
www.hertz.com

MAUI CRUISERS
www.mauicruisers.net

NATIONAL
www.nationalcar.com

ALOHA RENT-A-CAR
www.aloharentacar.com

Index

See also Accommodations and Restaurant indexes, below

Photo **Credits**